Self-Esteem and Meaning

SUNY Series in Transpersonal and Humanistic Psychology
Richard D. Mann and Jean B. Mann, Editors

Self-Esteem
and
Meaning

A Life-Historical Investigation

MICHAEL R. JACKSON

State University of New York Press

ALBANY

To my mother and the memory of my father

Published by
State University of New York Press, Albany
© 1984 State University of New York
All rights reserved
Printed in the United States of America

For information, address State University of New York Press, State University Plaza, Albany, N.Y., 12246

Library of Congress Cataloging in Publication Data
Jackson, Michael R., 1946-
  Self-esteem and meaning.
  (SUNY series in transpersonal and humanistic psychology)
  Bibliography: p.
  Includes index.
  1. Self-respect—Psychological aspects. 2. Self-respect—Psychological aspects—Case studies. I. Title. II. Series.
BF697.J26   1984   155.2′32   83-18248
ISBN 0-87395-852-7
ISBN 0-87395-853-5 (pbk.)
10 9 8 7 6 5 4 3 2 1

Contents

Acknowledgments

Many people have contributed to this book, and I would like to take this opportunity to thank at least some of them.

A number of those involved in interview research at the University of Michigan were particularly important, not only in helping me to define and shape my own ideas, but in clearing the methodological path ahead of me. First and foremost among these is George Rosenwald, whose critical acumen and dedication to the interview method were like a steady beacon illuminating the dark. Also of enormous help was Barnaby Barratt, who introduced me to the literature that provides much of the intellectual framework of this book.

Other people, too, made contributions in a variety of ways. Ellen Gross acted both as friend and teacher and supplied in her own work the model upon which this investigation is based; Tod Sloan provided intellectual camaraderie and a continuous stream of new ideas; Sue Miller combined a sympathetic understanding of interview research with a warm friendship; Joel Hencken played an important role as friend, critic, mentor, and gadfly; Bob Green, Rick Ochberg, Hank Greenspan, and Jeff Evans all gave critical feedback and support in the right proportions; and Debbie Jackson worked long hours as my most important critic and ally by offering a variety of comments and suggestions, helping me to prepare the final manuscript, and reinforcing my own self-esteem with her encouragement, support, and belief in this project.

Dick Mann played a crucial role in the publication of this book, and I wish to express my appreciation to him for the time, effort, and encouragement he offerred. I would also like to thank the members of my doctoral dissertation committee, Jack Meiland, William Rhodes and Howard Wolowitz, for their support of the project which led to this book and for the feedback they gave me in connection with it. I am particularly grateful to my committee chairman, Eric Bermann, who scrupulously respected my efforts to develop my own ideas, but who always demanded that I do so in a thorough and rigorous way.

The most important contribution of all, however, was made by a group of people who cannot be named. They are the subjects in the present investigation, who generously shared the most personal and painful aspects of their lives with me. They must remain anonymous for reasons of confidentiality. But their cooperation in this project is gratefully appreciated, for without it there would have been no project at all.

Self-Esteem and the
Problem of Meaning

A T THE END of the last century, William James expressed a sense of uneasiness. Although he himself was one of the founders of American psychology, James was disturbed by the trends he saw developing in the field. He warned against the tendency to treat human nature as a mere technical problem, and he suggested that the basic facts of inner life—the *meaning* of human experience— would remain untouched by experimental approaches. At one point he complained about "the humbugging pretense of exactitude...in psychological literature," adding: "what does a human being really learn from it all beyond what he already knew by the light of nature?" [1892, p. 96].

Experimental psychology went on to conquer the field, however, and in the century since James wrote the above passage, laboratory techniques have been applied to every conceivable aspect of human psychology. Tens of thousands of experimental investigations have been conducted in areas as diverse as motivation, development, learning, and counseling. Both the size and the diversity of this research establishment testify to the influence of the experimental approach in American social science. But the person who wishes to understand human psychology in a personal and meaningful way can hardly avoid an impression of another kind: a vague and persistent sense that, amidst the methodological and technical sophistication, something is very wrong.

American psychology seems to have lost its soul. Embracing the canons of prediction and control, it has failed to address human experience. Psychologists design complex experiments, but they avoid discussing ordinary behavior; they measure responses, but they do not talk to their subjects; they study variables, but they do not study people. Moreover, this is not a mere failure in values, a lack of a proper humanistic attitude. For in losing its soul, psychology seems to have lost a great deal of its "sense" as well. Research is conceptually disconnected from ordinary life, and the results of experimental investigations tend to be inconsistent, insubstantial, and difficult to apply in the real world.

These problems are not secret ones. They have been pointed out by psychologists and nonpsychologists for a number of years, and they have even been the focus of occasional public criticism. What is more difficult to see, however, are the underlying reasons for the problems—the reasons why experimental psychology has failed to develop a science of human behavior, why it continues to dominate the field despite the obviousness of this failure, and why no other research orientation has succeeded in replacing it. To gain some insight into these questions, it is useful to consider a specific area of psychological research, one which is especially representative of the problems in the field: the psychological literature on self-esteem.

Self-esteem would seem to be an important phenomenon. Not only would it appear to involve the issues of identity and value, but it would also seem to reflect how individuals feel and act in a variety of circumstances. It is not surprising, therefore, that a great deal of research has been focused on self-esteem and that this research represents a wide range of theoretical orientations. Self-esteem has been "operationalized" in a multitude of ways—as a score on questionnaires, as a coded behavior, as an intervening variable, as a "self-ideal discrepancy," as an evaluation of task performance, as a "buffer mechanism," and as a variety of other functions and tendencies. This multitude of approaches is complex and bewildering, but it is unified by a single overarching theme: the attempt to deconstruct a complex phenomenon, to identify its basic elements and correlates, and to accumulate objective knowledge about it.

After thirty years of intensive effort, however, there can be little doubt that this project has failed. What has emerged instead in the self-esteem literature is a confusion of results that defies interpretation. Hypotheses have been tested about the relationships between self-esteem and hundreds of other psychological variables.

Many of these hypotheses have been formally supported, but most observed trends have been weak and insubstantial. There are few replications or systematic extensions, and it is difficult to know which findings are worth pursuing. Moreover, because different investigators begin with different assumptions, their findings stand in obscure relation to one another. There is little consensus on just what this research as a whole signifies for clinical work or for the understanding of psychological development. On the contrary, reviewers of self-esteem investigations have noted massive inconsistencies and contradictions in the literature. For example, Wylie concludes a major survey of published research on self-esteem by pointing out the "striking incidence" of weak, null, and contradictory findings (1979, pp. 690, 692). The following passage, from another review of the self-esteem literature, illustrates the nature and scope of the problem:

> For many issues, empirical support can be found for each of the positions. For example, Cowen (1954), Bosheir (1969), and Larsen and Schwendiman (1969) find a negative relationship between self-esteem and authoritarianism.... In contrast, data described in Hamilton (1971) and Kayser (1972) suggest that there is *no* relationship between self-esteem and authoritarianism, and Wylie (1961) cites four studies obtaining positive relationships. In using the ability to admit negative but true information about oneself as an adjustment indicator, Taylor and Combs (1952) find a positive relationship—high self-esteem persons are more able to honestly admit unflattering descriptions—but Moore and Ascough (1970) find a negative relation, and a wide variety of studies have found that the high self-esteem person is more likely to use denial defenses against negative information. In persuasibility studies, the results have generally been complicated. Negative relations between self-esteem and attitude change tendencies are frequently found, but curvilinear and even positive relations occur....
> While self-esteem has generally been positively associated with sociality and social skills (e.g. Berger, 1955; Omwake, 1954; Rosenberg, 1965; Fitts, 1972b; Luckey, 1961), Achenback and Zigler (1963) report that persons with [low self-esteem] have higher "social competence" and Neuringer and Wandke (1966) find that high self-esteem persons have higher interpersonal instability. In moral behavior, the results are similarly mixed. Rudestam et al. (1971) reports no relationship between self-esteem and altruistic behavior,

and while Aronson and Mettee (1965) and Graf (1971) find a negative relation between self-esteem and cheating, Jacobson et al. (1969) report conflicting findings. Most research regards high self-esteem persons as more ambitious and confident; Pepitone et al. (1967) find them to be more competitive. In contrast, Faucheux and Moscovici (1968) and Graf and Hearne (1970) find low self-esteem persons to be more competitive, and Martire (1956) finds a negative relationship between self-esteem and achievement motivation. A strikingly discrepant set of findings is a pair of studies using direct measures of "adjustment"; Block and Thomas (1955) find a curvilinear relation between self-esteem and adjustment, with medium self-esteem representing the best adjustment; Chodorkoff (1954b) also finds a curvilinear relationship but reports that the middle position is the most maladjusted (Wells and Marwell, 1976, pp. 72-73).

Faced with results like these, one author has concluded an overview of the self-esteem literature with a brief commentary on "the utter bankruptcy of it all" (Diggory, 1966, p. 62).

Critics of the self-esteem literature have generally attributed these problems to lack of rigor. For example, Wylie (1974, 1979) cites shortcomings common to many self-esteem investigations and suggests a number of steps which could be taken to remedy these problems—primarily, the validation of a small number of research instruments and the use of these instruments in a consistent program of carefully designed and reported research. Wells and Marwell make similar recommendations and advocate the use of new experimental and statistical techniques. Recommendations like these, however, are little more than statements of faith in the experimental approach. While it is undoubtedly true that the quality of experimentation has often been imperfect in the investigation of self-esteem, there is little reason to believe that more experimental rigor will now lead to a better understanding of the phenomenon. In fact, there is good reason to expect just the opposite. Three decades of increasingly sophisticated experimentation has produced a divergence rather than a convergence of information about self-esteem; and the results of recent and rigorous experimentation are in many cases more difficult to apply to ordinary life than those associated with the less-sophisticated work of the past.

The problem seems rather to lie in experimentation itself—or, more correctly, in the application of the experimental method to the investigation of self-esteem. While the experimental method is clearly a useful device in many areas of human inquiry (the "hard" sciences like physics being the prime example), results such as the ones described above suggest that something is radically different here. Self-esteem is not a determinate process like the ones studied in the physical sciences; its nature lies rather in its subjective character and in its ever-changing manifestations and implications. Confronted by a phenomenon so elusive and so dynamic, the experimental method is, as it were, overpowered. Like an optical instrument buffeted in a storm, this method produces multiple and conflicting partial-images, unable to resolve them into a single picture.

These conflicting images seem to follow primarily from the reductionistic assumptions of the experimental method and the incompatibility of these assumptions with certain aspects of human psychology. Laboratory procedures are designed to reduce reality into constituent parts—that is, to break it down into simpler elements and to show how these elements affect each other in discrete cause-and-effect relationships. From the standpoint of experimental design, self-esteem is regarded as a "function" of such elements—a psychological "variable" which is part of our make-up and which interacts with other variables to produce our experience. As such, self-esteem needs to be studied by procedures that systematically reduce it to its simplest forms and manipulate its interactions with other variables to determine its underlying causal structure. But this conception—convenient though it may be for designing and justifying psychological experiments—overlooks a crucial fact about human experience, namely, that important phenomena like self-esteem are defined not by their causal structures but by their *meanings*.

To illustrate this point, let us briefly examine the following statement by a man named Jim. When he asked to describe the experience of self-esteem, Jim remembered certain events from his senior year in college:

> I was on the school newspaper and that was a time I felt very good about myself. The paper was important because it gave me a chance to comment on what was going on around me on the campus and in the world. And it was expressing certain aptitudes that I had, things I enjoyed doing. You know, writing editorials, the investigative side of it, interviewing someone, hitting the library, or whatever. One incident still stands out in my mind. The chancellor wanted to gain eminence for the university by establishing a medical school, which I thought would be expensive and

unnecessary and would end up sucking a lot of vitality out of the rest of the university. One of the pleasures of being a reporter is that you can choose what you're going to concentrate your energies on. So I wrote an article analyzing the medical school and why the arguments for it were false. The article was met with a lot of disbelief. To a certain degree, people were ready to buy my skepticism about its effects on the rest of the university, but no one believed my claim that the country and the state didn't need another medical school and that there was going to be a surplus of doctors in another decade or so. I felt a bit like an anachronism on a college campus, you know, a left-over student activist crying in the wilderness. It turned out I was right. Later on, the Carnegie Institute came out with a report that in a much more precise and solid way came to the same conclusion that I had. Boy, that was satisfying [laughs].

If we consider this passage in detail for a moment we can see that Jim's experience is a complex one. A variety of factors appear to have contributed to Jim's good feelings about his article: the challenge to a powerful authority, the use of his skills, the disbelief of his peers, and so forth. But Jim's self-esteem is not a "product" of these factors, like a mechanical process or a chemical reaction. His experience is important not because of its causation but because of the meaning that it holds for him. This meaning is defined by the entire story Jim tells, and by the unique and specific pattern in which the elements of this story are interwoven—for example, in the fact that Jim challenges authority *by* using his skills, in the fact that his peers disbelieve him *because* he is challenging authority, and in the fact that his challenge is validated *in spite of* their disbelief and *by virtue of* his skills. None of these elements could be removed without altering the story and the meaning of Jim's self-esteem. Nor, for that matter, could any of them be removed without altering the meanings of all the others. Together they form a complicated network of interdependent connotations, a field of significance which is intricate and complex, but which is simultaneously irreducible.

The meaning of a phenomenon like self-esteem, then, is more than a mere "function" of its constituents. It seems to reside in an irreducible pattern of experience and conception in a person's life. Any attempt to understand self-esteem must give recognition to this irreducible pattern. Such an attempt must identify the specific events and relationships that constitute the elements of self-esteem, but only in relation to the larger field of personal meaning which they collectively define. The reductionism of the psychological experiment, however, fails badly in this respect. Rather than exploring the natural contours of the field of meaning, the experimental method is quintessentially analytic. It is designed to sever lines of personal meaning, to remove human actions from their natural context, and to identify these actions as products and functions of conceptually discrete causal processes. The method provides no basis for the reconstruction of the subjective field which has been thus reduced. Nor can meaning be recovered by more rigorous experimentation, for this merely accelerates the reductive process. Increasingly sophisticated experimentation means increasingly refined surgical precision; the more rigorously the experimental method is applied to the field of meaning, the more thoroughly it succeeds in decimating this field.

But if the experiment is not the proper tool for investigating the meaning of self-esteem, what is? We seem to require a more naturalistic approach that can explore self-esteem in a living context. We must examine the themes that constitute self-esteem—the opportunitites, the problems, the triumphs, and the defeats that the individual encounters in the development of self—but without losing sight of how these themes are woven together into a person's own story. It would be best if we could ask about the details of such a story so that we could probe more deeply into the meaning of the phenomenon; but we would also want to allow a person freedom in responding so that he or she could cover the whole field of relevant events.

Why not study self-esteem, then, in a process of dialogue that would allow individuals to tell their own stories? In the give and take of an intensive interview we might explore the natural contours of self-esteem. This is an appealing idea in a number of respects—methodological, ethical, and philosophical. Before we consider it seriously, however, a note of caution needs to be sounded. The interview is not new to the field of psychology. It has traditionally been used by clinical workers to understand self-esteem and other psychological phenomena. By employing the interview, clinicians have avoided many of the pitfalls encountered by their experimental colleagues, but they have run into certain methodological and conceptual difficulties of their own. Some of these difficulties have been quite substantial and have contributed to doubts about the legitimacy of the interview.[1]

One particularly troublesome problem is that of how to conceptualize interview material. While clinicians have used the interview to explore the natural structure of self-esteem, they have frequently had trouble finding appropriate concepts for discussing this structure once it has been identified. The source of this problem is, once again, the irreducibility of the field of meaning. If meaning involves a variety of elements but emerges only at the level of the whole, then it presents a peculiar and paradoxical problem to anyone who attempts to discuss it theoretically. Such an investigator must consider the intricate themes that constitute the meaning of self-esteem, but in a way that maintains the integrity of the experience and preserves its existence as a coherent whole. Clinicians who have written about self-esteem have found such conceptualization to be a difficult task and have generally moved in one of two directions.

One group of investigators has approached the phenomenon in a primarily *analytic* mode. The models proposed by these investigators have usually postulated certain components of the personality and certain interactions among these components associated with the experience of self-esteem. These theories have taken a variety of forms—for example, Freud's (1914a, 1923) conception of self-esteem as the libidinal cathexis of the ego by the superego, and Sullivan's (1953) analysis of positive self-feeling as an outcome of a well functioning self "dynamism." Since models like these have tended to be rather abstract, they have sometimes been reformulated in more phenomenological terms. Thus, Freud's original conception of self-esteem has been largely replaced in psychoanalytic theory by the analysis of internalized social experience. This analysis focuses on the importance of developing an internally cohesive system of "self-representations" leading to a stable and mature sense of self-esteem.

The trouble with conceptions like these, however, is that they tell us little about the meaning of the phenomenon. They cut through the

---

[1]Perhaps the most substantial of these difficulties concerns the validity of the interview. Because of its unstructured format, the interview has often been regarded as a subjective, unreliable, and generally inferior method of gathering information. For a variety of reasons, this issue has not been discussed in the present section, but is considered in some detail in the appendix.

fabric of verbal themes woven in the original interview process and hypothesize instead agencies and forces functioning mechanically in the human mind. Like the technical procedures of experimental science, these theories are reductionistic in character; and their reductionism undermines their illuminative power, even in their more phenomenological versions. For example, the concept of a "cohesive system of self-representations" obscures rather than clarifies the meaning of self-esteem. The concept glosses over a variety of personal themes and reduces them to the status of interchangeable components. In so doing, it neglects the creative human subject who organizes experience in a unique life history.

Other clinicians writing about self-esteem have reacted against this reductive tendency. These investigators have assumed a theoretical stance which is more humanistic and *synthetic*. In general, these writers discuss the potentially integrative aspects of personality, stressing the importance of personal growth. Thus, Maslow (1950, 1970) views self-esteem as an aspect of a more general process of self-actualization, while a variety of other clinicians and humanists relate it to the striving for the "ideal self." In contrast to reductionistic approaches, these conceptions are holistic in their vision, and they recognize the creative human subject who attempts to establish a coherent way of life.

Just because of their holism, however, these theories are limited in another important respect. The same characteristics that free them from reductionism tend to curtail their conceptual power. While they preserve the sense of the human subject who strives for meaning in his or her life, these theories are often disappointingly close to folk conceptions, popular wisdom, and outright cliches. For example, they affirm the importance of aspiration and the necessity of learning who one is. What tends to be lost in these quasi-popular treatments is a critical analysis of the structure of meaning. The destructive influence of reductionism is gone, but little has been provided to take its place.

Clinicians using the interview, therefore, have had problems conceptualizing the meaning of self-esteem. They have tended to employ either reductionistic treatments like those used by experimental psychologists or *anti*reductionistic treatments which are popular or quasi-popular in tone. The former approach is respectably analytic, but loses sight of the coherent sense of self-esteem, while the latter approach is adequately synthetic but fails to investigate the structure of the phenomenon. If the interview is to serve as an effective research tool, something intermediate needs to be supplied. We seem to require another approach to the conceptualization of self-esteem—a nonreductionistic form of analysis designed to deal specifically with the structure of meaning. The particulars of such a method have yet to be specified, but we can assume they will be quite different from what has gone before.

If we wish to study self-esteem as a phenomenon with meaning, these are the kinds of adjustments that are necessary. The reductionistic machinery of experimental science needs to be replaced by a more naturalistic approach. People's accounts of their lives need to be collected, preferably through an intensive interview process. This process must explore the thematic lines that contribute to the significance of the experience of self-esteem, but it must do so in a free-ranging and open-ended manner that makes it possible for the subject to tell his or her own story. Moreover, the material obtained in the interview must be conceptualized in an appropriate way. It must be critically examined as a complex construction, but preserved as an account of a person's life. If the existing literature on self-esteem represents a classic "case study of • a variable" (Wells and Marwell, 1976, p. 250), then an investigation of this kind must take a different perspective more specifically suited to the study of human beings.

The remainder of this book is an attempt at such a project in that it describes a study of self-esteem conducted by the author between 1978 and 1981. The purpose of the investigation was to examine self-esteem as a psychological experience with personal meaning. To accomplish this task, interviews were conducted with a dozen subjects from a variety of backgrounds and social situations. These interviews were almost completely unstructured and covered most of the major events of each subject's life. Nevertheless, at the focus of each interview there remained a particular experience of self-esteem. Such an experience was initially described by each subject and elaborated in the context of the rest of his or her account. This technique made it possible to identify a structure of meaning which seems to underlie the phenomenon of self-esteem. In the following chapters, I will present this structure and examine it in a nonreductionistic framework. Before passing on to the presentation of these findings, however, it will be useful to say something about the procedures that were followed in this investigation.

•The study was conducted as part of a doctoral dissertation and was influenced by the work of the life-history research group at the University of Michigan. Subjects were recruited through informal channels—specifically, through mutual friends and acquaintances of both the subjects and myself. None of them were known to me personally before the interview.

A total of twelve subjects were interviewed. Although details of the subjects' lives are disguised below, some general characteristics of the group can be reported. Subjects ranged in age from twenty-nine to sixty-one and came from a number of different backgrounds. This group was not a "random sample" in any technical sense, but it was selected to include people from a wide • variety of demographic, social, and economic situations. Half of the subjects could be classified as coming from the middle or upper-middle classes; and the other half could be designated as working class or unemployed. Six of the subjects were males and six were females. Two of the subjects were black.[1]

Each subject was interviewed twice, in sessions approximately a week apart. The sessions lasted one-and-a half to two hours apiece, making the total interview time for each subject three to four hours. Interviews were tape-recorded, and generally occurred in the subject's own home.

For every subject the interview began with the same initial question. It was the only predetermined question and constituted the only formal structure in the entire interview. The subject was asked to tell me about a time or incident, occurring at least a year prior to the interview, during which he or she had felt very good about himself or herself. The period of a year was chosen somewhat arbitrarily to increase the likelihood that the remembered incident would be a significant one.

Reactions to this question varied, but most subjects had trouble thinking of an incident at first. When this problem occurred, I assured the subject that most people experienced the same difficulty and that something would probably come to mind. If the subject continued to have difficulty, I began asking questions about his or her life in general. Invariably my questioning brought a specific incident to mind, and in this manner all the subjects were able to recall an experience of self-esteem rather quickly.

Once we had identified a self-esteem experience, I inquired into it

---

[1]As it turned out, interviews with three of the first four subjects were useful only in a heuristic sense: they helped to define the direction of the study, but were insufficiently focused to provide formal case material. (The statement by Jim which is presented above is a composite of material drawn from one of these interivews.) The accounts obtained from the remaining nine subjects are written up below as formal case presentations.

in some detail. I asked the subject about the facts surrounding the incident, the events leading up to it, the people involved in it, the subject's feelings about it, and so forth. Ordinarily, this took between ten and thirty minutes and produced a detailed account of the subject's experience. This account provided a reference point in the subject's life and helped to define the rest of my questions.

After we had a reasonably clear and detailed picture of the subject's incident of self-esteem, I began to turn my questions to other aspects of the subject's life. I inquired into themes and events that seemed to bear some relationship to the original incident and into others that appeared to be more peripheral. Subjects frequently offered material from their early life histories, and I quickly learned that this material could be particularly useful in illuminating an incident of self-esteem. After the first few subjects, I began to inquire after such childhood material if the subject did not provide it spontaneously rather early in the interview. By the end of the first interview, therefore, I typically had both a well-described experience of self-esteem and a fairly large body of life-historical material in which to locate it.

In the second interview, the subject and I continued the broad-based dialogue we had begun the week before. However, there was a certain increment of structure in that I had a number of questions and hypotheses ready in my own mind. I looked for opportunities to put these to the subject, and whenever possible I shared my thoughts. Of course, I also followed up on new themes that seemed to be important. Near the end of the interview, I summarized my understanding of the subject's account and invited his or her comments and corrections. In general, these were minimal. I also asked the subject about his or her reactions to the interview process. This question elicited a number of positive comments, including some that suggested the subjects had experienced the interviews as therapeutic.

Originally, I had planned to present subjects with partial or complete versions of my write-ups of their cases so I could include their reactions in the final report of the study. During the course of the investigation, however, I decided not to do so. There were several reasons for this change. The most important of these was my realization, during the early stages of the analysis, that I was having trouble formulating some cases because I was concerned about hurting subjects' feelings. For a while I considered giving subjects edited versions of my analyses, but I soon concluded that this solution was unsatisfactory. Not only did such a plan seem unfair to the subjects, it also raised questions about the meaningfulness of the feedback since important parts of the analyses would remain unknown to the subjects. The comments of some previous investigators (e.g. Rubin, 1976) also gave me cause for hesitation. These reports suggested that subjects often find it painful to read over their own cases, and that they tend to respond to such write ups with a superficial agreement aimed more at distancing themselves from the material than at evaluating it. For all of these reasons, and a variety of practical considerations as well, I decided not to solicit feedback.

Anyone who has worked with transcribed material is familiar with the problems posed by the sheer mass of the data. The twelve interviews in the present study produced over a thousand pages of transcripts that had to be intensively analyzed. In reality, the analysis of interview material does not begin at any formal or specific point. My guesses and hypotheses during the interviews were an early stage in the analytic process, as was my original conceptualization of the study. There was, however, a particularly intensive analytic phase during the months following the completion of the interviewing. At that time I read very carefully through the transcripts and began to organize the material in certain important ways. One of these ways was to write up each subject as a separate case study. In doing this basic work I discovered a great deal of coherence in the material which had formerly eluded me. Simultaneously, I began comparing and contrasting the cases along every dimension that looked potentially significant; and this approach revealed a number of suggestive patterns and regularities. I found that these two processes—studying specific cases and theorizing across cases—supplemented each other in a very powerful way.

It has already been noted that meaning is irreducible and that it therefore requires special conceptual tools. Previous writers on self-esteem have given little recognition to this fact, and have generally tried to understand the phenomenon through the analytic mode of causal reduction. I was aware of this problem when I began work on the theoretical portions of the present study. Fortunately, I was also aware of recent work in the fields of linguistics and philosophy that appears to offer a nonreductionistic approach to conceptualizing meaning in human life. This approach views constellations of meaning as *systems of signification* or *languages*. By studying the rules of these systems or languages it is possible to examine their underlying structure in a careful and focused manner that nevertheless preserves their natural coherence. I have therefore discussed the material below as systems of linguistic and semiotic signifiers defined in the context of each account by the subject's verbal and nonverbal behavior. At this point I will not go into the details of this approach since it is formally introduced in the following chapter. Instead, I will conclude the present chapter with a brief overview of the rest of the book.

Chapter 2 will identify a general pattern of meaning which is evident in the accounts of all the subjects. This pattern will be illustrated by an initial case study (Esther) and then discussed in more theoretical terms. Accounts of two more subjects (Ed and Paul) will also be used to illustrate specific aspects of this pattern.

The third chapter will deal with psychological conflict and how the resolution of such conflict relates to the experience of self-esteem. Two modes of conflict resolution will be discussed: symbolic resolution, corresponding to defensive self-esteem, and genuine resolution, correspondong to nondefensive self-esteem. Two subjects' account (Denny and John) will be used to illustrate the former outcome, and a third (Anna) will be used as an example of the latter.

In the fourth chapter the pattern introduced in chapter 2 will be examined in a more critical light. The constructs of that chapter will be pushed to their limits by an examination of three cases in which the constructs appear to be minimal (Charlotte, Lou, and Ruth). This examination will provide specific material for comments about the nature of language and the alteration of meaning in processes such as psychotherapy.

The fifth and final chapter will serve as an overview and conclusion by using material from the previous chapters to discuss the nature and construction of the self. Particular attention will be paid to the interactional relationship between self and other. The perspective of Mead's symbolic interactionism will be used to critique some current concepts in the self-esteem literature and will provide the basis for some final comments about the organization and meaning of self-esteem.

TWO _____

The Dimensions
of Self-Esteem

In THIS CHAPTER, we will begin our consideration of actual
case material by reviewing the accounts of three subjects—Esther,
Ed, and Paul. Each of these subjects describes a different experience
of self-esteem, and their accounts together will serve to introduce
the phenomenon and to illustrate something of the variety of forms
it can take.

When we examine these accounts more closely, however, we will
discover certain commonalities in the structure of their meaning.
Although each account is based on a different incident of self-
esteem, each one displays a similar pattern of life-historical and
conceptual elements. In tracing the specifics of this pattern, we will
begin to obtain a general picture of self-esteem—a sense of what
the experience is like, how it functions in people's lives, and why it
seems to be especially meaningful.

Accordingly, we will consider elements of a theory in this chapter;
but we will not do so at the outset. Instead, we will begin by
examining one subject's account in full. Esther describes an
experience of self-esteem and a life-historical context in which this
experience is embedded. Her case will serve as an initial example
and will provide us with material for further discussion. After
examining Esther's case in some detail, we will consider three basic
constructs that will be used in this study—ideology, idealization,
and the central conflict. These constructs will be formally defined

and illustrated with material from Esther's account, and this, in turn, will lead to some initial comments about the nature of self-esteem and its structure of meaning. We will then consider the cases of Ed and Paul, which will serve to illustrate the first two constructs—ideology and idealization—in detail. The third construct—the central conflict—will be discussed in the following chapter.

We begin, therefore, with the case of Esther. Esther describes feeling good about herself during an especially gratifying period of her professional life. We can assume that such an experience would be positive for anybody; but as we explore the details of Esther's past we will uncover a context of personal history that gives her experience of self-esteem a unique and very specific meaning. In more general terms, too, the experience which Esther describes
• seems to be an important one because it represents the resolution of a major and recurring conflict in her life. We will see this pattern in the other cases of this study, and we will consider it further as we go along. For the present, however, let us turn to Esther's account as she herself presents it, without analysis or theory.

ESTHER: A SENSE OF COMMUNITY

Esther is a sixty-one-year-old white mother of three who works as an administrative assistant in a small liberal arts college in the western United States. Unlike many of the other subjects, Esther had no difficulty when asked at the beginning of the interview to describe a time when she had felt good about herself. She quickly recalled a period ten years earlier when she had worked as a secretary in the history department of the college. Esther initially described this period in terms of the affection she had experienced there:

> I worked for the historians, and that period I felt very good about myself. They showered me with gifts and I was really part of the department... I guess the affection that I got from the historians was a thing that made me feel very good.

The sense of affection that Esther describes extended beyond the work setting. She and her husband were included in social gatherings and regarded as peers by the historians:

There was not a member of the department—fifteen members—who did not invite me and my husband to dinner, to parties, to picnics, to all kinds of social events. I felt like part of a big family.

The history department was like a family to Esther in other ways as well. Esther and her husband spent holidays with the chairman of the department and his wife, and the children of the two couples became friends with each other. Moreover: "[Another] colleague used to love to come to dinner because he didn't have any children and he loved my kids."

On another occasion, when the chairman was going through a difficult period prior to a divorce,

[He] asked me if he could have a key to our house. [He said] that he was having difficulty sleeping and that he would feel more comfortable if he came and slept in our guest room when he was that uneasy. And I guess I was surprised at the lack of class distinction. And I guess I also interpreted it that he felt comfortable with me and that he looked upon me as a friend. It was the beginning of a long-term friendship.

Another manifestation of the familial atmosphere of the history department was the maternal role that Esther took on toward the students: "I was really close to that crop of graduate students for those four years. I keep in touch still with many of them.... One in particular teaches in New York. I spent time with him every time I went back to visit my children." Esther's involvement with students has continued in her present job, where her boss sometimes calls her "the mother of the college." She has mixed feelings about this title because, "I feel I have a dimension other than motherhood"; but Esther clearly prizes her special relationship with the students. During one of our interviews, we were interrupted by a long-distance call from a former student, and Esther and her husband identified him to me as one of their "children," a member of their "expanded family."

The familial atmosphere of the history department was very different from that of previous jobs Esther had worked. For example, she recalls a government job she had had years earlier: "[It] was a disaster. You sat in a loft, one desk after another as far as your eye could see—like a mile. And the supervisor walked down the aisles and looked at your wastebacket to see... how many blanks you wasted.... It was awful." More recently, she had worked in an engineering firm where "they were really only interested in what I could produce, but not in me as a person at all." The job with the history department, however, was different. Esther recalled in the interview how it had looked to her when she first applied. She and her husband were new in town and she was looking for a job:

> I was offered several and decided that I wanted to work for the historians because that office wasn't one where desks were lined up.... It looked like they were going to treat you as an individual, not as part of a machine.

To Esther, being treated as an individual means having one's potential recognized and being allowed to develop it. Her job in the history department was such an opportunity. She was able to accomplish a number of things no one else had been able to do, everything from getting the office painted to establishing an employment service for students. In addition, she experienced herself in new ways and began to see herself as someone with abilities she had previously not recognized:

> There were talents I had never explored in myself, for instance supervisory abilities. Writing ability. You know, the idea of not having to turn to the chairman for every letter that went out, but being able to write memoranda independently, to deal with the Dean's office independently.

Esther's growth in these new areas seems to have been closely related to the acceptance and encouragement she experienced in the history department:

> I think it's easier to prove youself when you're given encouragement to do so.... Being embraced as a member of the department really helped me to grow and to use whatever creativity I had in getting things that they wanted to see done.

In sum, Esther was able to develop a new set of abilities and a new perspective on herself in the context of the encouragement and support provided by the history department. This atmosphere of acceptance was very important to Esther. At several points in the interview she described the depreciatory attitudes toward secretaries she had encountered in other work settings, and complained about the lack of respect which people in lower-status jobs often experience. In contrast to these traditional attitudes, Esther elaborated a more egalitarian philosophy:

> You know, there's a whole different way to look at work, and that is...that human effort is something to be appreciated for its own sake, and when you clean the floors, [or] collect garbage, or when you work as a professor teaching, the human effort involved is the thing to be appreciated.

In connection with this, Esther described her "ideal" society:

> I don't think it's one that I can put a label on, but it's one in which human effort, no matter what kind, is valued, in which teamwork is an important thing. I strive for that in our working situation.

This idea is not new to Esther. During her youth she was passionately interested in politics and labor relations. She read widely and was influenced by a number of social theorists, including Henry George, Thorstein Veblin, and George Bernard Shaw. During the interviews, we discussed Esther's political interests and she articulated what she called a "social philosophy" based on community responsibility and respect for people in all social situations. Esther also talked about her attempts to apply this philosophy in her past and present work situations. For example, she has tried to "develop a sense of community" on her current job by getting to know the housekeeping staff on a personal basis. She has also tried to make the college a "nurturing" place in which clerical and other workers will have opportunities to develop their own special talents and abilities.

In attempting to understand the meaning of these ideals—and, indeed, the significance of Esther's experience of self-esteem—it is important to consider the larger context of Esther's life history. Esther was born and raised in an ethnically mixed suburb of New York City. Her parents were Jewish immigrants who had come separately from Eastern Europe in the early years of the century. After meeting through a common acquaintance, they had married and established a neighborhood grocery store in an area populated by first-generation Polish, Irish, and Italian immigrants. In this setting, Esther grew up along with an older and a younger sister.

Esther has many happy memories of childhood and of the people she knew in her neighborhood. Of greatest importance, however, was family life. One of Esther's most vivid childhood memories, for example, is the sight of her aunt's living room decorated for Passover seder with the smell of delicious food cooking in the kitchen. Jews were a minority in the neighborhood, and Esther's parents conveyed a strong sense of the importance of maintaining the family as a bastion of religious orthodoxy and identity:

> We were bound to family. The Rabbi was important. I went to Hebrew school every day. But we were really *held* to family. The fear was that you'd be contaminated if you broke out since your whole social life revolved around the family.

Esther's memories of her father are affectionate ones, and she describes a special relationship with him. She was her father's favorite child, "the fair-haired one," cheifly because they both shared a "sunny disposition." She remembers her father as a kind and generous man whose basic humanity was manifested more in practice than in theory: "He came from an orthodox Jewish background, and anybody who wasn't Jewish was bad.... And Yet, on a one-to-one basis he lived beautifully with them and he dealt with them in a really humane way." One of the ways Esther's father showed this humane side was on family outings. Every Tuesday afternoon he would close up the store and take his children to a local attraction or cultural event. Esther recalls that he would always put a soda box in the back seat of the car and take along a neighborhood child whose family did not have a car.

These outings reflected a larger value system in Esther's family that emphasized the importance of education. Esther recalls that her parents had "a real lust to see their children educated. It was *the* big thing in their lives, education was valued above all else." Her father, in particular, set an example in his own life:

> He never went to school. He went to the Educational Alliance on the lower East Side of New York City—night school—and learned how to read and write, but he never attended formal school.... My father read a newspaper in Yiddish and an English newspaper every day of his life, and he wouldn't let things like the New York Daily Mirror or the New York News in the house. The only newspaper we were allowed to read was the local newspaper and the Sunday New York Times. So he had—he had standards.

In connection with this, Esther recalls her father's political interests. The local newspaper was a socialist publication, and

Esther remembers her father reading it and talking about politics and the problems of labor. Some of her earliest memories are of "endless conversations" in which her father and a neighbor would discuss what American workers would have to do to improve their lot. Esther traces the origin of her political interests to these times and to her own conversations with her father about these issues. Although Esther came to connect socialist ideas with humanistic values and respect for all people, she realized that her father did not do so—at least not explicitly. His political views were "always on a cosmic basis," and he did not seem to want to extend them to all spheres. For example, he would criticize his immigrant neighbors for their illiteracy. Esther fondly remembers trying to "knock some sense" into him during long discussions in which he would criticize other immigrants and Esther would hotly defend their potential: "He would sit and talk politics with me for hours. I would disagree with him and get furious with him—but the fact was that he enjoyed talking about it."

Esther also expresses warm feelings for her mother, whom she characterizes as an optimistic, giving person. At one point in the interview, she described how her mother—who is now eighty-nine years old and living in another state—had been recognized by the mayor of her city and placed in the local Hall of Fame for her work with senior citizens in the area.

> My mom is a loving lady, and she's not only loved by her children, but also by her peers. She's outgoing, she's bighearted and sensitive to people.... She was head of her senior citizens' club and she can say things to them like "I know you all have aches and pains but if there's anything that turns a friendship off it's using a friend to constantly complain. Let's put a moratorium on our pain talk."

Esther describes her mother as an extremely hard-working woman who was taken out of school in the fourth grade to work in a factory. After marrying Esther's father, she worked with him in the store sixteen hours a day and took care of Esther and her sister in her off time. In addition to these burdens, Esther's mother also took care of some of her husband's relatives and an orphaned niece from time to time.

Not only did Esther's mother work long and hard, she also played the dominant role, both in the family business and in the home. If family life was "the hub of everything" in Esther's world, then Esther's mother was the hub of the family:

My mother was the stronger of the two [parents].
Psychologically—not emotionally so much—but she was
psychologically stronger. I think my mother also had an
edge on my father in raw intelligence.

Esther's mother was the decision maker, both at home and in the
store:

Mother was a woman who controlled her household all her
life.... She was really the dominant one in the relationship.
She had the smarts and...generally speaking my father got
along better with people but my mother had the
organizational skills in the business.... She basically made
the decisions and he carried them out.

This arrangement was usually acceptable to both parents. At times,
however, Esther's mother was a "nag" and even an "emasculator."
  During the interviw, Esther reflected on what the reasons might
be for her mother's controlling nature, and she talked about her
mother's family of origin. Esther characterized her maternal
grandfather as a "martinet," a "hard man," and a "disciplinarian"
who ruled a tightly knit family in which there was no room for
disagreement. Even at the present time,

[My mother's family] can drive you crazy because there are
moments when they hate each other and don't have the
guts to tell each other. It's all internalized and they have
ulcers, and they have high blood pressure, and they have all
kinds of stress diseases as a result.

One of Esther's aunts (her mother's oldest sister) had six children,
four of whom had ulcerative colitis. Esther attributes this to the
control which her aunt always maintained, even after suffering a
massive stroke:

From her bed in her hemiplegic state—she couldn't speak so
that outsiders could understand, but her family could
understand, and she controlled that whole family 'til she
died.

This aunt is an important figure in Esther's early memories. Esther
remembers her as a domineering woman who maintained a tight
control over Esther's mother and the other members of the family.
For example, Esther's family was expected to spend all holidays at

the aunt's house, and did so until Esther and her sisters finally rebelled. On the other hand, Esther also described her aunt's talents—particularly as a homemaker—with considerable admiration. The following passage is interesting because in it Esther seems to become aware of this second set of feelings about her aunt:

> (Did you have any positive interactions with her?) Oh, yeah, she was an enormously talented woman. She was a fantastic seamstress... She was the decision maker in the business—my uncle had a scrap-metal business that flourished, and she was the one that told him when to buy and when to sell. And she was a magnificent cook, and had a very good aesthetic sense; her home was beautiful, she had gardens. There wasn't a thing that woman—and she was literate—there wasn't a thing that she couldn't do. (Um-hm. Did you like her?) [Pause] I guess I did. [She sounds somewhat surprised.] I admired her. Hmmm. [Faintly.]

Esther's aunt, then, is the object of very mixed feelings, the center of a network of ambivalently experienced relationships in the family. She orchestrated the holiday celebrations; she was a magnificent cook, seamstress, and homemaker; and she was an intelligent and competent businesswoman. But she was also a domineering person who stifled the family through an oppressive system of emotional control.

If Esther was indirectly controlled by her aunt, however, she was directly controlled by her own powerful mother. And the problems associated with this state of affairs are particularly evident in an incident Esther described from the early years of her marriage.

Shortly after Esther was married, her father died. For a period of time thereafter, Esther's mother and younger sister lived with Esther and her husband. The situation, however, became problematic: having two extra people in the house put pressure on everyone, particularly Esther, who was trying to raise her own small children. In addition, Esther's mother presented special problems:

> Mother could not give up the control. In the midst of my disciplining a child she would say "Don't listen to your mother, she's crazy." She didn't really mean that but [it] would just infuriate me because she was denying me my prerogative as a parent.

Esther decided she could not continue to have her mother and sister stay with her, but she could not bring herself to tell her mother:

> I was afraid of her anger.... She would have been hurt and I would have felt very guilty; and I don't know how well I would have lived with that guilt....
> (Had it been hard for you to assert yourself with your mother before?) Yes. [Very quickly.] It's less difficult now, but I had a very, very hard time. That's probably been the biggest struggle of my life. (Mm. Even as you were growing up.) Yeah...I now know that no matter what children say a mother doesn't reject a child. But I didn't know it then, and I was just terribly, terribly afraid. (That she would reject you?) Yeah. (Why do you think you were so afraid of that?) [Pause.] It has to do with the whole family gestalt. They're so closely knit a family—not only my mother but her sisters and brothers.

Let us pause now and consider the themes which have emerged in Esther's life-historical account. One of the most salient of these themes is the importance of the family. In Esther's account of her childhood, family life is the source not only of affection and security, but also of religious, social, and cultural identity. The family stands above all other influences, determining the shapes and limits of personal life: "We were bound to family.... We were really *held* to family. The fear was that you'd be contaminated if you broke out since your whole social life revolved around the family."

Esther makes it clear that this was a gratifying experience and that she felt loved and protected in the confines of her family. But in describing these confines she presents a second life-historical theme, a dissonant one which begins to define a major dilemma in her life: the very closeness which made family life so satisfying and so secure also lent itself to a kind of oppressive control. In Esther's account this dissonance is personified in descriptions of her mother and aunt, strong and nurturant women who orchestrated the life of the family, but who did so in ways that seemed to disregard the needs and prerogatives of other family members.

This conflict is particularly clear in Esther's description of her adolescence. She describes herself during this period as a "slow bloomer." She had weight problems and was embarrassed about her body. She became sensitive, shy, and isolative, and she spent much of her time alone, walking in the woods or reading. When she was with her mother, however, Esther felt exposed to excessive attention and concern:

My mother would call her sister ritualistically every single day on the telephone, and she told my aunt everything about the three of us. I used to say to my mother hostilely "are you going to tell her how many times I went to the bathroom today?" There was a kind of indecency about it, you know? If I told my aunt about myself it was one thing, but if my mother did it it was like denying me my privacy as an individual.

Such problems were not limited to Esther's relationships with her mother and aunt. In the following passage, Esther describes the dilemma that she and her sisters experienced in their father's inordinate concern for them:

If anything we were too well loved. (What do you mean?) Oh, you know, Friday afternoons ritualistically we went to the public library and we were within easy walking distance. And my two sisters and I would start towards the library and my father would come with the car and pick us up and take us there. And we really, really resented it. We'd say "we wanted to walk, it's a beautiful day.... The trees are beautiful.... Why do you have to do this all the time?" And he thought he was being good to us. (What did you resent about it?) That we weren't allowed to do it on our own.

Esther's parents, therefore, seemed to ignore her needs as an individual. Even in the face of her active protests, they maintained a kind of insistent control, invading and interfering with the smallest of her activities. It is important to keep in mind that this controlling behavior stemmed not from a selfishness or lack of concern by Esther's parents, but rather from an *over*concern. This is the core of Esther's dilemma. She might complain about her parents' excessive attention, but she could not rebuff it or refuse it altogether. Such an act would have been interpreted by her parents as rejection, and would have entailed the risk of Esther's being rejected herself. This conflict was particularly true of Esther's relationship with her mother. Esther's mother "could not give up the control," and she dominated her daughter with an affection that Esther both appreciated and resented. Because it was her mother's love itself that was intruding into Esther's life, Esther was trapped in a double bind. She could neither accept nor reject her mother's controlling behavior, and she was "terribly, terribly afraid" that any attempt to set limits on it would lead to hurt, anger, and mutual abandonment. Esther describes this dilemma as "the biggest struggle of my life";

but more than this, her dilemma seems to be the prototype of a more general conflict between closeness and individuality which appears in her account in a variety of different modes and contexts. At several points during the interview, for example, Esther talked about the struggle she has gone through in her own role as a mother to find a proper balance between parental guidance and respect for her children's wishes. At other points she discussed her obligations to her husband and how they had conflicted with her attempts to achieve independence. More relevant to the present discussion, however, are the ideas that Esther developed about human relations in the workplace, for these ideas define her role in the history department and suggest the underlying meaning of her experience of self-esteem.

We have already noted Esther's special interest in socialist politics and the problems of labor. This interest began in conversations with her father and increased as she grew up during the Deppression and did her own reading and thinking about the subject. We can assume that Esther was excited and inspired by the political events which were unfolding around her; but it is also clear that she was developing her own ideas about human nature and social relations. Socialist philosophy was, for Esther, an expression of respect for all people and for their potential to improve themselves given the opportunity to do so. It defined a way in which people could work together in a cooperative spirit while maintaining a sense of individual dignity. If we consider this social and political ideology in the context of Esther's early history, we can see that it has a very important underlying significance: *Esther's ideology is organized along the same axis that defined the conflict in her own family—the wish to promote collective life while preserving the dignity of the individual.*

The extent to which Esther has defined labor and family issues in the same terms was illustrated at several points throughout the interview. For example, at one point she discussed the need to recognize individuality in one's children and one's co-workers:

I think that the family that really works well is the family where the parents recognize that each member of that family is an individual with separate kinds of talents [and] different kinds of drives.... You must always recognize that these are individuals who [you] should not be dominating. Dominating and nurturing are two different things.... And I feel that way about my co-workers at work, most of whom are younger than I am. And it does work. (Being nurturing instead of dominating?) Yeah.... If you recognize where everybody is at, what their ambitions in life are, you get to know them.... That doesn't mean that you invade their daily lives [but]... they [need to] get the feeling that you're helping them to build their skills so that they can help themselves. And the inevitability, you know, is that they're going to leave you. You have to face that too.... (Just like your children.) Yeah.

It would be impossible to understand the meaning of Esther's experience in the history department without understanding the close relationship that exists for her between relations at work and relations in the family. For Esther, the experience in the history department was, in some sense, a resolution of a salient and recurring conflict in her life. It was a compromise in which she was able to participate in a close and supportive community which resembled the nurturant family of her childhood but which respected her individuality and encouraged her to develop her own potential. This experience appears to have promoted Esther's self-esteem in two different ways or modes.

In an abstract mode, Esther's experience in the history department involved a putting into action of her ideals about work and human dignity. The history department was for Esther a humane working "community," one where low-status as well as high-status work was valued, where it was possible to be treated "as an individual, not as part of a machine." Esther herself made an important contribution to this community and helped to demonstrate that such a setting could be effective in promoting not only the goals of the job but also the dignity of her fellow workers and herself. This *abstract* meaning, however, would have been hollow and intellectualized were it not for the more personal, *life-historical* meaning which the experience had for her. In this more personal mode, Esther's experience in the history department represented the resolution of her own specific needs and aspirations. She was able to play a nurturing and maternal role toward other members of the department, just as her mother had once done in the family; but she also experienced a sense of mutuality and equality, and she was able to develop her own talents and abilities just as her father had once developed his own potential by educating himself. In this sense, Esther was able to reconcile the values she had seen demonstrated by her mother and her father and to put these values into action in an important sphere of her life.

Before passing from this case, however, it is worthwhile to consider an additional issue: To what extent does Esther's experience in the history department represent a *genuine* resolution of this conflict?

We might wonder, for example, whether Esther's solution is as successful as she presents it. Esther claims that "dominating and nurturing are two different things," and that she strives to promote the latter at work, but not the former. But there is a certain sense in which nurturant behavior has dominance built into it. It would be surprising if Esther—the "mother of the college"—did not wield some power through the granting or withholding of her approval. Moreover, there is a peculiar way in which nurturant behavior can lock the recipient into an unwelcomed position of compliance. Suppose, for example, that one of Esther's underlings did not wish to improve her skills, but only wanted to earn her pay and go home. Such a person might find herself in the same kind of double bind with repsect to Esther that Esther experienced in relation to her mother. This consideration is more than idle speculation, for it suggests that Esther's experience in the history department might be less a case of resolving a childhood conflict than of reenacting it, with herself in the parental role.

Similarly, there are reasons to question the accuracy of Esther's conception of the amount of power she wields. For example, at one point in the interview she talked about new faculty members in the college and their concerns about power:

> I have a lot to do with the faculty at the college and the new ones are extremely insecure until they find out what the structure of the college is and where the quote power lies, you know? (Um–hm.) [Pause] I laugh—I smile when I tell you that 'cause that's all illusion, you know. There is no power. But they think there is.

A few minutes later she described how she had been promoted to her present job as administrative assistant. She had originally been recommended for promotion, but due to the president's carelessness in following through on his recommendation, the promotion was denied to her by the board of directors. When she found out, she was furious and quit her job on the spot:

> I was never so angry on my job as I was then...because Lloyd [the president] was so peripatetic that *I* was actually running that college, and everybody around me knew that including the faculty.

Eventually the situation was resolved and Esther was given the promotion.

This incident leaves little doubt that Esther wields very real power on her present job. She herself tends to play it down, however, at least in ordinary circumstances, and to regard power relations in the college as an "illusion." While Esther's characterization may accurately portray her perception of the situation, there are reasons for believing that her perception itself may be inaccurate when it come to issues of power and dominance.

These considerations do not necessarily invalidate what Esther has told us about her experience in the history department. They do, however, suggest that we must regard such reports with caution, especially when we attempt to interpret the overall significance of a reported incident of self-esteem. Caution will be particularly important when we address the question of "real" versus "defensive" self-esteem. We shall return again to this issue below.

THE STRUCTURE OF SELF-ESTEEM: CONCEPTUAL TOOLS

Now that we have examined Esther's account, let us take a step back and view it from a more general perspective. We have considered a specific example of self-esteem and a network of verbal themes surrounding it. If we examine Esther's experience in the history department in the context of the rest of her account, the experience begins to take on a certain significance—a unique and specific pattern of meaning growing out of her past and present life, and her ways of thinking about herself and the social world. We are now ready to examine the details of this pattern—the particular combination of elements that defines the significance of Esther's self-esteem. At the same time, we will consider Esther's account as an illustration of a *general* pattern of meaning which seems to be present, in one form or another, in all the cases reported below. Esther's account, therefore, will serve both as a specific example and a general type representing the structure of meaning in the experience of self-esteem.

Before initiating this project, however, we need to consider an important question. In the previous chapter, it was noted that meaning is not a psychological "variable." It is not a discrete or measurable thing which exists in cause and effect relations to other elements of a subject's account. Rather, meaning seems to emerge at the level of the whole, in the entire story that a subject tells. But if meaning is not a psychological variable, if it emerges instead at the level of the whole, how can we understand its internal structure in a systematic and detailed way?

As indicated in the previous chapter, this problem has been a significant one, not only in the experimental literature on self-esteem but in the clinical literature as well. Meaning is a subtle and elusive phenomenon which has proven extremely difficult to conceptualize, and if we wish to think about it in a coherent way we need to develop some new ideas. These ideas must constitute an alternative approach to the conceptualization of psychological phenomena. To lay the groundwork for such an approach, let us briefly consider some major characteristics of meaning and what these characteristics suggest for psychological research and theory.

To begin with, meaning, as it occurs in the ordinary course of human life, is enormously *complex*. In Esther's case, for example, the experience in the history department is defined by a multitude of themes which extend, elaborate, and modify each other, and branch off in a variety of different directions. This kind of complexity is associated with the complicated events that collectively define a personal history and with the almost limitless situations and problems that an individual must comprehend in the course of such a history. In order to deal with these situations and problems, the human mind must employ a vast array of signifying elements—that is, images and symbols. Moreover, these signifying elements must be related to each other in ways that represent the individual's experience in something approaching its actual richness. The vast array of images and symbols, therefore, must be connected by an even vaster array of intricate and cross-cutting mental relations. Any aproach to human meaning must give adequate recognition to the complexity of this system. It must be capable of tracing the elements and relations that constitute a life-historical and conceptual field. In short, the approach must be powerfully analytic and function at the finest level of the structure of meaning.

At the same time, however, there is another characteristic of meaning which adds quite a different dimension to this task. As we have already observed a number of times, the field of meaning is also *irreducible*. We saw this in Jim's story in the previous chapter and we can see it again in Esther's account. A story like the one told by Jim or by Esther is a single gestalt of lived experience, and none of the parts that make it up can be meaningfully separated from the rest of the story. Such attempts to reduce meaning to constituent parts have caused endless problems in the psychological literature, and we must be very clear in rejecting these approaches and in preserving a more naturalistic and holistic perspective. In addition to being powerfully analytic, therefore, the investigation of meaning must be uncompromisingly synthetic. It must encompass meaning as it actually occurs in the natural context of psychological life—as an integrated and coherent gestalt of experience described or comprehended by a human subject.

Personal meaning, then, presents a character which is both *complex and irreducible*; and if we wish to investigate it in an adequate manner, we need an approach which is both *analytic and synthetic*. We must examine the intricate themes and relations that constitute the structure of a psychological phenomenon, but only in a way that preserves the irreducible sense and coherence of that phenomenon. Previous conceptions of self-esteem have generally favored one side or the other, analytic or synthetic. Experimental theories have treated the phenomenon in an essentially analytic mode,[1] attempting to reduce it to constituent parts in the hope that its full meaning could be recovered at some later time. Clinical conceptions have tended to be polarized between analytic reductionism and synthetic impressionism. What seems to be required is a more balanced approach, one which reconciles the modes of analysis and synthesis and which is capable of studying meaningful phenomena in a way that is simultaneously focal and comprehensive. What kind of approach might fit these requirements?

If we look beyond the field of psychology, some possibilities begin to present themselves. Sociologists, anthropologists, philosophers, and others have all grapled with the problem of meaning, and a number of them have developed approaches for understanding and discussing meaningful phenomena. These approaches are quite varied and none of them has won general acceptance. However, there is growing agreement across many fields on one important point: meaning seems to be deeply associated with a particular class of uniquely human behaviors—namely, the broad range of representational and communicative behaviors that we know as language.

---

[1]Actually, this statement is something of an oversimplification. The causal reductionism of the experimental approach does entail a synthetic principle—namely, the unifying continuum of space and time as defined by classical and modern physics. All causal theory is subordinated to this principle, which is, however, too sweeping and rudimentary to serve as an organizing framework for human meaning. In the present investigation, a synthetic principle will be provided, not in *physical* space and time, but in the *semantic* space and time defined by the subject's representational and communicative behavior.

It is useful here to define language broadly to include not only speech and writing, but other signifying behaviors as well, including thinking, gesturing, and picturing. Saussure (1916) has pointed out that the signifiers constituted by such activities are generally organized in regular ways to form *systems* or *languages*. According to Saussure, a language is any group of signifiers that define each other by the way they are used in practice. Each signifier is defined by its relationships to all the other signifiers in the system, particularly the ones with which it is most closely associated. For example, the different pieces in a game of chess exist in a set of changing relations. Each one is given meaning by all the other pieces on the board, and any time a particular piece is moved it changes the significance of all the others. Collectively, the pieces constitute a system of signification, a language in which the game of chess is played. Likewise, a group of memories in a life-historical account or a series of gestures in a social interaction can be regarded as a system or language of signification. We can apply this conception to Esther's account by identifying its most important images and concepts and determining how these signifying elements are related to each other in groups or systems. By examining the rules and details of such systems—the particular ways that particular signifiers are related to each other in actual practice—we can trace the specific elements of meaning that contribute to Esther's experience of self-esteem.

The examination of meaning as language-based systems of signification, therefore, seems to be an appropriate analytic tool for this study; as a tool, it gives full recognition to the complexity of human experience and the way in which this experience is systematically organized. But if the examination of language provides an analytic tool for conceptualizing meaning in human life, we need a corresponding synthetic device to accompany and supplement the use of this tool. Such a synthetic device must function to preserve the coherence and unity of meaning while nevertheless permiting the analysis of complex and intricate systems of language. Fortunately, such a device exists in Schafer's (1976) so-called "action" perspective.

Schafer's work is based on philosophical conceptions developed by Wittgenstein (1953) and Ryle (1949). These authors have demonstrated that meaning can be discussed in a comprehensive and consistent way as forms of behavior by an active individual, particularly when such behavior is described in its full social and life-historical context. Schafer extends this conception to encompass a wide range of psychodynamic phenomena like identification, conflict, and defense. The key to Schafer's method is to phrase statements about meaning in ordinary language describing *actions by people*. Thus, language is regarded not as an object or a mechanism, but as an unfolding gestalt of signifying behavior. From the standpoint of this perspective, for example, we would not say that Esther's self-esteem is "influenced" or "determined" by her social philosophy; rather, we would say that Esther *explains* her self-esteem in social and philosophical terms. Likewise, we would not characterize Esther's experience in the history department as a "product" or "derivative" of her early experience; rather, we would say that she *describes* this setting in the same way she describes her family of origin.

Because it is consistently nonreductionistic, Schafer's approach is a useful synthetic tool. It provides the terms in which language can be analyzed without destroying the natural coherence of its meanings. This procedure is possible because language is a form of human action, the signifying behavior in which meanings are expressed. A careful examination of this signifying behavior is an *analysis* in the full sense of the term; but such an analysis is not a *reduction* because it presupposes an active human subject in a social and psychological context. For these reasons, the structure of meaning in Esther's and others' life-historical accounts will be examined as linguistically and semiotically organized systems of signification defined by the subject's representational and communicative behavior. These concepts will be explained in more detail as we go along.[1]

---

[1]It seems appropriate at this point to make some comments about Schafer's "action language." Readers who are familiar with Schafer's work will find occasional deviations from his guidelines in this book. For example, the somewhat static "systems of meaning" is used rather than the more dynamic formulations that Schafer recommends (e.g. "acting systematically and meaningfully"). I have taken this license because I believe that Schafer's principles are best regarded as regulative rather than constitutive. That is, they serve as translation rules to which statements about meaning must be *capable* of yielding, but not as metaphysical truths about what meaning *is* in some thoroughgoing or exclusive way. In this respect, Schafer's system stands to interview research as Minkowski's space-time geometry stands to experimental physics. The interview researcher should be able to phrase theoretical formulations in the terms of action language, but he or she is not *obliged* to do so any more than a physicist must slavishly translate every theoretical formulation into the Minkowskian terminology of "event systems" and "world lines." At the beginning of chapter 5 further comments about Schafer's "action" perspective will be made.

THE STRUCTURE OF SELF-ESTEEM:
BASIC CONCEPTS

It is now time to introduce three constructs which will be
employed in this study. These constructs will be used as tools in
analyzing all the experiences of self-esteem which are reported below.
They will aid us in understanding how self-esteem functions in the
subjects' lives—and more specifically, how it represents the
resolution of a longstanding life-historical dilemma in each subject's
account. The three constructs which will be elaborated in this
section are *ideology, idealization,* and the *central conflict.*

In the pages that follow, these constructs will be defined and
illustrated with material from Esther's case. Some material will also
be drawn from the next two cases—Ed and Paul—in order to
further illustrate the meanings of the constructs. The cases of Ed
and Paul then will be presented in full to further clarify and
exemplify the constructs of ideology and idealization, respectively.
The third construct—that of the central conflict—will be treated in
more detail in the next chapter.

Before defining these constructs formally, some general points
need to be made. The first of these points is an epistemological one.
The constructs of ideology, idealization, and the central conflict are
not presented here as the only ones that could be usefully applied in
the study of self-esteem. It would be possible to generate a number
of such categories for a variety of different purposes. Indeed, the
psychological literature abounds with such categories. The three
constructs which are described below, however, have been chosen
because they are particularly useful for the major goal of the
present study—that of understanding self-esteem as an experience
with personal meaning. More specifically, each of these three
constructs can be said to designate a language-based system of
signification which represents and expresses meaning in a social and
life-historical field. Using the general formulation of Saussure
(1916), each can be understood as a collection of signifying elements
which define each other by their use in practice. As will be clarified
below, for example, ideology is a system of concepts defining each
other in the subject's discourse, and idealization is a system of
remembered images giving each other significance in the subject's
recollection. Each construct, therefore, maps out a region of
meaning in the subject's life—a region that can be analyzed as a

system of signifiers but which is also a coherent gestalt defined by the subject's expressive activity.

An additional point needs to be made concerning the question of universality. There is no guarantee that the three constructs which are discussed in this section could be meaningfully applied to every possible account of an experience of self-esteem. The phenomena designated by these constructs do seem to be present in some form in all the accounts collected in this study, but as we shall see, the constructs do not appear to be equally salient in every case. Later in this chapter, we will examine two cases in which certain of these constructs are highlighted; and in chapter 4 we will consider the opposite phenomenon—cases in which specific constructs seem to be minimally important. Let us begin, however, by defining the constructs and illustrating them in relation to Esther's account.

Ideology

An experience of self-esteem like the one described by Esther is often not as simple to understand as it first appears to be, because socially meaningful situations are rich and multifaceted and require interpretation. We need, therefore, to look not only at the "objective" features of a situation in which self-esteem is reported, • but at the "subjective" ones as well: the set of ideas which the subject has about the situation and his or her own role in it.

In Esther's case, the experience in the history department was not just a matter of being in a friendly, gratifying setting. What seems to have made this experience an instance of *self*-esteem for Esther is the fact that she occupied a central role in the history department, a role that was important in making the department a certain kind of place: a humane and familial working community. Esther has definite ideas about what is necessary to create and maintain such a • community and about the part someone like herself can play in the effort. A set of ideas such as this one can be called an *ideology*.

The term "ideology" is not intended here to designate political or philosophical ideas per se (although such ideas may be important in individual cases). Instead, the term has been chosen because it indicates a set of ideals and beliefs, with two specific additional connotations: systematic organization and social practice. The concepts which make up an ideology are organized into a coherent structure or system of meaning; and the individual who holds the ideology uses it to understand the social world and his or her possible social roles. Ideology is thus a set of principles that implicitly or explicitly guides an individual's expectations, plans, and actions in the social sphere.

Let us now give a formal definition of the term ideology as it will be used in this study: *An ideology is a set of general conceptions that an individual has about the social world and his or her place in it. This set of conceptions includes two overlapping components: (1) a system of beliefs about what the world is like, which includes, implicitly or explicitly, a theory of human nature; (2) a system of ideals—that is, a system of ideas about how things should be, which includes, implicitly or explicitly, a theory about what one can do to bring this about.*

The two "components" of ideology—the beliefs about the social world and the ideals that guide one—are separated here only for purposes of analysis. In actual ideology, the two always accompany and codefine each other. Thus, one's ideals concern the aspects of the world that one attends to and forms beliefs about; and a set of beliefs implicitly includes one's conceptions of the kinds of improvements that are possible and how they might be attained. The fact that these two aspects of ideology are interrelated reflects the two points which were made above: meanings are inherently complex in nature and are situated in the context of an irreducible field.

Esther's ideology demonstrates these characteristics. During the course of the interview, Esther expressed a number of beliefs about human nature and the social world. She talked about how people in lower-status occupations are not treated with respect and how this lack of respect interferes with their strivings to learn new skills and abilities. In addition, she discussed how things could be changed to reflect a more ideal situation—primarily by treating people in a way that is nurturing but not dominating, and encouraging them to increase their skills and become more creative individuals. It is clear that Esther's ideals and beliefs are organized into a comprehensible structure, a vision of how the world should be and what she can do to bring this about. Esther talked about this structure as her "social philosophy" and explained how she attempts to actualize this philosophy by creating a "sense of community"—a close and familial atmosphere that will nurture and encourage people without dominating them. It was in reference to this meaningful structure, this ideology, that Esther explained why her experience in the history department had made her feel good about herself.

In all of the cases reported below we will see ideologies operating to a greater or lesser degree. In general, a subject's reported experience of self-esteem is initially rendered meaningful in terms of an ideology of some kind. Ideology can therefore be considered a kind of first layer of meaning, one that is usually accessible to the subject as an explanation of why he or she felt good about himself or herself.

Later in this chapter we will see different examples of ideology. Although these ideologies will be very different from Esther's, we will see that they show the same basic structure of organized belief about the social world and about what one can do to make things better. In Ed's case we will see an ideology oriented around the theme of success in business. In explaining the meaning of his experience of self-esteem, Ed articulates a theory of social life and human nature that is organized around the concepts of success and respect. Being successful in business gains one the respect of the community, and this respect will be concretely measureable in terms of one's income. The way in which this success is achieved is through "playing by the rules"—professional conduct in business which earns one the reputation that brings repsect in the community and financial reward. Ed understands his experience of self-esteem as a specific application and confirmation of these principles which, for Ed, characterize life in society and what one can do to establish oneself in it.

A very different ideology will be uncovered in Paul's case. Paul says far less about society in an overt way; but in articulating the meaning of important relationships in his life, he too outlines a system of beliefs about the social world and normative rules consistent with these beliefs. For Paul, the world is a precarious place in which the resources necessary for emotional and physical survival are limited and unreliable. The only people who can get along in this situation are those who are "businesslike," who adopt clear regimens and consistent schedules. By associating oneself with people like this and exercising one's own self-discipline, one can obtain a measure of security and sustenance. The incident of self-esteem that Paul reports is an illustration of a successful application of this strategy, the return to a regimen that Paul had nearly given up on, and the achievement of a goal that had seemed impossible.

The concept of ideology which is used in this study is not without precedent in the psychological literature. Other researchers have discussed self-esteem as a function of the individual's system of ideals and beliefs. The current conception, however, differs from those of other investigators primarily in regarding ideology as a system of concepts that are *linguistically organized by an active human subject.* Some researchers have adopted this perspective in part, but the constructs they have used have generally been problematic due to the fact that, in varying degrees, these researchers have continued to adhere to the tenets of causal reductionism. That is, these investigators have attempted to *reduce* ideology to a set of determinant or predictive factors.

For example, Freud (1921, 1923, 1924), in his theoretical formulations about the structure and function of the superego, recognizes the phenomenon of ideology and its close relationship to self-esteem. According to Freud, the superego is a peculiarly ideological mechanism developed to guide the individual's behavior in the social world. The development of the superego begins early in life when the child "introjects" his or her parents by representing them intrapsychically for defensive purposes. These parental introjects become the nucleus of a system of internal representations which eventually grows to include teachers, authorities, and other models, and which is ultimately refined into an abstract code of ideals and beliefs. The individual experiences self-esteem to the extent that the conscience—the self-observing component of the superego—evaluates the individual's actions as conforming to this internal code of ideals and beliefs.

This quasi-reductionistic account has a certain degree of explanatory force, but it leaves a number of questions unanswered. For example, it is not clear how the superego determines whether the individual is conforming to its ideals and beliefs, nor by what mechanisms self-esteem follows from this determination, nor how the superego processes feedback to modify its ideals and beliefs in accordance with the individual's experience. Psychoanalytic theorists who have attempted to answer such questions have run into great difficulties, both of a technical and conceptual nature (for example, see Schafer, 1968). Problems like these are unavoidable because they are generated by the reductionistic logic of the theory in question. The study of ideology, therefore, tends to be deflected into a variety of side issues, obscuring and confusing the investigaton of meaning.

Other theorists who have discussed ideology have run into similar conceptual problems. For example, Skinner (1957) maintains that meaning resides in the independent variables that act as controlling stimuli for verbal behavior. According to Skinner, the rewards and punishments that accompany these stimuli during the process of development gradually shape the child's verbalizations into meaningful patterns of attitude and belief. Videbeck (1960) has applied this perspective to the phenomenon of self-esteem, suggesting that the self-concept be viewed as "an organization of discrete self-ratings which are unitized by the principle of stimulus generalization" (p. 359). But conceptions like these are far from adequate. As Chomsky (1959) has pointed out, meaningful phenomena like the conceptualization of self and world can be fit into the mold of learning theory only by doing considerable violence both to the meaning of the phenomena under investigation and to the terms of learning theory itself. In characterizations like the one above, constructs like "stimulus control" and "generalization" must be stretched to cover so wide a variety of linguistic and semantic phenomena that they become essentially meaningless. Moreover, the claim that language is systematically shaped by positive and negative reinforcement is contradicted by a variety of empirical evidence (for example, see Chomsky, 1959).

Probably the most sophisticated attempts to explain conceptual structures like ideology in technical terms have been made by cognitive psychologists and other researchers using computer models. For example, one line of research has treated meaning in terms of semantic networks of interrelated verbal elements (e.g. Quillian, 1969). This model is similar to the present characterization of ideology as a linguistically organized system of signifiers, but with one very important difference: the computer approach is aimed not at the discovery and exploration of new patterns of meaning, but at the systematic *reduction*, through cybernetic analysis, of familiar patterns of meaning to their underlying cognitive and neural mechanisms. This is an entirely different kind of task, and one that involves enormous complications. So great are these complications, in fact, that they currently appear to be insurmountable, except for the very simplest kinds of meaning.[1]

Yet none of these problems needs to concern us if we are willing to adopt a different perspective. By abandoning the tenets of causal

---

[1]To give one example, Norman and Rumelhart (1975) have developed a computer model which simulates the structure of meaning involved in the performance of some routine tasks in the kitchen (e.g. making a sandwich). The authors report that the data base required to represent this information is very large, consisting of over 5,000 nodes (or signifying elements) and over 21,000 links (or semantic relations) among these nodes. Even with this degree of complexity, however, the system is unable to make some very elementary distinctions—for example, the difference between a piece and a whole loaf of bread.

reductionism and focusing instead on linguistic usage we can study the structure of meaning directly. The present conception of ideology is particularly useful for such a project because of its affinity with ordinary language. Ideology is defined in terms that presuppose the signifying activity of the human subject in a social and life-historical context. This conception eliminates the need to reduce ideology to abstract terms and anonymous mechanisms. Instead, we can allow the elements of ideology to define each other in the context of their use by the subject. In Esther's case, for example, an ideology is defined by the general, socially relevant concepts that Esther uses—"nurturing," "individuality," "potential," and so forth—and by the particular way in which she relates these concepts to each other in the above account. For this reason, ideology can be regarded as a *linguistically organized structure* of the kind analyzed by Saussure (1916). By the same token it is an "open" construct, defined by the subject's creative activity and designating as many potential manifestations as there are individuals who construct ideologies.

Idealization

Esther's ideology is not an isolated cluster of ideas detached from personal experience. On the contrary, her account of her life suggests that she has shaped her ideology very much on the basis of personal events. This is particularly true with regard to the experiences Esther describes in her family of origin. Esther recounts a pattern of interactions and relationships that provide the experiential foundation for the ideals and beliefs which now constitute her ideology. Chief among these interactions are those which involve the *idealization* of important figures, especially her mother, her father, and her aunt.

Of course, there were also points in the interview when Esther expressed negative memories and feelings about these people. She emphasized that she was not happy with some of the things they had done and that she has tried to learn from their mistakes in forming her own ideology. But what is more important here is the fact that, whatever their faults, Esther remembers these people as admired figures who served as living examples of certain important ideals in action, namely, treating people in a nurturing way and respecting their potential for self-improvement.

In accordance with these thoughts, we can define idealization as follows: *An idealization is a memory or description in which an important figure in a person's life history serves as an exemplar of some particular ideal in action.*

him about the business world and how to succeed in it, and she herself demonstrates success that Ed can only describe as "rather amazing." In exploring the details of Ed's account, however, we will see another theme based on Ed's latent idealization of his father— the ideal of remaining an individual and "bucking the system," an ideal that Ed believes to be specifically illustrated in his father's words and actions.

In Paul's case, we will see another pattern of idealization in a life-historical account. Paul idealizes only one parent, his father. But the themes that define Paul's ideals—firmness, exacting demands, discipline—are described in interactions with a series of important figures outside the family as well. In Paul's account, therefore, idealization takes on a new importance; moreover, the descriptions of idealized figures in this case seem to serve some of the same functions which ideology serves in other cases. Not surprisingly, this pattern appears to have implications for Paul's self-esteem as a general phenomenon.

Just as ideology is not without precedent in the psychological literature, so idealization has been recognized, implicitly if not explicitly, by other writers on self-esteem. Once again, however, previous analyses have been problematic due to reductionistic assumptions.

For example, experimental psychologists have acknowledged the importance of idealization in the so-called "self-ideal discrepancy" (e.g. Rogers and Dymond, 1954). In studies employing this construct, self-esteem is theoretically conceived as the degree of similarity between the subject's "real self" and "ideal self." In order to measure this relationship, subjects are required to rate themselves on a variety of characteristics and then to rate an "ideal self" on the same characteristics. The degree of correspondence between the first and second rating is taken as a measurement of the subject's self-esteem. Since this technique requires that the subject imagine an ideal personality, it seems to presuppose a process of idealization something like the one described in the present study. Some important qualifications need to be noted, however. The "ideal self" of the psychological inventory is related to the idealized life-historical figure in only the most indirect and procedural way. The former is literally a "pale reflection" of the latter—pale because it abstracts information from a thematically structured life history, and a reflection because it transfers this information to the preestablished mold of an ideal-self inventory. This process of abstracting and transferring necessarily involves a substantial loss of information and is probably one reason why ideal-self ratings tend to be stereotyped across the population (Wylie, 1974; Wells and Marwell, 1976.) The concept of the ideal self is discussed further in chapter 5.

It has already been noted that idealization is defined differently in this study than in clinical theories like psychoanalysis. While psychoanalytic theory does recognize the idealization of life-historical figures, it focuses on a particular and primitive instance of such idealization—namely, the "all-good" parental introjects which form the ego ideal or core of the superego. This focus has been useful for understanding certain aspects of early development and psychopathology, but it has also obscured some important facts about self-esteem as an ordinary phenomenon in adult life. The present investigation suggests that self-esteem is organized around specific *thematic content* involving a particular constellation of ideological concepts and a set of corresponding idealized memories. The psychoanalytic definition of idealization,however, paints across this thematic complexity by proposing a uniform characterization based upon a single infantile process.

What is missing in the psychoanalytic account is critical—a recognition of *meaning* as the organizing principle of idealization and *signification* as the active process by which this principle is put into effect. One of the concepts in the psychoanalytic literature which tends to perpetuate this problem is that of the internal "representation" (Hartmann, 1950, 1956). It is easy to regard a representation concretely as a "little picture" of something. All representations, however, including images, are also *signifiers* which are related to each other in a context of meaning and anchored in a social and life-historical field. The dynamic principle which organizes this system is the individual's activity in the material world. Idealized images and other representations are neither the cause nor the effect of this activity. Rather, they *are* the activity—or more correctly, they are an essential aspect of it: the imaginal and conceptual signifying acts by which the individual shapes his or her conduct in the world.

Piaget and Inhelder (1966) have provided support for this contention. They report that the capacity for mental imagery develops only in conjunction with the semiotic function, that is, in conjunction with the ability to use such imagery to represent objects in the context of the "past perceptual experience of the subject" (p. 70). It is important to emphasize that the *semiotic* use of imagery is *not* the same thing as the *linguistic* use of words and other symbols. Piaget and Inhelder emphasize that the former is used to represent *objects* in the context of the subject's experience, whereas the latter is employed to represent *concepts* and provides the basis for (verbal) language. According to Piaget and Inhelder, both kinds of signification play a role in adult thinking.

Idealization, as the term is used in this study, involves a *semiotic employment of images*. The idealized image represents an object, for it reconstructs the subject's perception of a person; and it carries a meaning in relation to other images representing other objects in the subject's experience. The sum total of these images is the subject's life history, a semiotic network of signification which the subject organizes by imaginatively reconstructing his or her past interactions with the world. Idealization is part of this life-historical field, a subsystem of semiotically organized images which are defined and interrelated by a particular theme: the ideal demonstrated by the idealized figure. By virtue of this specific theme, idealization is related to ideology and to the larger field of life-historical and conceptual meaning which defines the experience of self-esteem.

The Central Conflict

So far I have defined ideology and idealization and related them to each other as regions of meaning in the experience of self-esteem. Ideology is a system of general concepts that represents ideals in abstract terms. Idealizations are the specific memories that illustrate the same ideals in concrete images. Both ideology and idealization are systems of signification. The former is a linguistic structure giving ideals a conceptual definition and the latter is a semiotic form defining them experientially. There is still something missing, however.

The central importance of ideals suggests that the experience of self-esteem involves the solution to some kind of less-than-ideal or problematic situation. For example, Esther describes a lifelong dilemma, a set of ambivalent feelings about relationships in the family and other social settings. She wishes for familial closeness but she fears the possibility of excessive control. The examples set by idealized figures and the "social philosophy" by which Esther has tried to make these examples programmatic are presented in her account as guiding principles by which Esther has tried to resolve this *central conflict*. Her experience in the history department represents a specific attempt at such a resolution.

Following the example in Esther's case we can define a central conflict as follows: *A central conflict is a set of memories and concepts in which an individual expresses painfully contradictory themes. In descriptions of early experience this conflict involves actual encounters with specific other persons, but in descriptions of more recent and contemporary experience it takes the form of a characteristic pattern of conflicting ideas in terms of which important events are understood.*

As this definition implies, a central conflict can be experienced as either external or internal, suggesting that such a conflict is prior, in some sense, to the experience of individual identity. The word "prior" here does not mean causally or developmentally antecedent. Instead, the word refers to priority of a logical or conceptual kind— that is, the experience of individual identity seems to *presuppose*, in some sense, the pattern of contradictory themes that defines a central conflict. A person's experience of self is given substance and meaning in terms of these themes. For this reason the central conflict can be said to delineate an *existential problem* in the subject's life, one that is "existential" in the most fundamental sense, for it concerns the subject's definition of himself or herself as an existing social person. *The experience of self-esteem represents the subject's attempt to resolve this existential problem in some specific situation.*

It is not clear at this point whether the central conflict is one of several conflicts which contribute to identity or whether it is "the" existential question for the subject in some ultimate sense. In chapter 4 we will return to this question and examine it in the context of a case that seems to illuminate it. For the present, however, let us turn to the case material for illustrations of this phenomenon.

In Esther's case, a central conflict is evident in descriptions of early family life. For Esther, family life was a mixed blessing. On the one hand, she describes her family as the "hub of everything," the source of all love, social support, and cultural solidarity. On the other hand, Esther says that she was "too well loved" by her parents and that the very things about family life that made it gratifying also made it excessively controlling. This conflict was a major source of concern in Esther's childhood and adolescence. Nor did it stop being a concern when Esther left home, for Esther conceptualizes her struggle to find her adult identity largely in terms of the issues raised by this conflict. For Esther, a major question has always been how to achieve the kind of closeness and affection she experienced as a child without recreating the intrusive control that so often accompanied it. The story of Esther's attempts to find a balance between familial closeness and individual dignity is, in an important sense, the story of her attempts to become a person in her own right. Her failures to do so—such as the episode which occurred when her mother was living with her—have been devastating because they have struck at the core of her identity. Her successes—such as the job in the history department—have stood out as high points in her life because they have brought with them a sense of being a complete person in a meaningful social world.

We will see another example of a central conflict in Ed's descriptions of his life. Ed describes a relationship with his mother in which she seemed to take a special interest in him. Yet when Ed tried to win his mother's approval he found that his accomplishments were never good enough for her, that she always expected more. Ed's mother seems to have conveyed the sense that only when Ed achieved sufficient success would she regard him as a worthwhile person; yet, simultaneously, Ed came to suspect that his mother could never be satisfied. Nevertheless, Ed has continued to try to win the kind of success that would convince his mother (and himself) that he is truly a person of worth. His ideals are oriented around the theme of success in business, and Ed describes "high" and "low" periods during which he has moved closer to and further away from such success. The incident of self-esteem which Ed describes involves one of these "high" periods.

In Paul's case we will see an entirely different kind of central conflict. Paul describes an unhappy childhood characterized by overt rejection and neglect. Paul's central conflict is defined in the discrepancy between his need for a sense of basic security and the message conveyed to him by his mother that he was not worth taking care of. In his current life, too, Paul experiences the world as an uncertain place in which even the simplest need-satisfying activities can easily be undermined or disrupted. Paul's ideals, therefore, have involved strategies by which a minimum degree of security and sustenance might be guaranteed. His experience of self-esteem concerns a time when these strategies were successfully applied and he was able to return his life to a more certain course.

Some comments are in order here about the status of the central conflict as a signifying structure and its relationship to ideology and idealization. I have already characterized ideology as a linguistically organized structure, that is, a system of concepts that define each other in the context of their use by the subject. Similarly, I have described idealization as a semiotic form, that is, an image of a real object (in this case a person) that is given meaning in relation to the other images of the subject's life history. Both of these characterizations follow Saussures's (1916) analysis of meaning, which regards the definitions of the various signifiers in a system as residing in their relations with each other. We can now extend this analysis to the pattern of conflicting themes which has been labelled the central conflict. Like ideology and idealization, the central conflict can be regarded as a system of signification which is given meaning by the relations among its elements. Unlike ideology and idealization, however, the central conflict includes organizations of meaning at *both* the imaginal and conceptual levels. The central conflict, therefore, has a *double structure*, that is, *both a semiotic structure and a linguistic structure.*

The semiotic structure of the central conflict is the system of images from the subject's early history in which conflicting themes are played out in specific family interactions. The linguistic structure of the central conflict is expressed in the subject's conceptualizations of his or her past and present experience in terms of these conflicting themes. Idealization and ideology refer to the semiotic and linguistic structures, respectively, which a subject presents as general guidelines for solving the existential problem defined by his or her central conflict. Idealizations are the semiotic paradigms that provide elements of a solution to the central conflict at the level of concrete images. Ideology is the system of general beliefs that supplies the framework for a solution to the central conflict at the conceptual level. A reported experience of self-esteem represents an application of the guiding principles of idealization and ideology in order to resolve the central conflict in a specific situation in the real world.

As in the case of ideology and idealization, there are certain constructs in the existing psychological literature which correspond to that of the central conflict. The first and best known of these is Freud's (1914b) "repetition compulsion." Freud states that patients in psychoanalytic treatment seem to be compelled to repeat certain patterns of behavior—specifically, disturbed interpersonal relations that closely resemble conflicted interactions in the patient's early family of origin. This compulsion to repeat is evident in a wide variety of social situations, but it is particularly visible in the transference reaction of the psychoanalytic patient to his or her analyst. According to Freud, the patient must confront his or her transference on a repeated basis so that it can be worked through in all of its important manifestations. In this manner, the patient can achieve a better degree of functioning and (we can assume) a more complete self-esteem.

The repetition compulsion is an interesting conception and it raises a number of important theoretical questions. Some of these questions will be considered in the next two chapters, so a discussion of the topic is postponed until then.

Subsequent authors have developed similar and related conceptions. For example, Berne (1964, 1972) has analyzed the "games" and "scripts" in which people repetitively and systematically act out certain unconscious life plans; Lichtenstein (1977) has discussed the "identity theme" which is established in the early relationship between mother and child and which subsequently serves as the guiding motif in the individual's efforts to define a self; and Sartre (1960) has examined the lifelong "project" of the human subject attempting to transcend prestructured roles through action in the social and material world. Perhaps because they have been developed in close association with case material, all of these formulations are relatively free from the assumptions of causal reductionism. However, the above formulations differ in certain important respects from the present concept of the central conflict. The latter is conceived of as a constellation of life-historical and conceptual conflicts which are organized as semiotic and linguistic systems, respectively, and which the subject attempts to reconcile in the present through specific actions and reconstructions of meaning. This formulation gives greater emphasis to the role of conflict in psychological life and to the importance of human signification as the specific tool for resolving such conflict. Some of the details of this process of resolution will be clarified in later sections of this book.

Let us now consider two cases which further illustrate the constructs that have been discussed in this section. These are the cases of Ed and Paul, to which certain allusions have already been made. In the following pages we will see each of these cases as a coherent whole in which the regions of meaning associated with ideology, idealization, and the central conflict are organically interrelated. Of course, this is how meaning actually occurs in people's lives, and these cases will illustrate how no one region of meaning can be fully appreciated in isolation from the rest of the field.

Nevertheless, it is possible to focus attention more fully on one region or another, especially when the case material lends itself to such an emphasis. The cases of Ed and Paul have been chosen because they present this advantage. In Ed's case the phenomenon of ideology is particularly salient, and in Paul's case idealization receives special emphasis. After considering these two constructs in the accounts of Ed and Paul, respectively, we will move on to a detailed consideration of the central conflict in the case material of the next chapter.

We begin with Ed's case, in which a particularly clear example of ideology is evident. In this account it is possible to see how a set of ideas, different from the kind ordinarily thought of as an ideology, functions as one in the sense of the term as defined above. In addition, this case will give a clear illustration of how ideology is constituted life-historically in interactions with an idealized figure. In so doing, the case will raise an important theoretical question: To what extent does ideology actually have to address the issues of the central conflict? Since there are reasons to think that Ed's ideology does not address his central conflict in a straightforward way, we will consider the question of real versus defensive self-esteem once again. It will not be possible to answer this difficult question at this point, but raising it here will serve to prepare the way for a fuller discussion which will be undertaken in the next chapter.

ED: PLAYING BY THE RULES

Ed is a thirty-one-year-old white salesman for a small company that manufactures electronic equipment. He lives alone in an apartment complex in a middle-sized midwestern city. Although Ed was interested in the prospect of being interviewed, we had some difficulty making contact and scheduling interview appointments because Ed's work schedule on most days extends from early morning until nearly midnight.

When asked to describe a time when he had felt good about himself, Ed recalled another job that he had held. Several years earlier, after five years as a salesman in a men's clothing store, he had been promoted to manager and buyer for the store's collegiate section. Not only had this promotion meant an increase in salary and responsibility, but it had also represented to Ed the recognition of his potential. In the year following the promotion Ed had gone on to prove this potential in a rather spectacular manner by reversing a declining trend and setting a new sales record for the store. Ed describes the year that he held this job as "a time that was a real high for me in my life."

> Things were going very smoothly. I was just really enjoying life, I felt self-confident. I guess the way to put it [is] that I felt that there was nothing in the world that could lick me at that time. I had the world by the tail and I was fully and well aware of it.

Ed refers to his positive feelings during this period as a "business high":

> If business is going well, really, really well, I don't care what's going on outside, it all goes well... I'm probably a rather obnoxious person because I'm probably pretty cocky. Personally, I just am on a super high.

Success in business, then, is very important to Ed. During the interview he described it as the "primary" influence in his life which can raise his spirits to a "super high" even if everything else is at a "low." Moreover, the meaning of this kind of success seems to go beyond material considerations. As Ed and I discussed his business activity, he made it clear that his conception of success involves adhering to a certain set of standards. Tracing the particulars of these standards, we began to discern the outlines of an ideological system in Ed's life, one that is closely related to his positive feelings about his performance in the manager's job.

To begin with, Ed emphasized that it is important to him to be successful "by the rules." Being successful by the rules means treating fellow salesmen fairly and not "stepping" on them on the way up. For example, Ed explained that he could probably have advanced more quickly to the manager's position if he had been willing to steer customers away from another salesman who was his main competitor and to "press" the merchandise in his own part of the store. However, he chose not to do so:

> I guess I wanted the store to succeed. You know, I felt that for me to be a success the store had to be a success too, which means he's also got to be a success.

Not only are a saleman's interests tied to those of other salesmen; they are also tied to the interests of the customer:

> As far as feeling good about myself...I feel very good when I can help somebody, especially if it helps them make a decision whether or not to buy something. The good salesman is not necessarily always the person who sells something. He may sell the idea of not buying at this time, because in some cases it really is against the better interests of the person, and in the long run [the salesman who does this] is going to have a much more profitable business.

Ed discussed this reciprocity of interests in terms of reputation and trust. Customers want an "even exchange" of "dollars for services," and they remember when they do and do not get it:

> [A good salesman] is not going to get complaints, not going to have a bad reputation. He's going to have the reputation that—if you go into a store and with some good, logical reason someone talks you out of buying something, and as you get down the road you see "gee, you know, they were right," you'll go back because when you walk in there and they tell you you *should* buy something, you'll have a much greater trust.... That's the kind of principle I've operated on: no single sale will make or break me, and if I'm honest to people I'm selling to I feel very good about it.... I really feel good about making a sale I think will help somebody.

According to Ed, therefore, it is to the advantage of the salesman to promote the interests of the customer. Ultimately, this practice will pay off in a good reputation. More than this though, Ed seems to be saying in the above quotations that the mere act of helping people is satisfying. But things are not quite so simple. At one point in the interview I asked Ed if he valued helping people even when there was no prospect of making a future sale:

> Definitely. And—though—it puts it back in a financial role again...Even if they don't buy from you again you will receive financial success from that also, simply because of the fact [that] I couldn't buy the advertising that they can give me. (Mm-hm.) So yeah, it comes back to the financial. (They are not necessarily separate from each other.) No, they—I have a very difficult time in business dividing financial success [from] the respect of success because I think they go hand-in-hand.... I don't think that one can go without the other. It may be that the financial success is a little more concrete measure of the respect-type thing.

Clearly, Ed is not talking about altruism. Helping customers is inextricably related to advancing one's own financial career, even if there is no immediate return, because it is through customers that one's reputation in the community grows. This kind of reasoning is what makes Ed's conception a true *ideological structure* rather than a mere set of goals or values. Ed is not simply talking about what he wants to achieve—financial success, for example. He is laying out a *theory* of human nature and social life; and the elements of this theory give him direction in the social world. Being respected by one's customers is important *because* it leads to financial success; financial success is socially meaningful *because* it is a "concrete measure" of respect. Profit and public standing are inseparable in the ideological structure that Ed presents.

In the previous section, I characterized ideology as a linguistic structure—a system of concepts that define each other in the context of the subject's discourse. In the present account we can see how this kind of definitional system works. Ed uses a number of terms, and each of these terms helps to locate, articulate, and differentiate the meanings of other concepts in his ideological system. As each new term is introduced, the others are given clearer and more specific meanings in the developing context of the whole. For example, *good salesmanship* means *helping* the customer to make the right decision, and therefore gaining the customer's *respect*. Respect, in turn, contributes to one's *reputation* in the business community, and is also a form of *advertising*. All five of these concepts—salesmanship, helpfulness, respect, reputation, and advertising—are closely related in Ed's ideology, and they all designate elements that contribute to *financial success*. At the same time, financial success is a "concrete measure" of one's respect in the community, and, as such, it bolsters one's reputation and serves as a form of advertising; and advertising of course, makes it possible for the salesman to help other customers. All of these concepts, therefore, elaborate each other in the linguistic structure of Ed's ideology; each concept has specific relations to the rest, and together they constitute a system of principles that defines the shape of Ed's social aspirations.[1]

---

[1]It is interesting to consider the terms and metaphors which provide the content of Ed's ideology. In contrast to Esther's political language, Ed invokes the terminology of business and finance—not only in his statements about salesmanship, but in much of his auxiliary language as well. One manifestation of this is Ed's tendency to invoke the metaphors of quantity and measurement (e.g. "even exchange" and "concrete measure"). Another example is Ed's description of his feelings in terms of "high" and "low" periods, which he explicitly linked, on at least two occasions, to fluctuations in the nation's business cycle. Such metaphor systems are essential to ideology and constitute what may be called an individual's *linguistic style*. As this case and the previous one both illustrate, linguistic styles are often supplied by particular subcultures or by the culture as a whole. Lakoff and Johnson (1980) have compiled a number of examples of metaphor systems that are dominant in our culture, which collectively contribute to what might be called a culturally shared core linguistic style.

As noted above, Ed's ideology prescribes certain kinds of behavior toward fellow salesmen as well as toward customers. This is evident in Ed's account of "playing by the rules" with other salesmen:

> I want to be successful by the rules. I'd just as soon not have to step on anybody going up. I really—I really sort of feel—there's an old saying, "you don't want to step on too many people going up because you may have to come back down some time." I don't quite believe in that saying, but I don't want to step on too many people coming up...because they may eventually be up there too and you'd just as soon not have them using you for things.

This statement, however, introduces a new consideration: To what extent does Ed *actually* subscribe to the ideology which he has laid out? There are significant qualifications in the above quotation. Ed states that he would "just as soon" not "have to" step on "too many" people going up. In another part of the interview, Ed made a similar qualification when he commented that he "usually" doesn't feel very good if he has pulled the wool over a customer's eyes. These momentary disruptions seem to represent intrusions of another part of Ed's personality, a part that is much more concerned with immediate success, which he tries to integrate into his public self-conception. Keeping this consideration in mind, we must wonder about Ed's actual commitment to his ideology and about what success really means to him if not the attainment of his standards.

It is not difficult to identify the life-historical roots of Ed's ideas about respect and success. Ed describes a close relationship with his mother, and he attributes both his love for sales and his abilities in this area to her influence:

> I think my mother was more the pusher in our family. Dad is a pretty easy-going guy who sort of takes success as it comes. You can tell when he's proud about something, [but] you can't tell real easily when he's disappointed.... Mom, on the other hand, you have no trouble telling either way.... She pushed for success in everything.

One way in which Ed's mother pushed for success was in her own sales work. During Ed's earlier years his mother did not work, but when he became a teenager she took a job as a real estate broker. Ed recalls his mother's success in her work:

She was...rather amazing in the real estate business. She's definitely where I got my love for sales, I'm sure. She never really worked at it full time. She wondered how some of the people who were in [her] office made a living at it.... She was doubling the sales of several of the people who were supporting famillies...and she used to say "I just can't understand how they're making it." She did a really tremendous job.

Besides doing well, Ed's mother set an example of professionalism:

I think most people have a rather low opinion of [sales work].... There are not a great deal of people out there who would even consider a sales position. And that never even was a question with me. Mom was in sales and it was good, you know, she was very professional about it. She was really concerned about what was going to happen to [the buyer] afterwards, and that's the type of professionalism that I mean. So I guess I always equated sales people to an extent with her because she was that way.

Ed remembers his mother encouraging his own attempts to be enterprising as he grew up. For example, when he was eight years old he showed rented films in his basement every Saturday afternoon; the other children in the neighborhood would pay a nickel to watch.

I'm sure Mother absolutely hated it, but she always backed that. She seemed to think that was good that [I] had the ambition.

Later, Ed acquired a paper route which he owned for several years. By the time he gave up the route he had nearly quadrupled the number of customers on it. This increase was not directly attributable to his mother, but her influence in the background is clear:

(Did she push you to expand the route?) No, but...she always would ask you when you came back, "Did anybody new move in?" Those weren't the exact questions. But she'd just basically find out how it had gone that day.

Ed's mother also helped him to understand the principles of good business as they applied to his paper route:

She really taught me how...if you do a good job for
people how they will bend over backwards to do a good job
for you. One of my best customers happened to be one of
the local bars...and he took three papers a day for
patrons.... I always made sure that his papers got
inside...so they'd never get wet.... I always bagged the
papers. I never threw papers, it was always delivered. And I
had an awful lot of customers who appreciated that. This
one guy, he'd tip me at Christmas and special times.... In
the summer on the hot days I always knew [that] when I
got back, sitting on top of the papers would be an opened
Coke or something like that. And so that type of stuff—
Mom just really emphasized the fact to me and drove home
[that] why that type of thing happened was because I was
doing something, you know, going out of my way to make
sure that the guy always got the papers on time.... Mom
just explained that sometimes you have to go a little bit
out of your way but it always gets rewarded.

In this recollection we can see, in the finest detail, the life-
historical framework around which Ed's ideology is constructed. Ed
describes a set of relationships that serves as an illustration of the
mutually respecting business community; but more important in
this memory is his mother's commentary, shaping and defining the
situation, interpreting its meaning, articulating its implications. A
theory of social relationships, a system of values, and an agenda for
action are all presented in this commentary in prototypic form.

In other memories, Ed describes how his mother responded to
his work achievements with pride and acclamation. For example, as
a teenager, he acquired a sales job in a clothing store:

She always used to ask, once I started selling, "Well, how
much did you sell today?" And it got to the point [that]
she didn't really have to ask. If it was worth bragging
about I did [laughs].... You started setting goals for yourself
because you knew what her standards were, and eventually
I think my standards got higher than hers.

As Ed grew older, however, he began to feel burdened at times by his
mother's advocacy:

She was always pushing for improvement, and it caused
some problems for a while. There's a point, I guess...that
you feel comfortable at and you feel successful at, and you
want to lay back a little bit; and Mom just didn't allow for
that very well.

This conflict is illustrated by an incident that occurred when Ed was a senior in high school. Because he had shown exceptional interest and ability in science, Ed was chosen as one of six students in a large metropolitan area to receive a summer scholarship. He and his parents were invited to an honors convocation in recognition of this accomplishment; also present at the ceremony were other exceptional students, including one girl who received a school pen for participating in more activities than anyone else. Ed recalls that his mother's response to the convocation was to ignore the scholarship he had been awarded and to ask him why he had not won the school pen.

> She couldn't be satisfied with—she couldn't recognize the success I'd had....
> I just...kind of looked at her and said, "Well, to hell with you, then," and my senior year...I just kind of rebelled.... It wasn't really until about the start of the second semester in college that we started getting back together again.

Ed and his mother did get back on good terms, but not entirely. Ed continued his rebellion in his attitude toward college. After some difficulty deciding on a major, he reduced his attendance to part time, and finally quit altogether. His mother tried to persuade him to return to school, but the more she did so, the more resistant Ed became. Significantly, the year of Ed's "high" on the manager's job occurred shortly after his dropping out:

> I said, "Chuck it, I'm...having a great deal of success at what I'm doing, I don't really need school." And I was really still of the belief [that] I could buck the system, do it without a degree. In fact, I'm still not sure that I don't have that belief in the long run.

During the interview Ed denied that his good feelings about the manager's job had had anything to do with his quitting college. There are reasons, however, for believing that there may have been a connection. To understand why, let us consider Ed's relationship with his father.

Ed's father had immigrated to the United States from England during the Depression. After some very difficult times, he was able to secure work in a large industrial firm as a design engineer. He remained with the firm for the next two decades and became a supervisor, a notable achievement in light of the fact that he had only a sixth-grade education. After becoming a supervisor, however, Ed's father was unable to advance any further, primarily because of his lack of educational credentials. This problem had repercussions within the family:

> (How did your mother feel about his situation?) The thing that bothered Mom was the fact that she knew he was better than where he was, and yet there was nothing she could—there was nothing he or she could do about it.... It's one of the things I think she hid from him fairly well. He was in a dead-end street and he was at the end of it.... It probably has something to do with...why I feel that [college] degrees are such a waste and ridiculous.

Ed believes one reason his mother pushed him toward success was because she wanted to see him avoid the "dead-end street" of his father's situation. It seems, however, that her actions created a very painful dilemma for Ed. Although he states that he is closer to his mother than to his father, it is clear Ed has affectionate feelings for his father as well. At several points in the interview, Ed made comments like the following:

> He was always there if I needed to talk to somebody....
> Dad liked the paper route; Dad liked to walk. And that was one of our good times together. Dad and I would always deliver the Sunday morning papers together.

But Ed's father was judged in the family as a failure, a man who had never equalled his potential. The pressure Ed's mother put on Ed to succeed was a constant if implicit reminder of this assessement. Moreover, Ed's mother appears to have conveyed that Ed's success was to compensate for his father's shortcomings. The fact that Ed deeply resented this situation is evident in his resistance to returning to college, especially in light of the following comment:

> Something that my dad taught me is the futility of our measurement system when it comes to education.... Our society has moved so far away from [recognizing] what the individual is capable of—if you're capable of doing something why in the world should a degree or anything else have any bearing on it?

The question of the importance of college degrees is one on which Ed's parents took opposite stands; and on this issue Ed chose to stand with his father. In Ed's ideology, this choice is represented as an individualistic twist, the belief that one should still be able to prove oneself, to "buck the system, do it without a degree." In the world of life-historical meaning, however, Ed's stand on this issue seems to involve a refusal to side completely with his mother, a refusal to surpass his father in a clear and direct way, and an affirmation of and idenfication with his father through a recreation of his father's situation in his own life.

In many other ways, however, Ed did try to live up to his mother's expectations. We have seen these attempts in his memories of trying to please his mother, in his acceptance of her ideology, and in his wish to live up to the values and tenets of her system. But Ed's attempts to meet his mother's expectations seem never to have been wholly successful because Ed sensed that he could not really satisfy his mother: "She couldn't be satisfied...she couldn't recognize the success I'd had." Moreover, Ed seems never to have received the one thing he really wanted from his mother: acceptance of himself for who he was. There is little in the interview material to suggest that Ed ever experienced unqualified love for his mother. Her esteem and affection are always described as conditional, dependent on his accomplishments, directed toward his career:

> I enjoyed sports.... But she [didn't] look at that as...a big success goal.... She was much more interested in things like [school clubs].... [She would say] "You really should be working on those instead—they may introduce you to some people that you'll need for the future...
>
> Mom just really—she was always concerned about the type of people we had for friends, which sometimes bothered me too.... I guess I like to judge my friends more by the fact that they're people that I can count on.... And I think that Mom adds the other quality in there that they also need to be positive influence on my career....
>
> Mother was always concerned about the people that I went with. [When] I dated Marsha about five years ago...I think my mom wished that we [would] get married.... Half of Mother's like for her, I think, is that Marsha as a business wife would be excellent.

Consistently missing in these descriptions is any indication that Ed's own wants and needs are important to his mother. It is only his career and his potential success that seem to matter to her;

anything else is regarded as irrelevant—or worse, as dangerous. The consequences of this problem were made particularly clear near the end of the interview when Ed described how his plans for marriage had been disrupted in the year prior to the manager's job.

Ed and Kathy had begun dating while he was working at the clothing store. As their relationship became more serious, Ed realized that his mother was not happy about it. One of her concerns was that if Ed married he would never complete college. More than this, though, Ed's mother believed that Kathy would be a hinderance to Ed's career because she was uncomfortable and shy at social functions. Ed's mother made no secret of her disapproval of Ed's engagement. Ed recalls that when he called home and told his mother about the engagement, her reaction was to drop the phone. From that point on she pressured Ed to delay the wedding date. Meanwhile, Kathy's parents were pressuring her to make it sooner. These forces began to take their toll on the couple, along with the other anxieties associated with getting married. Ed and Kathy began to fight about little things, and as time went on the fighting got worse. Eventually, it culminated in a disastrous episode in which each of them attacked the parents of the other. According to Ed, this confrontation was the final event which "just literally destroyed the relationship."

This incident, more than any other, seems to capture the central dilemma in Ed's account—a dilemma that can be described as a conflict between the themes of acceptance and success. Ed's relationship with his mother presents the prototype of this conflict. Ed describes a series of idealized interactions in which his mother plays the role of both friend and mentor. She conveys the sense that Ed can achieve the kind of acceptance and appreciation that his father never earned; but as time goes on this promise seems to recede like a mirage. Ed does win approval from his mother, but only on a contingent basis—only as long as he pursues the activities that she believes to be essential for his career. Eventually, Ed senses that, like his father before him, he cannot gain his mother's acceptance in any deeper sense, for she is too single-minded, too driven by her own sense of priorities for Ed. It is always Ed's success and not Ed himself that is the primary focus of her concern.

Nevertheless, Ed continues to hope for the kind of acceptance his mother has never been able to give him. At many points in the interview he alluded to the importance of social support and reliable relationships, including long-term friendships he has had with some women:

She was...somebody who you could talk to.... I think I dated her more out of just the idea [that] she was a good friend and never having it, you know, go into anything all that serious.... She was just a really, really good friend.... If you happened to be seeing her that night, you knew you were going to be picked up by the next morning, you were really going to be ready to face the world again.

Although Ed wishes for success, therefore, he continues to seek the acceptance and affirmation that his mother was never able to give. His central conflict is the struggle to find a balance between two priorities—the establishment of himself as an independent and successful person and, simultaneously, the achievement of a sense of security and acceptance. And as Ed confronts the complications of the social world, his ideology is the means by which he attempts to attain this balance.

Ed's ideology concerns the nature of the business world, but as Ed himself indicates, his ideology involves a great deal more as well. On the one hand, Ed's ideology prescribes *a plan for achieving financial success*. This aspect is evident in a cluster of concepts which prescribe particular rules and forms of conduct in the business world and which are associated with Ed's idealization of his mother. These rules include cooperating with other salesmen and helping customers in ways that promote one's reputation in the local community. Enriching and extending this group of ideas is another ideological cluster associated with Ed's latent idealization of his father. This cluster concerns the importance of establishing oneself on the basis of one's own merits rather than by virtue of a college degree.

At the same time, Ed's ideology addresses the other side of his central conflict, *the wish for acceptance and affirmation*. Financial success is offered as a "concrete measure" of social acceptance and public respect—the respect of customers who know that they can trust him, the respect of salesmen who know that he will "play by the rules," and the more general respect of the community at large. Moreover, success means *self*-respect to Ed, for it attests to all of these things in a clear and measurable way. It means that Ed has established himself as a success in the community as a person of worth in the social world.

Ed's ideology, therefore, presents a plan for resolving his central conflict. The plan reconciles the demands of success and affirmation and presents a strategy for attaining them both. By proving himself in the sphere of business, Ed attempts to validate himself in a way that he—and his mother—cannot doubt. Esteem and acceptance may be conditional in Ed's life, but his ideology specifies what the conditions are and serves as a kind of linguistic map, guiding him through the ambiguous terrain of the social world. This characterization is not the kind usually associated with the word "ideology," but, as noted above, the term is useful because it connotes an organized constellation of belief and social practice—aspects which are salient in the account Ed presents.

Once again, however, we must consider the question of whether Ed's ideology offers a "real" solution. Like Esther, Ed seems to be reliving the past, at least in certain important respects. His ideology seems to repeat his mother's expectations more than to offer a real solution. Moreover, Ed himself seems to reject the tenets of this system, even while laying them out. We saw this contradiction in certain intrusions in Ed's discourse—a kind of ruthlessness that sometimes pierces through his ideological language as though this language were a mere ornamentation or rationalization to which he is only superficially committed.

There appears to be an important sense, therefore, in which Ed's ideology is not entirely relevant. It lays out a theory of social relations but it seems to bypass some of Ed's most important concerns. We would seem justified in asking whether Ed can ever attain the kind of validation he wants from success in business. We might guess, instead, that a more genuine transformation—a reworking of the terms of the central conflict—would bring Ed to a fuller and steadier sense of self-esteem. In the next chapter I will address this question and the extent to which an ideology like Ed's can be related to the concept of "defensive" self-esteem.

In this case we have seen some of the general features of ideology. We have considered ideology as a system of concepts that guides an individual in attempting to deal with his or her central conflict. But these concepts are not developed in a vacuum. As this case and the previous one both illustrate, ideology is related to life-historical events, particularly idealized interactions with important people in the subject's life. The memories of these idealized interactions provide a concrete ground for ideology by supplying illustrations of specific ideals in action. If we wish to understand the meaning of self-esteem in something more than abstract terms we need to consider this concrete level.

Let us turn, therefore, to another case in which the phenomenon of idealization is particularly salient. Paul describes an experience of self-esteem that represents the resolution of a central conflict. In Paul's account, however, ideology plays a relatively minor role.

Much more important are specific individuals who Paul remembers guiding his efforts. In some respects, these individuals seem to function as a *substitute* for ideology; and although this gives Paul a mode of action for dealing with the problems of his central conflict, it also imposes certain limitations on his possibilities and his sense of self-esteem.

PAUL: FINISHING THE JOB

Paul is a forty-eight-year-old white maintenance worker for an aeronautical engineering company in the Midwest. He is a father of three, but he has been living alone since he and his wife were divorced approximately eight years ago. There is something subdued about Paul's appearance. His drawn features and deliberate manner give him a melancholy air; but this quality is offset by a matter-of-fact style of speaking, occasional ironic comments, and a frequent dry laugh.[1]

In selecting an incident of self-esteem, Paul reached further back in his memory than any other subject: he recalled his graduation from high school. Primarily, this event seems to have represented to Paul the completion of a task that he had nearly given up on:

---

[1]Such nonverbal and paraverbal behaviors are extremely important in the representation and expression of meanings. Specifically, they serve to organize current situations in ways that resemble and extend previous ones. As will become evident below, for example, Paul's manner of describing his childhood recreates in the listener some of the sadness and dismay which he himself must have experienced at the time. Likewise, his matter-of-fact demeanor is, in part, a behavioral reconstruction of the activities of the idealized figures he describes below. A nonverbal system of this kind can be designated an individual's *semiotic style*.

Semiotic style is the concrete counterpart of the metaphor systems of linguistic style, and, in general, these two modes of expression supplement each other and operate together. Semiotic style represents in *action* what linguistic style represents in *words*. In Ed's case, for example, the linguistic metaphors of business and salesmanship are reinforced by a particular (semiotic) style of delivery. In laying out his ideology Ed gives a kind of formal yet earnest presentation, as though he were attempting to *sell* this philosophy to the listener. In the present case, too, and in the other cases of this study, the reader will detect similar correspondences between linguistic and semiotic styles.

When I graduated, that was a big thing. I didn't think I
was going to make it [laughs]....(So that was a time when
you felt really good about yourself?) Yeah. (What do you
remember about that time?) Well, actually, the fact that I
was real late in graduating.

Paul went on to explain that he had fallen behind his classmates
because academic difficulties had led to his being held back several
times previous to high school. He remembers his feelings about
seeing his friends graduate before he did:

Every year that we went through I seen them at
graduation. I was always kind of, you know, felt sad that I
wasn't there 'cause I was—well, then I finally made it
[laughs]...
(Do you remember how you felt when you went to the
graduation?) Well, I felt sort of sad in a way, but...I felt
good that I'd accomplished that thing that far.

There was good reason for Paul to feel proud. He had had
learning difficulties ever since the first grade, when he had been
held back for the first time. As he went through grade school Paul
feels he learned little, that "they were passing me along at that time
just to keep things moving." In fifth grade Paul flunked again. After
this failure he received extra help from a teacher and was able to
acquire sufficient skills to get him through the next two years. In
eighth grade he was held back again when his family moved twice
during the school year. For the rest of the time he was in junior
high school Paul consistently failed his classes, but was advanced
anyway.

There is little reason to think that Paul would have done any
better in high school had it not been for an auspicious turn of
events. On the second day of school Paul was assigned a counselor,
whom we shall call Miss P. Miss P. seemed to take a special interest
in Paul. She began meeting with him from time to time to see how
he was doing in his classes. At first he did not do well, but with
Miss P.'s interest and encouragement Paul began to improve. By the
end of the first semester he had achieved a C average. During his
subsequent years of high school Paul became more and more
involved with Miss P. His grades continued to improve and he failed
no more classes. By the time he graduated Paul had nearly achieved
an A average, an accomplishment which he attributes mostly to
Miss P.'s influence: "It was a struggle. I had a good counselor. But

that's the only thing that pulled me through.... (The couns—) The counselor, right. She just kept after me."

The change during high school which Paul describes is a dramatic one, and it points to the importance of specific relationships in promoting an individual's self-esteem. Of course, we do not know what Paul and Miss P.'s relationship was "really" like; we have only Paul's retrospective account. There can be little doubt, however, that in Paul's own mind Miss P. plays a crucial role in his experiences in high school. More generally, the presence of an encouraging and helpful person who "just kept after" him seems to have been critical. To understand why this is so, let us consider Paul's history.

Paul recounts an unhappy childhood fraught with images of bleakness and rejection. He was born in the sixth month of his mother's pregnancy when she tried to abort him. Many of his earliest memories feature his mother's indifference:

> From about the time I was five or six I was pretty much on my own.... I'd come home for lunch. A lot of times my mother wouldn't be home....
>
> I guess I got to the point where I felt that I couldn't really depend on her being there. If she couldn't be there for lunch then I couldn't depend on her for much else....
>
> Myself in particular—I don't remember too much about my younger brother—but it seems like we were sort of ignored.... It was raining. I had started school and I remember walking home in the rain. When I got home my mother changed my clothes, or had me change my clothes. But then we got in the car and she went to pick my older sisters up from school 'cause it was raining; and I had walked home [laughs]. You know, things like that.

Overshadowing the bleakness of Paul's memories at times was the deadly manner in which he reported them. Sometimes he did so with a perfunctory laugh, as in the above quotation. At other times he described depressing events in an offhand and matter-of-fact manner, and at still others he betrayed a searing rage in his use of understated or ironic language. The following comments came just after Paul had explained that not only he, but his younger brother as well, had been born in the wake of an attempted self-abortion by his mother:

> My mother was quite famous for that afterwards. She tried, uh, she talked a couple of young people into trying

abortions, kids they didn't want. This, of course, was after I was up and married, and I didn't know about one of them until later. I guess the woman almost died. (And she also tried to abort it when she was pregnant with your brother?) My brother, right. Yeah, you see, at that time they wouldn't do it in the hospitals.

There are some indications that Paul's mother did try, at times, to show him love. For example, Paul has a vague sense that his mother cared for him more when he was very young and became indifferent both to him and his brother after his brother's birth when Paul was three. In general, though, the picture which Paul paints of his mother is that of a depleted and depressed woman, barely able to function in the maternal role or to contend with her ambivalence toward her children. In Paul's account his mother is characterized as gradually deteriorating into a severly alcoholic condition which required institutionalization at least once when he was a teenager.

Paul describes his father as a taciturn man who was a harsh and rigid disciplinarian. For example, when Paul's oldest sister became pregnant out of wedlock, his father made her leave home, saying "If you're old enough to get prenant...you're old enough to support yourself." In his own case, Paul was locked in the closet or whipped by his father for offenses such as getting lost or having something that another child had stolen.

In some ways, Paul's father seems to have given him little more than his mother did. For example, Paul never received a birthday present from either parent. Yet Paul has positive memories of his father:

When it come to certain things I felt I could go talk with him more.... He always had a way about him that you knew that it was businesslike, and I sort of enjoyed that part of it.

What Paul appreciated about his father's "businesslike" manner seems to have been that it signified firmness and reliability, traits that were very important to Paul. Paul recalls his father's attitudes about work:

You always had the feeling that if you didn't do your job...he would come down on you for that....
He always...gave us the impression that anything you

done was important. Especially to finish it.... (Mm-hm. Did he, in his own life, make it a point to finish things he started?) Most generally, yeah. And everything was—it had to be right, as far as put away. He was always neat about everything. But he always tried to finish everything he done. He never left anything undone.

Paul's father had acquired his attitudes toward work early in life. He had grown up on a farm where he had learned to live by a strict and demanding schedule. Later he had worked as a shoemaker and had eventually become a leather cutter in an automobile factory. Throughout his whole life, however, he always maintained the kind of rigorous schedule he had lived by on the farm. Paul remembers his father's regimen and his own reactions to it:

There was always a set schedule, which I think has affected me today. Supper at six, up at seven in the morning for breakfast, off to school by five to eight.... It was a good, solid schedule, which I enjoyed quite a bit. (You liked that.) I liked that, yeah, the schedule was my game [laughs]. (What did you like about that?) Well, you always knew that things were—where you were going to be at a certain time and that things were always, uh—seemed to fall into place better.... If we had to be at a certain place at a certain time it always fit, we knew what time we could plan on having supper.

Especially noteworthy in the above quotation are the allusions to meals. Images of food and hoped-for nourishment appeared at many points in the interview as Paul related the story of his life. It was as though he has always been acutely aware of any source that might provide him with basic sustenance. At one point, for example, Paul remembered that as a teenager he had wanted to have his own restaurant. While discussing this he added that working as a dishwasher would be no disgrace, for "if you can get a meal and some money, well, what difference does it make what you are?" At another point, Paul described how his father had regulated money during hard times, doling out enough to Paul—if he earned it—for a candy bar. Later, when Paul tried to explain why he had always preferred adults who were strict disciplinarians like his father to those who were more lenient like his mother, he said:

You remember incidences about those people; whereas somebody that's just there, you don't remember as having done anything. There's nothing, really, to remember them for. It's like getting a candy bar, you know. You remember getting that candy bar, but who gave it to you, that's soon forgotten.

This passage begins to suggest the outlines of a central conflict in Paul's account. Paul describes his life as a struggle to acquire the basic supplies necessary for physical and psychological survival. In Paul's account, the need for food is not simply a symbol for the wish for love; it is a constant reminder of the precariousness of life itself, for Paul knows what it is like to come home hungry to an empty house. In his earliest memories Paul describes a mother who cannot be trusted to provide for his needs: "If she couldn't be there for lunch then I couldn't depend on her for much else." Under such circumstances, an adult who is "businesslike," who retains a reliable schedule and clear demands, is to be preferred over anyone offering mere gestures of love or kindness. At one point Paul clarified this preference when he explained why he had liked teachers who had refused to give "imcompletes":

> [An incomplete] was a "maybe"—maybe I'll give you a better mark, maybe I won't. (...[Did that have anything] to do with your experiences with your parents?...) Uh, this is possible, 'cause I felt that when [my mother] wasn't strict I was never sure where she stood.

In Paul's account, therefore, a central conflict emerges around the question of whether others can be trusted in even the most minimal way. This conflict is represented concretely in Paul's descriptions of early childhood. On the one hand, Paul longs for security and nurturance, and he describes a search for sources of sustenance. On the other hand, his mother is unreliable and Paul concludes that he is "on his own." It is only in his father that Paul sees a possible solution. Here is an adult who knows what he wants, and demands it in a clear and uncompromising way. By complying with these demands and conforming to his father's schedule, Paul can expect to receive a degree of sustenance and care.

In this light it is not surprising that Paul has adopted his father's attitudes toward work and that these attitudes constitute the core of an ideology that emphasizes discipline, setting and keeping a schedule, and finishing what one starts:

> Today...I look back and I see so many kids—the way things are handed to them today, and they just don't appreciate what they got....

[Having a schedule is important] because you have some sense of direction. I mean, you know when you start out that you're going to finish it, you've got someplace where you know you're going to step.

At several points in the interview Paul emphasized the viability of these ideals and the fact that they "pay off," ultimately, in a number of ways. For example, he described how his children have acquired self-discipline and how his oldest son is now profiting by working his way through college on a difficult part-time schedule. Like the tenets of Ed's and Esther's ideologies, those that Paul describes present a strategy for succeeding in the social world.

We can see Paul's ideology operating in the incident of self-esteem that he initially described. Above all, graduation from high school represented the completion of a task that Paul had nearly abandoned, the return to a schedule he had not kept for many years:

Every year that we went through I seen them at graduation...then I finally made it....
I felt good that I'd accomplished that thing that far.

But Paul's account differs from those we have already seen. Paul's ideological statements tend to be brief, and they are usually presented somewhat implicitly. While Ed and Esther lay out abstract systems detailing the workings of social life, Paul's characterizations are generally more concrete, moving from one life-historical event to another. Furthermore, in elaborating his experience of self-esteem, Paul does not give a central role to ideology. Instead, he emphasizes specific interactions with specific individuals. It will be recalled, for example, that Paul believes he was able to graduate only because of the help he received from his counselor, Miss P. Let us consider, therefore, the role of idealization and idealized figures in Paul's account.

I have already discussed the importance of Paul's father to him as a guarantor of stability and security. Even though there are many indications that Paul sometimes felt neglected by him and often experienced him as severe and rigid, it is clear that Paul knew he could depend on his father. In the following passage, for example, Paul describes how he knew exactly what to expect when he helped his father paint the house:

He'd make sure that we knew we'd have to get up every day at a certain time, and that was 'cause we had to do the house 'till it was *done*. And the quicker we got it, the quicker we could do what we wanted to do, and this type of thing.

But his father's demands meant more to Paul than a mere sense of stability. They also seem to have signified a belief in Paul's abilities and an expression of caring between father and son:

> He always, like I say, gave us the impression that anything you done was important. Especially to finish it. And even maybe that it wasn't as good as it should be, but if you started something, if you stayed with it, it eventually could amount to something....
>
> My dad always encouraged me with little things that I'd try to finish, and just—the interest was always there.

In the demands his father made on him, therefore, Paul detected a genuine interest. What seems to be crucial here, what makes this interest different from the occasional interest displayed by Paul's mother, is the particular context in which it occurred, the nature of the relationship between Paul and his father. Interest and attention could not be meaningful to Paul unless they were accompanied by some kind of *assurance*, a guarantee they would not evaporate. This assurance was provided by his father's strictness, by the system of demands which he imposed on Paul. Paul trusted his father because his father's demands were clearly spelled out, clearly communicated, and rigidly and reliably followed in practice; and because of the security provided by these demands, his father's interest had substance for Paul. This interpersonal context is what makes Paul's appreciation of his father an *idealization* as the term has been defined above. Paul idealizes his father not as "all good" or as "perfect," but as demonstrating a specific ideal in action. In the context of Paul's life-historical account, the ideal of discipline provides a solution to Paul's central conflict and defines a way of life in which some trust is possible, in which a minimum of sustenance can be expected and obtained. Paul's father shows how this ideal works, both in his style of living and in his attitude toward Paul.

Let us note, once again, that idealization is not the same thing as ideology. Although both of these structures represent a subject's ideals, idealization represents them in semiotic rather than linguistic terms. Idealization is a systematic employment of specific images representing specific objects and events in a person's life; and the way in which these images are organized as a whole establishes the meaning of the idealization. In the above passages, for example, Paul describes his father doing a number of different things—acting in a businesslike manner, imposing a schedule on the rest of the family, encouraging his children to finish what they start, and so forth. Each of these descriptions presents a specific image, a particular shapshot of discipline in action. Each represents the ideal in a different mode or situation, and collectively they form a composite image that portrays discipline as a living reality. Moreover, the larger context in which they occur further elaborates the meaning of the ideal. The images of bleakness and overt rejection which Paul describes in connection with his mother coalesce into a critical background or foil. Against this background his father's inflexibility assumes a significance that can be clearly appreciated: it becomes an island of stability in an otherwise chaotic world. In this manner, all the images of Paul's life history contribute to the meaning of the ideal of discipline; and in particular images of his austere father, this idealized theme is concretely crystallized.[1]

Paul's father is not the only adult who is idealized in Paul's account of his early history. Another important figure is the wife of the doctor who delivered him. In many ways, this woman was a substitute mother for Paul. She lived across the street, and on some occasions when Paul came home at lunchtime and found his mother gone, he would visit the doctor's wife, who would feed him. Paul also remembers this woman giving cider and doughnuts to the neighborhood children every Halloween. But the doctor's wife is more than a nurturant figure in Paul's account; she also embodies many of the same qualities of firmness and strictness that Paul admired in his father:

---

[1]It may be somewhat misleading to refer to these life-historical elements simply as "images." When Paul says that his father "always had a way about him that...was businesslike," he is probably referring to an array of memories, some of which would be easy to describe and others of which would require a great deal of reminiscence and reconstruction. We can assume that such a descriptive statement ordinarily calls to mind a condensatory image something like those described by Freud (1900) in connection with dream formation. In fact, it is likely that imagistic processes similar to the ones discussed by Freud underlie the construction of all thought and discourse. On the other hand, it is probably not *logically necessary* to make any assumptions about actual images. We can simply regard descriptive statements as linguistically constituted semiotic elements which—*like* images—refer to specific objects and events in the context of the subject's life history.

When you worked for her everything had to be done a
certain way, and if you told her you was going to be there
at seven and you were late, you could always plan
on...having a few words when you got there.... Like I
say, everything had to be done just about right, or...she'd
say "Well, you better do it over again.";...I guess she was
right.... It paid off in the long run, 'cause I always had
jobs cutting bushes, cutting grass for people in the
neighborhood....
    (What was she like?) Well, very [pauses] oh, should I say
dignified in some ways?...Should I say arrogant? Uh,
aristocratic—not arrogant but aristocratic, perhaps. She
always carried herself quite proud.

But the doctor's wife receded as an influence in the later years of
Paul's childhood. He saw less of her, and eventually she moved to
another city. Another important figure, however, emerges at this
time.
    During most of his childhood Paul was having trouble in school.
By the time he reached the fifth grade he still lacked basic skills such
as reading and arithmetic. His fifth-grade teacher, however,
determined to change the situation:

She was an old-maid-type teacher, uh, very dedicated....
Starting in January after the Christmas session, she was
keeping me after school on the average of three nights a
week, and gradually increasing the amount of spelling words
that I had to learn, plus she was giving me extra math.
Well, I felt discriminated against at the time, I thought she
was being a little too hard on me, you know. Because, gee
whiz, here's all these other kids, these all-A students—they
ain't getting half the math that I was getting, you know. I
was staying after school to get it.

Undoubtedly the situation *was* confusing to Paul; but he could
hardly have failed to notice that he was receiving a great deal more
interest and attention than the other students. Paul's next words
suggest that he was aware of his teacher's interest and measured
his parents' interest against it:

And my parents never wondered where I was at, I mean it
just—they knew if I wasn't home at supper time I was at
school. Of course, she might have called them, too, I mean
she might have made sure that they knew where I was at.

By the time Paul finished fifth grade he had learned a great deal:

> I learned more in that one year than I think I did all
> through...junior high school in a lot of respects....
> Because when I came [to a new school in seventh grade]
> with all this that she had given me...they were just
> teaching stuff that I had gotten there. (In fifth grade?) In
> her class, yeah.

Paul's characterization of this woman as "as old-maid-type
teacher" is not as pejorative as it may sound. On several occasions
during the interview he made fond allusions to "old-maid teachers"
and indicated that these older women choose teaching as a
substitute for family life. The implication would seem to be that in
the relationship to an "old-maid teacher" Paul might find the
mother-child bond he had never known. Paul recalls the maternal
qualities of one such teacher:

> I had an English teacher—an old-maid English teacher—that
> kind of stands out in my mind.... She liked music and she
> liked cats. (Cats?) Yeah [laughs]. Her cat had kittens and
> she sent around birth announcements.... Those things kind
> of tickle you, you know. Birth announcements for a cat.

Unspoken but immanent is the contrast between this woman and
Paul's mother, the inducer of abortions.

In the later years of junior high school, Paul did very poorly once
again. He put little effort into his assignments and began to fail
classes on a regular basis. Publicly, he assumed a posture of apathy;
but in private he remained acutely aware of the attitudes of his
teachers, as the following comments suggest:

> None of my teachers in junior high ever talked to me
> about staying in school. I just—they just didn't seem to
> —you know, I went to class day after day without any
> homework even [laughs], and I was getting E's and there I
> was...I'd get my E and I'd still keep coming to school.

It is in this frame of mind that Paul entered high school and had
his first contact with his counselor, Miss P. Paul recalls his initial
impressions of Miss P.:

> She reminded me a lot [of]...the doctor's wife. Well, she,
> of course, had never married. She was one of the old-maid

teachers.... She always dressed the same. I mean, her hair
was always the same....
    She was, I think, a lot on the same order [as] my dad
[in] temperament.... She was very—well, I'd say a dignified
type of person. She always carried herself—well, she always
gave the impression of being a disciplinarian and this type
of thing. And she always gave you the feeling that you
could ask her a question and she always had a straight
answer for it.

Miss P. made it clear to Paul that she was going to be more active
than his other teachers had been. She monitored his performance,
and when it began to fall she called him in to talk about it.
Moreover, Paul recalls that "a couple of times she came looking for
me and wanted to know why my mark dropped in a certain class."
Paul's grades began to improve, but Miss P. continued to keep an
eye on him:

Sometimes—like we had a trial in American government.
We were having a kind of jury trial...I was supposed to be
the lawyer. She came in there and sat through the whole
thing. There were just different times you felt that she
knew where she had to be at a certain time.

But it was more than a mater of Miss P. keeping an eye on Paul; she
came to be someone he could rely upon, someone who "gave you
the feeling that she was *interested*."
    Like other important figures in Paul's life—his father, the doctor's
wife, the fifth-grade teacher—Miss P. was a strong person who
showed her commitment to Paul in her resoluteness and reliability.
Like these other figures, she demonstrated a way of being that
promised a better life and suggested a solution to his childhood
dilemmas. By setting goals, disciplining himself, and finishing what
he had started, Paul might be able to ensure a more secure existence
for himself.
    But there is something wrong here; for in some basic way, this
ideal never completely "took root" in Paul's life. In Paul's account of
his history it is always someone else who imposes the discipline,
someone else who sets the schedule. He himself seems to have been
unable to do so, except when others have supported his efforts.
This dependence on others has left Paul feeling frustrated and
helpless when such external support has been lacking or inadequate.
The extent to which this dependence has created problems in Paul's
life is evident in his description of the difficulties he encountered in
his marriage.

Shortly after marrying, Paul began to realize that he could not depend on his wife to do things when she was supposed to. At first this problem was not a major one, but as the children got older there were more activities that had to be coordinated. Paul tried to organize things, but his wife refused to budget her time and "the schedule just seemed to fade away." Paul was angry that his wife's behavior led to their always being late, especially when it was to PTA meetings and other events that involved showing an interest in the children. At one point he began setting the clock ahead so that his wife would be on time, but this did not work for long. Finally he began leaving without her. Meanwhile, he felt that he was being forced to take on a greater and greater share of his wife's obligations:

> Your work comes first if you've got to support a family, and I was trying to work part time also along with the reserves and—and then it got where I was trying to keep house too, and it just—I couldn't keep up with it [laughs].

Eventually, this and other problems led to the dissolution of Paul's marriage.

A similar pattern is evident in Paul's experience in the military. Paul joined the reserves when he was seventeen. At first he did not like the discipline and demands that it placed on him, but as time went on he began to feel differently:

> You'd get more of a sense of doing it for yourself. Just, uh, I guess it builds up your confidence or whatever...'cause in order to make the routine work I had to help myself, and then I had to do things myself in order to really get into it.

Paul reenlisted and eventually worked his way up to second lieutenant. During most of this time he was in a tightly disciplined "snap outfit" in his home town. Later, however, he moved to another city. The reserve unit there was undisciplined and "sloppy," a state of affairs Paul found very frustrating:

> They'd wait until everybody got there and come at any old time. Then they'd fall in. Sometimes the first class would get started late. Sometimes we'd be out by midnight, sometimes we wouldn't. [There was] just no system.

Paul transferred to a better unit for a brief period of time, but he was soon transferred back to the poor one again. The situation was intolerable to Paul, and finally, with sixteen years of service and five years left until retirement, he resigned from the reserves: "I was having trouble with my ex-wife at that time. I was just sort of giving everything up [laughs]. I dropped out."

From the day of his birth Paul was defined as unwanted. His mother conveyed to him that he was not worth feeding or caring for. In his early memories he searches for security amidst signs of desolation and rejection. Paul's father taught him that some trust is possible, at least in a context of rules and discipline. But this kind of trust can only be maintained as long as the system of rules is maintained. If someone presents a challenge to the system, the trust on which it is based is ruptured. The system itself may continue to function, but the security it provides is seriously compromised. Paul experienced this dilemma both in his marriage and in the military. In both cases Paul began with a certain security, based on a sense of shared obligation. In both situations, however, other people refused to be bound by the rules that Paul believed to follow from these obligations. The challenges presented by these people were devastating to Paul because they fragmented the *trust* he had managed to secure and undermined the foundations of his emotional life. Once this fragmentation had occurred, Paul felt he had no option but to "walk away"—to withdraw into self-protective isolation:

> A lot of people, they can just go from day to day and take things as they come, but if it gets too far out of line I just can't seem to hold everything together. (How do you react if the schedule starts breaking down?) I just walk away from it. [Laughs].

In Esther's case we saw that the love of a parent can be a mixed blessing, but that a second parent can demonstrate ideals that provide a modifying or corrective influence. In Ed's case we saw how conditional parental love can lead to the idealization of themes that may be disconnected from the actual needs of the individual. Paul's case, however, illustrates a different kind of problem. Paul was not loved in an oppressive or a conditional way. Instead, he was subjected to gross neglect. It was only in his father's strict demands that Paul detected any caring and attention at all. Given the lack of validation in Paul's life, the most he has been able to hope for has been a recurrence of similar situations. The idea of establishing a different kind of trust is almost inconceivable to Paul. Instead, he must be assured that others are dependable, that they will support and promote the rules. This need is one reason why idealized figures play such an important role in his account; and it also explains why they contribute to his self-esteem in a certain recurrent and predictable way.

For the same reason, these idealized figures are presented in sterotypic terms. To a large degree they are all alike—firm, demanding, disciplined, and attentive—and they are defined more by what they do for Paul than by who they are. Paul does not convey a sense of these people as real individuals with peculiarities and weaknesses of their own. It would be difficult for him to do so, however, for his own situation has always been precarious, close to the original conflict in which the question of his identity was posed; and Paul has always been in need of immediate solutions. In a struggle for psychological survival, a sophisticated understanding of other people is a luxury:

It's like getting a candy bar, you know. You remember getting that candy bar, but who gave it to you, that's soon forgotten.

This completes our initial consideration of self-esteem and of the roles played by ideology and idealization in constituting the meaning of this experience. The third concept introduced in this chapter— the central conflict—has not been highlighted in a particular case for two reasons. First, unlike the phenomena of ideology and idealization, the central conflict tends to be relatively prominent in every life-historical account. For this reason there is less need to make it the focus of any one case. Second, the theoretical issues raised in connection with the central conflict and its resolution are very broad. They include the question of the difference between genuine and defensive self-esteem—a question already raised above. Because these are large issues and because it seems advisable to discuss them in the context of more than one case, a full chapter has been devoted to this topic. In the next chapter, therefore, we will give closer consideration to the central conflict which underlies ideology and idealization, and to the defensive and nondefensive modes by which the individual may attempt to resolve this conflict.

THREE

The Central Conflict: Defense and Resolution

SUBJECTS' ACCOUNTS of their lives are thematic—that is, they are oriented around specific life-historical themes which recur in various forms and contexts. In examining the regions of meaning designated as ideology and idealization, we have seen certain of these themes expressed in a subject's ideals—concepts and images defining how the subject can play a positive role in a meaningful social order. When people are asked about experiences of self-esteem they describe living up to these ideals.

As we inquire more deeply into the meaning of self-esteem, however, we find that ideals can best be comprehended not as isolated elements, but as guidelines for resolving a *central conflict* in a person's life. It has been suggested that the themes which define such a conflict lie at the core of an individual's identity and that the employment of one's ideals to resolve the central conflict in a specific situation is the existential act which seems to bring with it the experience of self-esteem.

Certain difficulties are created, however, for we are presented with the question of what actually constitutes a resolution of a central conflict. In the last chapter we saw situations that seemed to represent resolutions, but it was suggested that things had not really changed or that the central conflict was as active as ever. These situations were characterized by inconsistencies and contradictions in the subjects' accounts, and it was further suggested

78

that such disruptions in meaning might be taken as indications that the subjects were expressing aspects of *defensive self-esteem*.

In this chapter the question of real versus defensive self-esteem will be discussed. This problem is a difficult one and raises unavoidable paradoxes from the start. For example, I have suggested that defensive self-esteem is signified by disruptions in meaning. We have already encountered such disruptions in Esther's contradictory statements about her own power on the job and Ed's inconsistent locutions about "playing by the rules." Yet, another point was also emphasized in the last chapter, one basic to the very study of life history: meaning is a contextual phenomenon, and to understand something in a life-historical account we must examine that thing in the context of the rest of the account. In fact, it is even necessary to examine the *disruptions of meaning* in the full context of such an account in order to understand their *meaning*. Defensive self-esteem, then, seems to involve *divisions in a field of meaning which is nevertheless indivisible in some basic sense.*

A second and related paradox concerns the relationship between conflict and self-esteem. It has been suggested that self-esteem involves an attempt to resolve a central conflict in an individual's life and that a true resolution of such a conflict is associated with genuine self-esteem. Yet it was also suggested in the last chapter (and this suggestion will be extended below) that the self is defined in terms of the central conflict. Genuine self-esteem, then, would seem to be aimed at *cancelling out—in some sense—the very terms in which the self is defined.*

Rather than attempting to solve such paradoxes it would seem wiser to regard them as cautionary principles. They warn against the simplistic application of ordinary definitions and distinctions in trying to understand the relationship between defensive and nondefensive self-esteem. Instead, we can use these paradoxes to define a different perspective. Let us hypothesize that disruptions and coherence always coexist in the field of meaning, that conflict and resolution continually interplay, and that *no experience of self-esteem is ever entirely defensive or entirely nondefensive.* Accordingly, the question of the relationship between real and defensive self-esteem becomes the question of how these two phenomena coexist and how one or the other seems to dominate in certain accounts and situations.

In the pages that follow, we will explore these questions in the accounts of three more subjects. The first two cases—those of Denny and John—will illustrate resolutions in which defensive elements are readily apparent. The third case—that of Anna—will serve as an example of a more genuine resolution. In all three accounts we will consider the quality of the resolution in terms of the ways in which groups of signifiers are organized—that is, the ways in which subjects exploit the semiotic and linguistic characteristics of ideology, idealization, and the central conflict in order to bring about a resolution, even while defending themselves against the effects of such a resolution. Let us begin with the case of Denny, which will introduce the important characteristics of defensive self-esteem.

DENNY: A DIFFERENT KIND OF LIFE

Denny is a twenty-nine-year-old white male who is currently working as the chief foreman of a furniture manufacturing company owned by his father. A resident of a large western city, Denny lives with his wife and son in an attractive suburban home. During the interview Denny presented a somewhat inconsistent picture. The first impression he gave was that of a rather brusque man. For example, when I got lost on the way to his house and called to clarify his directions, he retorted, somewhat curtly, "West, the direction of the setting sun." Once we sat down and began the interview, however, Denny seemed to unwind and become more personable. He talked in a free and expansive way, often adding persuasive phrases like "really," "believe me," and "I tell you." At other times during the interview he seemed to be somewhat abashed by my questions and answered them carefully and with qualifications.

When asked to recall a time he had felt good about himself, Denny remembered a project he had undertaken three years previously. He had planned and built onto his house an extension which consisted of a combination greenhouse and sunroom. Denny's recollection of this project and some of his feelings about it unfold in the following passage, which occurred at the beginning of the first interview:

> Uh, I would say the last time I felt good about myself was when I finished the sunroom outside that I added onto the house. (Was this more than a year ago?) Yeah, it was probably about three years ago. (Okay, can you tell me more about it?) Well, actually I didn't do it all alone. My wife helped, [her sister] helped, my father-in-law helped, uh, but basically I did it, actually. It was just a sunroom, a greenhouse sunroom like you see in a lot of houses, with

a—uh—it was more than a sunroom. It was really a kind of total environmental—[pauses]—concept.... It was to give the house an extension from the living room.... Before, [the living room] left you with the feeling that the room was too narrow and you would wish you could expand it, perhaps, make it look different.... [He describes the physical structure of the sunroom.] When I was done I thought to myself, you know, Denny, that really wasn't that hard.... Two hundred years ago every Tom, Dick, and Harry could do that, you know, that was no big thing for some guy to make a sunroom out there [laughs]. And yet somehow I really felt good about it.

This passage, which introduces Denny's incident of self-esteem, carries with it a number of indications of uncertainty and conflict. At the beginning, for example, Denny characterizes the sunroom project—which occurred three years previously—as "the last time I felt good about myself." This may have been a function of Denny's expansive style which involved a tendency to overstate things. It seems unlikely that this was actually the last time Denny had felt good about himself, especially since he talked in the interview about more recent positive accomplishments. The choice of these words is notable, however, as is the fact that they appear to emerge in a spontaneous and natural way when Denny begins talking about the sunroom project.

Moreover, describing the sunroom and his feelings about it seems to propel Denny into the realm of conflict. He is uncertain how good the sunroom is and how much credit he should take for it. He confesses that he did not build it alone, that he had help, but he adds that it *was* he who built it "basically." He minimizes the product as "just a...greenhouse sunroom like you see in a lot of houses," but he asserts that it was "more than a sunroom," that it was "a total environmental concept" expanding and extending the house. A moment later, however, he retreats again, admitting that the sunroom project "really wasn't that hard," that anyone could do it, and that it was "no big thing."

Denny seems torn, therefore, between regarding the sunroom as a genuine accomplishment and belittling it as "no big thing." This attitude suggests a central conflict around the theme of individual achievement and the degree to which Denny can take credit for such achievement. Although the details of such a conflict remain obscure at this point, the importance of individual accomplishment is readily apparent as Denny continues to talk about the sunroom project. In his next words, Denny extends the theme of the loss of frontier self-reliance which he introduced in the above passage. So begins the elaboration of a detailed ideology:

> I think it's because more and more people now, they don't really do anything for themselves like that. Like they rent from a landlord, they pay money for a car, and maybe they go eat their food out at fast-food places all the time, and they don't make their own clothes, of course, anymore, or their own shoes. So it's a different kind of life now.

In contrast to this are the basic instincts of human nature:

> I just think that it's a kind of an instinctive thing to make things for yourself, your family, especially in the way of shelter and protection....
> If you look...at any primitive culture—Eskimos are pretty primitive, I think. I'm sure that they—there's a certain feeling of satisfaction when they build their igloos or whatever.

Just as fulfilling this instinct feels good, Denny believes that not fulfilling it can lead to trouble. For example, he suggested that some people do "socially negative things" because they do not accomplish other things that would give them a positive feeling of achievement. In addition, personal accomplishments are the basis for being respected and having rights:

> If you don't do anything, then I say shut up.... I mean if you're not doing anything, my God, you hardly even have any rights. Unless you're paralyzed. (What do you mean?) Well, if you're not doing anything you don't have much right to complain about anything or to criticize anything.

At several points in the interview Denny talked about the forces that suppress the natural instincts:

> The reason [people] are not that way is because of society and what it does to people. Especially urban societies, city societies, you know....
> Sometimes I feel kind of melancholy about it.... I just think how much better things could be if people would remember, and if institutions and groups and TV and all kinds of things would stop blotting those things out.... (If they would remember what?) Oh, if they would remember some of the natural instincts and...the ways that people

should be and ought to be rather than trying to make everything artificial and, uh, take the spontaneity out of things.

Denny characterizes the forces suppressing the natural life as a trend toward "group think, group do." Large institutions, especially the government, are taking over more and more of the functions of life, creating a world of "strangeness" in which the individual is alienated from environment and self. In contrast, the building of the sunroom was an expression of the instinctive, natural life:

What I did, basically, is something that people five hundred years ago did.... You know, it was the earth, the environment, the natural things that were there before me and will be there after me.... I think certain things can be timeless...because they are part of what it is to be a human being.

The ideology which Denny lays out is explicit, not only in presesnting a theory of human nature and social life, but in analyzing the trends that have disturbed the current world. The building of the sunroom represents a rejection of these trends and a return to the simpler life of individual accomplishment in a natural setting. But there are certain inconsistencies in Denny's account. These inconsistencies raise questions about the function of Denny's ideology and the extent to which it is actually operative in his ordinary life. For example, while Denny emphasizes the desirability of the simple and natural life, it is also clear that he is very attached to the products of technology. At many points during the interview he indicated their importance to him as measures of the good life:

[My father's car is] a Ferrari 246 GTS. This is like a $26,000 car. It's a beautiful car, it really is. Knock-off mags, leather interior, handling, the whole shot....
    I could say "Here. Here's a Sony push-button color TV set," boy, that would make anybody happy....
    [The social sciences] are really nice accessories to have; they're kind of like, maybe, the electric windows on your car.

Another inconsistency exists in Denny's attitude toward history. As noted above, Denny is unhappy with current social trends toward institutionalization and the suppression of the individual. Yet Denny, who majored in history, has complex feelings about the modern era which are not reflected in his ideological statements. For example, he stated that the modern era is his favorite historical period:

I think I liked it because...there was a lot of things that just, uh, definitely changed the flow of history. I mean they were big things, and some of them were fascinating.

At one point in the interview I asked Denny about this seeming contradiction—that his favorite historical period is one of mass social movements and changes he deplores. He replied that studying these processes can help one to understand why they have taken place:

If you like good honey and you notice that the honey started to go bad at a certain time, you start looking at the period of time to find out why it went bad.

But this does not account for the intense fascination which these modern movements seem to hold for Denny:

The Russian Revolution and Hitler—now those were my two favorite things.... They were just so interesting because they were almost unreal to me. And Hitler. Sometimes I almost think, God—a person like that really ever lived?.... It's just amazing...how this one guy could do this—just the whole, you know, repercussions from that. And the Russian Revolution, the same thing.... You realize in a sense that this thing started almost with, I think, a few people. But it was an idea-oriented thing, the whole thing.

Let us pause at this point and take stock of Denny's account so far. In reviewing Denny's experience of self-esteem and his ideology we have noted a number of inconsistencies and contradictions. Describing the sunroom, for example, Denny oscillates between presenting it as a genuine achievement and playing it down as "no big thing." This seems to be part of a general pattern that runs throughout much of his account. During the interview Denny alternated between making expansive comments and backing off to qualify what he had said, frequently using words like "I mean," "believe me," "really," and "you know." More than this backing off, however, there are significant contradictions in the content of Denny's account, especially between his ideology and some of his apparent interests. Denny talks about the natural life, but he seems to be very fond of the products of technology; and although he expresses dissatisfaction with government and "group think," he is fascinated by powerful leaders and mass movements.

I have already suggested that such inconsistencies and contradictions seem to be connected with defensive self-esteem; and, indeed, Denny does seem to be defending himself when he describes his good feelings about building the sunroom. It is not clear, however, *why* Denny would feel defensive about this project or *what* he might be defending himself against. In order to throw some light on these issues, let us turn to a consideration of Denny's life history.

Denny is the oldest of four children born to parents of German ancestry. Denny's paternal grandfather was a first-generation German-American who worked as a salesman all his life. Times were hard when Denny's father was growing up, and Denny's grandfather had to take a job selling vegetables from a bicycle cart. Nevertheless, Denny's father jokes about these times and talks about how the family managed to make money anyway. After high school Denny's father went to work for a furniture manufacturing firm. He remained with the business until five years after Denny was born, at which time he founded his own company. The company was successful, a fact Denny attributes in large measure to his father's financial acumen:

> He knows what money is, what you got to do to get it, what you got to do to keep it, the different ways a person can spend it.... [He watches] its ebbs and tides and flows, you know, like the way a weatherman watches a barometer.

Denny describes his father as an extroverted and strong-willed man who dominates situations through political tact and manipulation. This is true inside the family as well as outside, and Denny characterizes his father as getting his way through the force of arguments in which "he'll stretch things a little bit, get into more of the gray areas of lying." Although it is clear that Denny has positive feelings for his father, he also characterized him as being somewhat "insensitive."

Denny describes his mother as a nurturant woman who is also very demanding. At various times during the interview he characterized her as a "mother-philosopher" and a "watchdog-teacher." Her parents were German immigrants who, despite hard times and economic limitations, raised her with high standards of honesty, morality, and workmanship. Denny recalls her teaching him these ideals as he grew up:

> She was always the first person to tell me if I wasn't fair to somebody, first person to tell me if I wasn't honest to somebody, first person to tell me if I didn't really try as hard as she knew that I could try.

In particular, Denny recalls his mother condemning poor workmanship and hypocrisy in people with whom she came into contact.

More than any other subject, perhaps, Denny describes a pleasant childhood. He states that he was close to both parents and that his experience with them was "in balance, definitely positive." Of particular interest is Denny's relationship to his father. Denny recounts a number of idealized interactions in which his father teaches him, helps him, and fosters his abilities and achievements. For example:

> Any time I wanted to make anything, you know, he'd be there to help me. When I was younger I can remember him doing that a lot.... I can remember his voice telling me, you know, do this, do that...
>
> He was always there when you needed him, you know, like if you were making something and you got into a little hot water...you knew that you could find out, you could ask him. Something good would happen, you know?...
>
> Different ideas that we would have to make money as kids, for instance, he always got enthused about that.

But as noted above, Denny also describes another side of his father, a side which is domineering and manipulative, and sometimes insensitive. The way in which Denny has experienced this side of his father was evident when he discussed what he called his father's "Depression syndrome":

> I realize now he's just the way he is because in a way, I tell you, it's—it's, I think, the Depression syndrome, a lot of men his age have this. Really. "You got a hole in your shoe? Put a piece of cardboard in there."... Maybe one of the girls would bitch about—uh, see we had to walk like a mile and he'd say..."That's okay, *walk* five miles!" Um, "You don't need new shoes." "That bike's okay—what's wrong with that bike? Oh, let me ride it around the block.

Eh, I rode it, nothing wrong with that bike, go ride that bike." You know?

If Denny resents this kind of behavior, there is also a peculiar way in which he has been silenced by it. For he must agree that his father knows whereof he speaks: he *did* have it harder than Denny, and Denny's life *isn't* so bad.

[My parents say] "You've got nothing to complain about, Denny." You know, that was always—("We had it harder than you"?) And they did, let's face it. I don't know how you were brought up, but I know that I didn't have it that hard...
    Everything was just nice, pleasant, you know?... So that's why now you wonder to yourself, God, is something going to happen, or how can you be that lucky, you know? Well, maybe that's getting paranoid or something to think that. (You mean—) Well, you've had so much good luck and so many good things have happened, my God, something bad's going to happen.... I have nothing to complain about, not really, I mean, I could complain about my shoes that are too tight—but [laughs] what's that in the face of the world?

Denny's ominous feeling that "something bad is going to happen" suggests a certain sense of guilt about his own favored position. In this connection, it is worth recalling the importance to Denny of individual accomplishment:

If you don't do anything, then I say shut up.... I mean, if you're not doing anything, my God, you hardly even have any rights. Unless you're paralyzed.... You don't have much right to complain about anything or to criticize anything.

Denny's favored position means that *he* has not done things, has not proven himself through individual accomplishments. We can assume from the content of his own severe standards, then, that Denny is uncertain whether he *himself* has any rights. This inference is consistent with some of the trends we have already noted in the way Denny presented himself in the interview. His oscillation between expansive comments and self-depreciating qualifications suggests doubt about the legitimacy of his achievements. It is as though Denny feels himself to be at a disadvantage and must keep himself covered on all fronts, lest he be challenged by someone like his father who *has* been proven.

Related to this problem is a series of intense feelings which Denny describes in connection with figures representing power and authority. We have already noted that Denny seems to be fascinated by historical figures who wielded great power. There is an opposite trend, however, in Denny's resentment of persons wielding authority in his own life. For example, at one point in the interview Denny talked about his dissatisfaction with his high-school teachers, characterizing them as "a lot of jerks." At another point in the interview he talked about his own brief interest in teaching and how it had ended because he would not "suck up" to the principals who did the hiring. At still another point he described how he had managed to get a medical discharge from the service because he had found the harassment of the instructors in basic training intolerable.

Denny's feelings of self-doubt and his ambivalence about powerful individuals seem to be related to a central conflict around the meaning of his favored position. Denny feels untested in life and unsure of his own abilities. Moreover, he feels unequal to his father, who *has* been tested. Unlike his father, Denny has not lived through hardship, earned his way, or proven himself. Both his mother and father remind him of these facts, especially his father, who periodically implies that Denny's interest in material products and luxuries is something to be scorned. There is a subtle betrayal here, for Denny's father, who loves the things that money can buy, is the very person who gave Denny these benefits, who modeled Denny's desire for them, and who showed him how they can be appreciated and enjoyed. In a very real sense, Denny has been given a set of needs and values by his father and then condemned by his father for having those needs and values.

Yet Denny does not believe that he is in any position to protest this injustice, because the major charge leveled against him is true: just as his parents say, he has not endured adversity, has not proven himself, has not matched his father's achievements. The ideals of fairness and honesty which Denny acquired from his mother force him to admit that this is the case. Moreover, it is not clear how Denny *could* prove himself, given the advantages he has received. Even if he were to renounce his material situation and deliberately test himself in the face of adversity, he would lay himself open to the charge of being a rich kid on a lark. Denny is caught, therefore, in the double bind of having to prove himself worthy and equal to his father in a life situation that has been defined by his father as too easy.

THE STRUCTURE OF DEFENSE: SYMBOLIC RESOLUTION

Let us return now to the question raised above, that of defensive self-esteem. We have already noted that there are reasons for suspecting that Denny's self-esteem is structured defensively in the above account. But we have yet to determine the details of this structuring and to draw general conclusions about the relationship between defense and self-esteem. The following pages will discuss defensive self-esteem as a general phenomenon by illustrating certain characteristic features as they appear in Denny's account. Throughout this discussion, however, it is worth keeping in mind the postulate adopted at the beginning of this chapter: *no experience of self-esteem is ever entirely defensive or entirely nondefensive.* Thus, while we will focus on the defensive aspects of Denny's experience, we can also assume that it involves elements of genuine resolution and real self-esteem. This point will be clarified as we proceed.

Let us begin by considering a general definition of defensive self-esteem: *An experience of self-esteem can be regarded as defensive insofar as it involves an attempt to resolve a central conflict without changing the way in which one's identity and one's world have been defined in terms of that conflict. This occurs when an individual achieves a limited resolution of a central conflict in a circumscribed region of meaning, a resolution which may be regarded as primarily symbolic.*

This definition suggests that defensive self-esteem involves an attempt to live out a contradiction. An individual tries to resolve a central conflict without changing the contradictory stamp it has imposed upon his or her own person or the way it has structured his or her reality in general. In order to accomplish this goal, the individual divides the field of meaning in some way and resolves the central conflict in a highly limited and circumscribed portion of his or her life. This operation is basically a defensive one, for it is aimed at keeping the reorganization which solves the central conflict from spreading to include a painful reevaluation of self and world. Such a resolution can be considered primarily symbolic since it addresses the central conflict in a highly visible region of an individual's world without carrying the process through to a more comprehensive and lasting reorganization. The particular way this resolution occurs in an individual case will depend on how the individual exploits the semiotic and linguistic characteristics of ideology, idealization, and the central conflict in organizing these structures vis-a-vis each other. As we shall see, different individuals organize these structures in substantially different ways. What remains true in all cases, however, is that the field of meaning is in some way divided and that this division keeps the resolution of the central conflict isolated and symbolic. A divided field of meaning is evident in *gaps and disruptions in the coherence of a subject's account.*

Because a symbolic resolution is aimed at solving a central conflict without changing the way in which the individual has defined self and world in terms of that conflict, such a resolution typically has two consequences. First, a symbolic resolution usually involves a reversal rather than a true reconciliation of a central conflict. The individual tries to undo or deny the painful aspect of a central conflict while maintaining the basic terms in which it defines the problems in his or her life. He or she therefore attempts to *reverse* roles or to live out a theme *opposite* to one which was experienced in the past; but it does not occur to the individual that the conflicting themes might themselves be made compatible. Second, a symbolic resolution usually does not involve real and lasting change in a person's life. Because it involves a circumscribed region of meaning, a symbolic resolution does not lead to an examination of the larger field of ideas and experiences in terms of which a person defines self and possibilities. Things therefore remain *essentially unchanged* and the individual continues to live out the same patterns as before.

Before discussing how these characteristics are manifested in Denny's account, it is necessary to extend some of what was said in the previous chapter about semiotic and linguistic systems. In chapter 2 a rather clear distinction was drawn between semiotic and linguistic structures, the former as a system of images or other signifiers representing *objects* in the context of the subject's life history, and the latter as a system of words or other signifiers representing *concepts* as they are used by the subject. However, researchers in the fields of semiology and linguistics have noted that these two kinds of systems are not entirely separable. For example, Coward and Ellis (1977) point out that semiotic systems depend upon verbal language for their intelligibility, and Piaget and Inhelder (1966) state that ordinary language must be supplemented by semiotically organized images representing "objects as such" (p. 70). It is best to regard these two kinds of structure as essentially continuous. What were identified in chapter 2 as semiotic and linguistic structures are more correctly regarded as interrelated organizations of meaning in which either experiential or conceptual elements are predominant, respectively. For similar reasons, patterns of meaning in semiotic structures tend to be reflected in linguistic structures, and alterations in linguistic structures can be used to reorganize semiotic structures. This dialectic is merely another manifestation of the principle emphasized at the beginning of this chapter, namely, that *meaning is indivisible*.

To give a concrete illustration of the above, let us consider the case of Esther. In Esther's account, semiotic and linguistic structures are generally organized in ways that presuppose each other. For example, Esther describes a "social philosophy" which is given experiential substance by both the idealized and the conflicted interactions she remembers in her family. It is not necessary for Esther to spell out to herself exactly what it would mean to take a nurturant or respectful role in a social community because she can remember the examples of her mother, aunt, and father. In this manner, the linguistic structures of Esther's ideology are developed in ways that presuppose (and extend) the themes which are presented in the semiotically organized imagery she describes. The reverse is also true. The particular experiences Esther describes, the way she describes them, and perhaps even the way she reconstructs them in her memory are all influenced by the way she conceptualizes them, namely, as instances of "closeness," "family," "control," etc. Esther's ideology and other linguistic structures, therefore, influence the way she organizes the semiotic structures in her account.

In order to see how Denny's experience of self-esteem is defensively circumscribed, let us consider the relationship between semiotic and linguistic structures in his account, particularly with reference to his interest in history.

I have already suggested that Denny is caught in a double bind. The double bind has been defined (Bateson, et al., 1956) as a pair of contradictory injunctions accompanied by a constraint which makes it impossible to leave the field. In Denny's case the contradictory injunctions consist of his father giving him an easy life while simultaneously demanding that he prove himself, and the constraint which keeps him in the field is the sense of honesty which forces him to admit that he does have it easier than his father. A major way Denny has dealt with this double bind is by adopting a *historical perspective*. This strategy has given a particular character to Denny's ideology—a historicized and intellectualized quality which expands the ideology as a linguistic production but simultaneously attentuates its relationship to the semiotic structures of idealization and the central conflict. We will now consider some of the specific ways this pattern is manifested in Denny's account.

As is true in other cases, Denny's ideology gains experiential substance from certain idealized images. Specifically, the ideals of individual accomplishment and making things for oneself and one's family are reminiscent of idealizations in which Denny describes his father building up his own business and teaching Denny how to make and fix things. But the historicized and intellectualized character of Denny's ideology embeds his ideals in an elaborate linguistic context that distances them from their life-historical origin. Rather than talking about doing well in business or taking pride in the quality of one's work, for example, Denny talks about a "natural instinct" for accomplishment in the context of primitive cultures and historical trends. The effect is to obscure the connections between Denny's ideology and the semiotically organized images which define idealized and other interactions between Denny and his father. The meaning of Denny's ideology thus becomes disconnected, to a certain extent, from his own *personal* history. Denny's ideology becomes a social critique on a grand scale, and is related to the semiotically represented themes of Denny's past in only the most indirect and insubstantial ways.

The effects of this defensive strategy can be seen in a number of areas, but let us take as an example Denny's attitudes toward money and power. Some of Denny's idealized descriptions of his father involve the theme of making money—indeed, this arena is the chief one in which Denny's father has proven himself. However, there is little in Denny's highly intellectualized ideology that addresses this issue on a mundane basis. Denny seems to lack an ideological framework relevant to his *own* work and potential financial success; consequently, he alternates between idealistic statements about the natural instincts and spontaneous expressions of enthusiasm for material luxuries. A similar problem exists with regard to the issue of power. Denny's ideology is phrased in terms that define power as a disruptive influence in social life. What is not given representation is a wish that can be inferred from Denny's descriptions of his relationship with his father, the wish to establish himself as a potent person equal to his father. This wish appears to be represented, indirectly, in Denny's fascination with powerful figures in history and in a certain tendency during the interview to assert himself inconsistently. Both of these issues, therefore—money and power—present themselves from time to time in Denny's account as images and characterizations that are not integrated with the rest of his account and, in fact, contradict his ideology and the meaning of his self-esteem incident.

When it comes to Denny's incident of self-esteem, the symbolic function of his ideology becomes most clear. The sunroom incident is described as an example of individual accomplishment in a world of technology, a reenactment of what people have done throughout history. This linguistic construction augments the significance of the sunroom project, but it also insulates and removes the project from the concrete semiotic structure of Denny's central conflict. Yet meaning is never completely divisible, and some of the traces of Denny's wish to prove himself in relation to his father remain and are evident in his advocacy of individual achievement in an era of governmental domination. Building the sunroom therefore represents the affirmation that Denny wants, but it does so *primarily by analogy*. Carrying out this project is *like* overcoming adversity through individual accomplishment. By virtue of this analogy Denny can fulfill his wish in a limited way. The conflict he experienced growing up—having an easy life but wanting to prove himself—is resolved not through a reconciliation of the terms of the conflict but through a symbolic recreation and reversal of them. In this manner, Denny's ideology creates an abstract arena in which he can symbolically break with his past, even while using conceptual terms from that past to structure his break from it.

Denny also uses the historical perspective of his ideology to curtail the possible use of semiotically represented life history to explore the full extent of his feelings about his father and himself. For example, Denny introduced the notion of his father's Depression syndrome when I inquired about the details of his father's insensitivity. Denny could have responded to this line of questioning by filling in more of his past history, describing incidents and interactions which would have conveyed the substance of Denny's relationship with his father. But such a response would have entailed a painful reconstruction not only of his father's past behavior but of Denny's own hurt feelings and disappointment with his father and himself. Instead, Denny chose to discuss his father in the context of *world* history, and in so doing retreated to the aloof stance of social commentator and historian once again. In this manner, the language of Denny's ideology, with its historical and sociological cast, serves to undercut its integration with the semiotically organized experiential details of Denny's central conflict. In so doing, it undercuts the exploration of self and the likelihood of real change in Denny's life.

In Denny's account, therefore, the field of meaning is disrupted and divided at a number of points. Many of these disruptions have to do with Denny's historicized and intellectualized use of ideology and his corresponding failure to integrate the semiotic structures of his central conflict and idealizations with the linguistic structures of his ideology. The result is that the incident of self-esteem Denny describes involves a circumscribed and relatively peripheral event which is given a symbolic meaning by the language of Denny's ideology. The sunroom incident does not involve a true reconciliation of Denny's contradictory relationship with his father, nor does the incident really fulfill Denny's wishes for successful achievement and recognition. But in the language of Denny's ideology, building the sunroom has meaning because it represents an instance of individual achievement in an institutionalized world. The task harkens back to an era when things were not as complicated and an individual could really accomplish things, just as Denny was once able to share and accomplish things with his father. In this manner, Denny's incident of self-esteem negates his central conflict in the detached realm of his ideology, a realm organized along the same formal lines as the semiotic structures of Denny's life history, but which is largely disconnected from these structures. Denny is therefore able to avoid a full reexamination of the experiences in terms of which his identity is organized, and his experience of self-esteem remains circumscribed, symbolic, and largely defensive.

This account should not lead the reader to assume that other instances of defensive self-esteem will follow the same pattern as Denny's. The fact that the field of meaning is disrupted in this case at the interface between the linguistic structure of ideology and the semiotic structures of idealization and the central conflict is a characteristic of Denny's style. This characteristic is primarily attributable to the historicized and intellectualized cast of his ideology. In the next case, that of John, we will see another example of defensive self-esteem which, like Denny's, is characterized by disruptions in the field of meaning. In John's case, however, the disruptions occur between specific incidents, each one of which involves closely related life-historical and conceptual (semiotic and linguistic) elements. For John, ideology, idealization, and the central conflict are intensely interrelated, but as a series of tightly organized incidents that stand isolated from each other. As we shall see, this defensive strategy presents itself in John's account as a recurrent theme that manifests itself again and again in his life without leading to change.

It is worth emphasizing again that no instance of self-esteem is ever entirely defensive or entirely nondefensive. I have emphasized the defensive aspects of the sunroom incident. But it can also be assumed that this incident and others like it in Denny's life have had positive effects on the way he feels about himself and his accomplishments. Even in relation to his father, the sunroom project probably has genuine meaning for Denny. The fact that he is capable of building something for his family and that he chose to do so in this case does demonstrate that Denny has initiative, that he is not someone who is "paralyzed." But the defensive aspect of the sunroom incident is more salient, and this is perhaps most evident in the fact that this accomplishment does not seem to involve any changes in Denny's work life, his family relationships, or his social world.

To further emphasize this point, let us consider Esther's case once again. We noted that Esther's job in the history department represented the resolution of her conflict between familial closeness and mutual respect. We also considered the question of how much things had really changed, since Esther appears to exercise control despite her protestation to the contrary. To this we can add the observation that Esther's incident of self-esteem occurred outside of her family, the primary arena in which her conflicts over nurturance and respect have usually manifested themselves. Nevertheless, there are reasons for believing that Esther's experience involves a genuine resolution in a way that Denny's does not. Esther describes the job in the history department as a pivotal experience, one that not only made her feel good about herself but also changed the way she thinks about herself. Moreover, there is evidence to support this statement in the fact that Esther's role and self-conception seem to have been different in the jobs she held after working in the history department, particularly in the one she has at present.

Esther's experience, therefore, shows a different combination of defensive and nondefensive elements. There can be little doubt that there are discontinuities of meaning in Esther's account and that her experience in the history department was in some ways encapsulated and symbolic; but it also seems that this resolution was more comprehensive than the one which Denny describes, and therefore represents a more thoroughgoing and genuine expression of self-esteem.

The interplay between defensive and nondefensive self-esteem has presented great problems for existing psychological research and theory. Studies of the relationship between defensiveness and self-esteem have produced a variety of contradictory results (Rogers and Walsh, 1959; Beloff and Beloff, 1959; Rothstein and Epstein, 1963; Taylor and Combs, 1952; Moore and Ascough, 1970), and there are a number of indications that these two factors cannot be measured independently. To give one example, Silber and Tippett (1965) report an investigation in which subjects were interviewed and classified into several different categories according to the type of self-esteem which they seemed to be exhibiting. These categories were: (1) defensive high self-esteem, (2) nondefensive high self-esteem, (3) ineffective defensive self-esteem, (4) inconsistent self-esteem, and (5) low self-esteem. Of particular interest is the relationship between the first two categories. The authors report more difficultly distinguishing between defensive and nondefensive high self-esteem than between any other two patterns (p. 1029). Moreover, when subjects were given standard psychological tests measuring self-esteem, those who had been categorized as exhibitng defensive and nondefensive high self-esteem tended to score similarly. These results suggest an intricate relationship between defense and self-esteem, one which may elude both the classificatory activity of the clinician and the psychometric technology of the experimenter.

Above all, previous conceptions of defensive self-esteem have failed to give recognition to the *synthetic* dimension of meaning, the way in which the field of life-historical experience and understanding is organized as a whole. As I indicated in analyzing Denny's account, even a disrupted and divided field of meaning still retains a kind of unity. One manifestation of this unity is a formal similarity among the various constellations of signifiers—for example, the similarity between Denny's wish to prove himself in relation to his father and his advocacy of individual achievement in an era of governmental domination. Patterns like this one indicate that an individual must use existing constellations of signifiers as guidelines for organizing each other, *even if he or she only does so by association, analogy, and reversal.* The fact that meaning is synthetic in this way, that it is never completely divisible, means that relatively isolated conceptual and experiential arenas of a person's life can become *symbolic of the whole.* In these arenas a person can effect a partial and primarily symbolic resolution of a central conflict, the kind of resolution I have characterized as defensive. Such a resolution will leave the individual's identity essentially unchanged; but some reorganization of the self will always occur because the field of meaning in which the self is defined is never completely disrupted. Defensive and nondefensive self-esteem, therefore, exist in a dialectical relationship. It is possible to distinguish instances in which self-esteem is primarily defensive or primarily nondefensive, but to do so requires an investigation of the thematic particulars in a given case.

So far we have examined a case in which defensive self-esteem is evident in the resolution of a central conflict in the symbolic arena of an intellectualized and historicized ideology. We will now consider another case. Like Denny, John describes a resolution that is primarily symbolic. In John's case, however, the resolution is accomplished in a very different way; John uses a close interplay of semiotic and linguistic structures to organize a series of experiences which represent resolutions of his central conflict but which remain essentially detached from each other and from the rest of his life. Juxtaposed with Denny's case, this one will give an idea of the variety of ways in which a symbolic resolution can occur. In addition, John's case will lead into a discussion of the repetition complusion, a clinical phenomenon which seems to be closely related to questions about the central conflict, defense, resolution, and self-esteem.

JOHN: INVISIBLE CURTAINS

I first met John when he waited on me in a men's clothing store in a western suburban city. John's slight build, glasses, and thin gray hair give him the appearance of an intellectual, an appearance further promoted by his use of elegant, though often catachrestic, turns of speech. A fifty-seven-year-old white father of three, John is a second-generation American of Lithuanian descent.

At the beginning of the interview, John had difficulty thinking of a time when he had felt good about himself. He commented that he does not hold himself in high esteem, by which he meant that he does not "pat himself on the back." Instead, he explained, he tries to set an example for his colleagues and family and feels good when he is regarded highly by others. I asked John if he could give a specific illustration and he recalled an incident that had occurred many years earlier.

At the age of forty John had been laid off from the manufacturing company at which he had been working as a precision machinist for twenty-one years. He had been very depressed at the time and very worried about the future. John had been with the plant for such a long time that he feared it was too late for him to go anywhere else or to break into a new career. At the time of his termination John went to the personnel department and requested a letter of recommendation for prospective future employers. The man in the personnel department received him very warmly, and a few days later John was given a most laudatory letter, crediting him with "everything that was good":

Character and attendance and responsibility and knowledge in [my] work. And I felt very, very good.... I thought that at least my labors were appreciated and there were evidently files kept on [it]. I would say that was one of the good feelings that I had during that time....
(Were you surprised at all when you got the good recommendation?) Not really. I didn't know if I would get it to that high level, and I was elated that I did.

In exploring his feelings about this incident, John and I discovered the outlines of an ideology, one which emphasizes the importance of doing good work and winning the respect of one's co-workers and family:

(It sounds like being recognized for doing well...was something that was very important to you.) Definitely is. (Has that been important all your life?) All my life, even unto the present day. I always try to do a little better tomorrow, a little better the day after, and...to me, that is life, always something better, an improvement...and that's how I tried to raise my offspring. I have three children...and I feel good that I have set a good example.

Setting a good example is important because it is not self-esteem but the esteem of others that John wishes to win:

I don't really hold myself in high esteem in life. I try to set very good examples to my colleagues and immediate family, and those to me are achievements in life. (Setting examples?) Setting examples and trying to the best of my abilities to present myself in a manner that's acceptable to other people that this man is of high esteem.... I notice in my own thoughts that people think highly of me, which is my goal, really, within my own level.

One way John has tried to set an example at home is by practicing reserve and self-restraint. He explained that he has always controlled his emotions and has refrained from getting angry because "to me it's not the intellectual thing to do." At work, too, John has attempted to perform in an exemplary manner. At one point in the interview he described how he has tried to avoid mistakes that the "average individual" would make. John feels that his dedication has led to his being "highly respected," not only for the work he does, but for the "quality of an individual" that he is. At another point in the interview John expressed the hope that when he retires he can continue to work part time "as a respected, elderly gentleman."

In sum, doing one's job to the best of one's ability, setting good examples, and winning the respect of one's family and one's co-workers are major tenets of John's ideology. The letter of recommendation seems to represent a specific instance in which John earned and received this kind of recognition:

> It's a very good feeling that people from personnel who have evidently looked over the past records think that much highly of you. So I felt very, very good.

Let us turn now to a consideration of the life-historical context in which John developed this set of ideals and beliefs.

John's father was a Lithuanian immigrant who came to America before the First World War and who, after several years in this country, married John's mother, the American-born daughter of a Lithuanian immigrant. John was the third of four children and the only boy. John describes his father as a man who was very conscious of his responsibilities to his family and who worked very hard. Much of the time John was growing up his father was away from home, working. There does not seem to have been much direct communication between John and his father, who was "never a man to express himself openly," but John describes himself as being aware of his father and learning from him "by observation and analyzing."

> Through my observation and knowing him as much as I would think he knew me...I think he accepted [manual labor] as a fact of his generation. And everybody thought highly of [my father] and they still do. He is a personal man that has never lost his temper and never would shun to work for the benefit of the family.

John's observation of his father appears to be the basis for an idealization of the themes of work and responsibility. In the following passage John describes how his father tried to get work to support his family:

> He loved to work. He still loves to work. (Did he communicate that to you?) No. (How do you know that—) 'Cause he would get up [at] three, two o'clock in the morning to stand in line at the local factory in the middle of winter and maybe be in line four or five hours. And

then the policemen would come on horseback and disperse
the group. But he did this day after day. He knew it was
his responsibility to go out and work to bring some income
to the family.

In the early years of John's life his father had worked in a coal
mine and a steel mill. Later, the family moved to the city, where
John's father tried to obtain factory work, as described above.
Eventually he was given a job, but this was soon followed by the
stock-market crash and unemployment again. The Depression years
were very difficult ones for the family, and John recalls his father
taking odd jobs of any kind to earn whatever he could.
  John's childhood was difficult in other ways, too. Because he was
the only male child he was under a great deal of pressure to succeed
in areas where his father felt inadequate—particularly school. He
recalls his father standing over him with a ruler, tapping him on the
ear, and calling him a "dummy" because he was having trouble
learning. For the most part, however, John's father was not directly
involved in teaching him; this and most other child-rearing duties
were left to his mother. Although John was restrained in making
negative comments about his parents, it is clear that he resents his
father's leaving so much of his upbringing to his mother:

> My father did not take too much of an interest in bringing
> up of the children....
>   He would always be working, and I was home alone
> domineered by women.

John's memories of his mother are generally unhappy ones, and
the image of her which emerged in the interview was that of a
severe and punitive woman who actively humiliated her son. For
example, John remembers one time when she whipped him in his
wet underwear because he had gone swimming and allowed
someone to steal his new blue jeans. Far more humiliating,
however, was the punishment that John's mother regularly applied
for minor infractions throughout much of his childhood:

> If I would displease my mother she would put my sister's
> clothing on me. It was a form of punishment and I was
> compelled to wear my sister's clothes. Not underclothing,
> but [it] just could be the topping like a dress.... I was so
> embarrassed. I may have resented it at that time and
> psychologically it may have had an effect on me.

John believes that these episodes affected his feelings about women:

It more or less embedded a feeling of male chauvinism and a disrespect for the opposite sex to a degree where...as I was growing up into adulthood I did not have the respect for the female species as much as I should have.

In connection with this, John explained that he has never experienced feelings of romantic love for a woman.

Not surprisingly, John's sense of his own self was not entirely clear as he grew up. His father's absense and his mother's behavior toward him appear to have left him uncertain and confused about his own male identity, as is indicated both by the content of the following passage and the overtones of some of the wording:

When I was about sixteen years old I had such an urge, I felt so inadequate.... I did have a hunger for knowledge of life. So I personally selected men that were twelve, fifteen years older than I was.... I felt that they [had] lived a life that I would—through their companionship and them trying to guide me—I would progress myself to a point of adulthood...and they accepted me in their group.

John states that he used these older males as models of "established adulthood" and tried to learn from their examples about proper social conduct and adult behavior.

Another part of John's search for identity was his attempt to come to terms with his Lithuanian background and to enter into the mainstream of American society. As he grew up, John felt that he was at a great disadvantage because of the limitations of his ethnic upbringing. During his early years his social experience had been confined entirely to the Lithuanian immigrant community. At the age of fourteen, however, he entered high school and experienced cultural shock:

Here I was finally mixed in with other nationals, which I did not experience before. Then I began to realize I was living in the past in a shell with these invisible curtains around me. I did not know the outside world.

The terms "shell" and "invisible curtains" appear several times in John's account of his upbringing, and they underline the extent to which he experienced contact with the larger society as a painful exposure. In addition, John frequently used another term in connection with his ethnic background. On numerous occasions during the interview he referred to immigrants as the "foreign element." Presumably, John, as a precision machinist, is familiar with the other referent of this term—namely, a bit of dirt or some other substance which infiltrates a machine and disrupts its functioning. This usage suggests a fear on John's part that his entry into the social mechanism would be regarded as a kind of noxious intrusion by something base or contemptible.

The above considerations bring us to the central conflict in John's life-historical account. Embarrassment and shame play an important role in John's story, and, as he grew up, a major question for him seems to have been whether or not he could be the focus of attention without being humiliated. Expressed in John's account as a tension between concealment and exposure, this conflict is captured in the paradoxical image of "invisible curtains." Life historically, John's struggle with this conflict is evident in his attempt to achieve a compromise between remaining hidden and exposing himself to the larger "outside world." This conflict is also evident in John's ideology as a preference to remain inconspicuous and to do reliable, good work which he hopes will, nevertheless, be singled out by those around him as exemplary. Some of the relationships between this ideology and John's early experience, however, have yet to be elaborated.

In Denny's case, we saw how the field of meaning was disrupted at the interface beteen semiotic and linguistic structures. This disruption was accomplished primarily by Denny's construction of an intellectualized and historicized ideology, a strategy that elaborated this ideology on a grand scale but simultaneously attenuated its connections with the life-historical central conflict and the idealizations that gave it experiential substance. In John's case, a different strategy is employed, but once again it is a strategy that simultaneously organizes and divides the field of meaning. Rather than attenuating the connections between semiotic and linguistic structures, John repeatedly brings semiotic and linguistic elements *together*; but he does so in a way that produces a series of life-historical structures, each of which is organized according to the same highly specific theme while remaining essentially disconnected from the others. To put it crudely, John splits the field of meaning along vertical rather than horizontal lines. This strategy is accomplished by the development of a relatively *constricted* ideology which closely reflects idealized paradigms and is used to organize certain other memories and experiences according to the same pattern. Let us now consider this strategy in its specific details.

I have identified John's central conflict as a set of ambivalent feelings about exposure, a question of whether or not he could be observed without being humiliated. One side of this conflict is given semiotic representation in John's description of being left "home alone domineered by women" and subject to humiliation at the hands of his mother. The other side of this conflict, however, as well as the idealization which offers elements of a possible solution to it, is represented in John's description of his relationship with his father. John describes a relationship in which he and his father did not communicate directly but knew each other "by observation." It should be added that John used the term "observation" a number of times during the interview to describe his relationship not only with his father but with a number of other people as well. In fact, the concept of "observaton" is a key one in John's ideology. John describes a social world in which people observe one another and lood for "good examples" of "acceptable" behavior. John's idealizations of his father involve interactions in which he observes his father setting examples of such behavior. In this context we can infer that John's description of his father's observing *him* expresses the wish for a reciprocal affirmation, the wish that his father might see *him* as exemplary and give him the positive attention that was so painfully lacking in John's childhood. In this manner, the semiotic structures of John's life history and the linguistic structure of his ideology are closely interrelated. It would be difficult to understand John's central conflict over possible humiliation or the meaning of his idealized descriptions of his father without understanding his ideology of reciprocal observation; and likewise, it would be difficult to appreciate the significance of John's wish to set a good example in the social world without understanding his past experiences of shame and humiliation and his longing to receive positive attention from his unexpressive father.

For the same reason, John's ideology has a constricted character. Rather than elaborating his ideals in terms that go very far beyond the issue of observing and being observed, John's ideology stays close to the original concerns which give it experiential substance and emotional reality. The constricted character of John's ideological language and the proximity of this language to the semiotic structures of his early life history are particularly evident in John's use of his ideology to select, organize, and reconstruct subsequent experiences in his life to fit the same thematic pattern that has already been described. Specifically, John reports a number of incidents, each of which follows the same pattern: a respected, usually older, male figure comes forward and reveals that he has been observing John from a distance; this male figure commends John for the qualities or example he has displayed, particularly as a good and conscientious worker. These experiences seem repeatedly to fulfill John's wish to receive positive attention and affirmation from an idealized figure like his father. At the same time, they do not change John's experience of himself in any larger way—rather, they merely "happen" to him from time to time, whenever such an idealized figure is available and acts in a way that can be interpreted to fit certain requirements. This set of experiences therefore constitutes a series of essentially unrelated *symbolic incidents*, each of which represents the resolution of John's central conflict in a specific and isolated interaction but has little effect on the rest of his life.

There are a number of such incidents described at various points throughout John's account. For example, at one point in the interview, John mentioned with pride how the mayor of his city had come to know and respect him "as an individual," as evidenced by his greeting John whenever they pass each other on the street. At another point, he related how he had decided to change occupations at the time he was laid off from the precision-machinist job:

> I happened also to work with an elderly gentleman who years past owned two or three clothing stores of his own. I respected him and he took a liking to me. He worked for this firm also and he was also laid off, but it didn't mind to him too much because he was getting to be retirement age anyway. But he saw that I was very much despondent, and he approached me and he says "Through my observation of your personality—I own clothing stores and I think if you don't like this work you could learn to be a clothing salesman."...So through thinking it over...I decided to do that.

At still another point in the interview, John described how his good work as a precision machinist had been recognized by his supervisors:

> I was highly respected and I was asked to go out on social functions with people that I thought were very knowledgable in their field...the higher supervisory personnel, or the people working in the personnel offices, where even to this day they do not mingle with people in machinery or productivity. There seems to be a birds-of-a-feather-flock-together situation, which always did exist and exists today. But I seem to have overcome that barrier. (In what way?) By being recognized as an individual, of not really what he is doing for a living, but the quality of an individual.

Most dramatically of all, John related the following story about his maternal grandfather:

> Rather than having any of his sons at his dying bed he requested that I come, and he wanted to foretell me his whole life—why he married his wife and what his goals in life were. He did tell this all to me on his dying bed, rather than selecting any of his children he selected me. (You must have been very close to each other.) I did not realize it at the time. Evidently he was observing me all these years and he took a liking to me. I did not realize it.

What is common to all these incidents is that John is observed and singled out by a more-established male figure who recognizes and affirms John's worth, particularly as a dedicated worker.[1] Among other things, this pattern appears to be a confirmation of the values of hard work and responsibility which John idealized in his father. But these incidents also reveal the thematic matrix in which John's values are organized—each bears the stamp of John's ideology of exemplary behavior and each represents a resolution of John's central conflict in a specific interactional context.

The letter of recommendation which John cited as his original incident of self-esteem follows the same pattern. Like the other incidents we have considered, this one represents a resolution of John's central conflict in a specific set of circumstances. Respected male figures—the supervisors and the people from personnel—reveal to John that they have been observing him all along. They commend him for the good work he has done and give him some measure of the affirmation he never got from his father.

This incident, like the other ones John describes, exemplifies what has been defined above as defensive self-esteem. Occuring in a carefully circumscribed region of meaning, the incident does not lead to changes in other aspects of John's life, nor does it involve a true reconciliation of the themes of John's central conflict. John does not discover, for example, that he can feel self-respect *without* being acclaimed by an observing male. Rather, the incident reproduces the structure of John's idealized relationship with his father and other

---

[1]Another manifestation of this pattern was John's reaction to me. At certain points he indicated that he experienced my request to interview him as a singling out of his life for examination and judgment. At one point he compared it to the television program "This Is Your Life," and at another point he said that because he was going to be interviewed he had known that I would be his "confessor."

males, the structure of reciprocal observation and affirmation which reverses the humiliation originally associated with John's central conflict. In fact, the semiotic characteristics of the letter incident seem to be selectively chosen and interpreted to produce this effect, to confirm that John has been recognized and appreciated by respected male figures, *despite evidence to the contrary.* This conclusion is suggested by the fact that the letter incident is actually part of a larger contradiction of which John is apparently unaware.

John interprets the letter as evidence that he had not been forgotten by the company, that his "labors were appreciated" and "highly" regarded. Yet John received the letter in the context of a very real and potentially disasterous abandonment: after twenty-one years of responsible and reliable work, John was being turned out to begin a new career somewhere else. The writing of a letter of recommendation was certainly a minimal obligation under the circumstances, yet John focuses on this gesture in a way that eclipses the significance of the larger situation in which it is embedded. John's interpretation of the letter incident, therefore, seems to give it undue significance by making the letter the vehicle of a symbolic resolution, an ideologically organized semiotic structure which closely resembles other semiotic structures in John's life—interactions with certain idealized males—yet which remains relatively detached from other important life events, including the abandonment by his employer, of which the letter itself is actually a component.

THE COMPULSION TO REPEAT

One of the most striking things about John's account is the recurrent nature of the theme represented in the letter incident. At least *nine times* during the course of the interview John talked about incidents that involved being observed and affirmed by respected males; yet, none of these episodes was overtly related to any other, nor did John show any awareness of a repetition. In other cases, too, important themes recur in various ways: Esther describes playing nurturant roles in a number of settings, Ed recalls a series of "highs" and "lows," Paul describes a number of demanding individuals who helped him during his childhood, and Denny reveals a series of problematic encounters with authority figures. In light of these patterns, it would seem worthwhile to consider the question of repetition in more detail and to investigate what it might signify about the phenomenon of the central conflict and its resolution.

The phenomenon of life-historical repetition has been recognized since the early days of psychoanalysis. In 1914, Freud described what he called the "compulsion to repeat" as a regular and predictable part of every analysis. According to Freud, certain infantile memories and impulses exist in an "unbound" state because they have been repressed. The unbound status of these repressed memories means that they cannot form connections with ordinary (secondary process) thinking. The result is that people act them out again and again, which is to say that action itself becomes a mode of remembering. The task of analysis is to create a special arena in which this action occurs—the transference—so that the analyst can help the patient to bring these experiences back into the realm of ordinary thought and conscious control.

However, Freud encountered certain difficulties with this formulation. The chief problem was the question of why people *needed* to remember these experiences. It was difficult to attribute this need to wish fulfillment because clinical experience showed that the repetitions usually led to painful and unhappy results. As Freud observed:

The compulsion to repeat the events of [one's] childhood in the transference evidently disregards the pleasure principle in every way (1920, p. 66).

In order to explain this and other related phenomena, Freud hypothesized a death instinct. This instinct was conceived to be an entropic tendency in biological life, "an urge...to restore an earlier state of things" (1920, p. 67), ultimately leading to the dissolution of the physical organism. The death instinct was thus opposed to Eros, the life instinct, and provided the motivational counterbalance that could encompass self-defeating phenomena like the repetition compulsion.

Freud's theory of the life and death instincts has never been widely accepted. It posits overarching principles that seem more appropriate to a mystic philosophy than to an empirical psychology. Moreover, it is aimed at reducing complex phenomena to a simple pair of biological forces, the kind of reduction that has already been criticized a number of times in this book. Nevertheless, Freud's adoption of a death instinct is understandable and even compelling. It *is* difficult to explain why people repeatedly engage in futile and self-defeating behaviors. In the following pages, therefore, an attempt will be made to reinterpret Freud's theory of the repetition compulsion in terms more compatible with the present study. Let us begin by considering Freud's account in terms of recent advances in the theory of the self.

Freud never said much about the nature of the self, but when he did his remarks tended to be somewhat obscure. One reason is terminological. When Freud wrote about human identity he frequently used the term "ego" in an ambiguous way. Most often, Freud characterized the ego as a biologically based psychic apparatus concerned with the regulation of impulses. This usage was not problematic in itself, but Freud also employed the word "ego" in another, quite different sense from time to time. On these occasions, he used the term to designate the individual's *image* or *concept* of self (what was referred to in the last chapter as the self-representation). This latter characterization is very different from the former characterization of the ego as regulating apparatus. While the biologically based ego apparatus can be thought of as the *source* of mental activity, the image or concept of self refers to the *content* of mental activity, part of the individual's field of meaning. Contemporary psychoanalytic theorists have found it useful to distinguish between these two senses of the word "ego," preserving the term "ego" to refer to the first sense and formalizing the word "self" to refer to the second.

Following this terminological distinction, Schafer (1976) has pointed out that the self is not a motivational structure; rather, it is a way of thinking about one's actions in a social context. The specific understanding which a person develops about his or her place in the social world defines a concept of self, i.e. a concept of who he or she is. This concept does not "regulate" or "channel" wishes and impulses. In fact, the situation is almost the reverse: the self is constructed to represent how the individual has acted upon his or her wishes and impulses and how others have responded to these actions. But there is a paradox here, for this characterization is not unequivocally true. An individual never simply "acts" on a wish or impulse. Such action is always organized and directed by the individual's understanding of the situation he or she is in, and this understanding includes, implicitly or explicitly, the individual's concept of self. Despite the essential correctness of Schafer's analysis, therefore, there appears to be a certain respect in which the self concept *is* a motivational structure. The extent to which it is a *limiting* structure will depend on the extent to which the field of meaning is disrupted. As long as the individual attends freely to the larger field of meaning, including those parts which are associated with the painful aspects of the central conflict, his or her concept of self will remain open to modification, even as it guides action. Such *reflective* behavior, therefore, and the self-concept associated with it, will remain *motivationally open*. An example of this kind of behavior is Esther's attempt to act in a less controlling way as she discovered the extent to which the maternal role she had learned was an intrusive one. In cases where the field of meaning is more disrupted, however, the individual's concept of self remains implicit and unarticulated. The result is *unreflective* behavior which makes the existing self-concept a static motivational structure *by default*. An example is John's unstated fear that he is inherently shameful and his consequent attempts to get the kind of recognition he never got from his father.

Freud's conception of the ego as regulator of impulses bears a formal resemblance to the motivationally closed, unreflected self. As an apparatus, the ego acts automatically in a given situation and is not changed by its own actions. For this reason, the ego concept has always been more useful in accounting for pathological phenomena. By treating the ego this way, however, Freud played down the constructive role of the individual and the essential continuity between reflective and unreflective behavior. In turn, Freud's conception of the repetition compulsion was limited. The repetition compulsion can be seen as a kind of unreflective behavior in which an individual acts on the basis of life-historical themes without understanding the full extent to which his or her concept of self is based upon them. Such an individual's understanding will be characterized by the kinds of disruptions of meaning we have already seen in Denny's and John's accounts. Freud recognized the importance of such disruptions in his contention that the repetition occurred because certain memories were not available to secondary-process thinking. What Freud's account failed to emphasize, however, is that the field of meaning is never completely divided, and that unreflective behavior always has within it a certain reflective aspect. If it were not so, psychotherapy would be impossible. The reflective aspect of the repetition compulsion is evident in the fact that such repetition always involves at least some degree of purposefulness. In fact, the repetition compulsion is not a "compulsion" at all; it is the individual's repeated attempt to find the solution to a problem, the existential problem of the central conflict.

Freud's emphasis on the pathological aspects of the repetition compulsion, however, dovetailed with his mechanistic analysis of the ego, and this in turn required external motivating forces. In looking for such forces, Freud was led to posit the life and death instincts. As has already been noted, this conception is untenably reductionistic and it directed Freud away from the thematic complexities of the central conflict and its resolution. Whatever its problems, however, Freud's instinct theory offers an important insight: the concept of life and death instincts pitted against each other in eternal battle implies something which has already been suggested above, namely, *the cental role of conflict as an organizing principle of human identity.*

Conflict has often been recognized as a developmental influence in the construction of the self (e.g., Freud, 1915, 1923; Jacobson, 1965; Kernberg, 1966). However, as noted in the last chapter, there are also reasons for suspecting that conflict is a *logical prerequisite* to the concept of self. Let us take a closer look at this idea by extending certain ideas from Lacan's (1953, 1966) analysis of the repetition compulsion.

Lacan's analysis is based on a particular incident reported by Freud (1920) in his discussion of the repetition compulsion. Freud describes how his grandson engaged in a certain form of repetitive behavior which seemed to represent an attempt to gain mastery over his mother's intermittent absences. The child would throw a toy away from himself, calling out the German word "fort" ("gone"), and having done so, would then pull the toy back, crying out the word "da" ("there"). Lacan discusses this incident as a prototype not only of conflict and repetition, but also of language acquisition. He emphasizes that the dialectic of the conflicting themes of presence and absence is reflected in the child's simultaneous acquisition of a *pair* of words, "fort" and "da."

This observation could serve as the basis for a hypothesis about development, namely, that words are learned in opposed pairs which correspond to conflictual themes. But the significance of Lacan's observation goes beyond developmental speculation. What is interesting about the so-called fort/da incident is that it illustrates and illuminates a certain characteristic of signification which was originally discovered by Saussure (1916). As was noted in chapter 2, Saussure observed that the meanings of the elements of a semiotic or linguistic system need to be established in terms of their relations with other elements in the same system. This characteristic has been summarized by Lacan (1966): "No meaning is sustained by anything other than reference to other meaning" (p. 498). In accordance with this perspective, the crucial consideration in establishing the meaning of any particular word is not how it resembles but how it *differs from* or *stands in opposition to* other words. As Saussure succinctly put it, "In language there are only differences" (1916, p. 120).

The fort/da incident illustrates that the difference or opposition between two signifiers is inherently related to the experience of actual and potential conflict. Lacan suggests something similar, but his analysis remains obscure, partly because he does not make the important distinction between semiotic and linguistic elements, both of which are present in the fort/da incident. The words "fort" and "da" are the linguistic elements that represent the concepts of absence and presence, respectively. But the child also needs an "object language" to represent the application of these concepts concretely, which is accomplished in this case not by mental imagery, but by throwing away and pulling back the toy. By alternately performing these actions, the child understands that the absence and presence of the object are irresolvably conflicting themes. At the same time, however, he gains some measure of control over this conflict by repeatedly reversing its terms. Repetition, conflict, and signification, therefore, are all inextricably combined in this incident.

What the above analysis suggests, and what the fort/da incident concretely illustrates, is that *meaning and conflict are deeply interrelated.* Semiotic and linguistic systems are structured isomorphically to actual and potential conflict in an individual's life.[1] In general,

---

[1]It should be emphasized once again that this is not a causal or developmental theory but a statement about the characteristics of signification. A strictly developmental analysis of the relationship between conflict and meaning would probably run into difficulties. For example, it might be possible to show that a child could not learn the meanings of words like "spoon" and "fork" without understandng the *differences* between them, but it would still be unclear how such differences relate to *conflict.* The present analysis, however, is based on a consideration of what meaning *must entail* in order to be coherent in the context of the subject's total experience.

This point can be clarified by considering Mao Tse-tung's famous dictum, "All political power comes out of the barrel of a gun." Mao's dictum could be taken as a causal analysis of how the world's political leaders came to power. But a more likely interpretation is that this is a statement about what political power *entails*—that it can be understood, ultimately, in terms of the actual and potential use of guns.

The relationship between meaning and conflict is similar to the relationship between political power and guns. Semiotic and linguistic terms take their meaning, ultimately, from actual and potential conflict in the subject's life. Thus, a child who knows the difference between a spoon and a fork understands that the function of one is incompatible with the function of the other, but this will not present an overt conflict unless the child actually tries to eat soup with a fork or meat with a spoon.

semiotic elements are given meaning in the context of actual life-historical conflict, whereas linguistic elements reflect conflict indirectly and gain their significance for an individual only insofar as they correspond closely to important semiotic structures and the life-historical conflicts with which these structures are associated. All along we have seen this dialectic in the relationship between ideology and idealization. The former offers conceptual tools for dealing with the potential manifestations of the central conflict, but it gains experiential substance only from the latter, which provides the concrete elements of a solution based on the positive side of the ambivalent relationships associated with that conflict.

The constellations of signifiers that constitute personal identity, therefore, are organized in terms that are highly sensitive to and reflective of conflict. The complex of contradictory themes that has been defined as the central conflict can be considered a group of especially salient elements in the vocabularies of the semiotic and linguistic systems used by the subject. If these systems are inherently tied to conflict, however, they also offer the tools for overcoming such conflict. This statement presents us with another paradox, but one that will have to wait until the next chapter for discussion.

So far we have seen two examples of defensive self-esteem. The accounts of Denny and John illustrate very different—in some respects opposite—strategies for dividing the field of meaning. We will now consider a case that shows elements of *both* these strategies. In Anna's account, ideology is highly developed and somewhat removed from ordinary life; but there is also a tendency to structure ordinary situations to recreate idealized interactions in a recurring way. Anna's case, therefore, shows a more complex and balanced strategy than either Denny's or John's. But Anna's case is balanced in another way, too, for along with these defensive elements, Anna presents evidence for a nondefensive and genuine resolution of her central conflict, at least in some important respects. We will therefore conclude this chapter with a consideration of nondefensive self-esteem as it is manifested in Anna's case. At the same time, this example will serve to illustrate once again that no experience of self-esteem is entirely defensive or entirely nondefensive and that these two aspects of resolution always go together in a particular instance.

ANNA: CROSSING BOUNDARIES

Anna is a thirty-one-year-old black woman who is currently

engaged in theological studies preparatory to becoming an ordained mnister. She lives with her husband and three daughters in a large city, where she is involved in a number of community, social, and religious activities. When I asked Anna about an incident of self-esteem, she recalled something that had happened in connection with one of these activities the day before.[1] Anna teaches a Sunday-school class for the teenages in her church, and on the day before our initial interview she had made a change in the format of the class.

Previously, Anna had taught the class in a spontaneous and unstructured way. She had conducted informal discussions, encouraging the students to be "philosophers"; she had invited guest speakers; she had taken the class outside the church to play raquetball and to "hang out" downtown. This unstructured format had appealed to the teenagers, and Anna's class had been successful and lively. But Anna had not been content to remain with a completely unstructured format because she had also felt an obligation to give her students "solid" knowledge, knowledge that would "put together head and gut" and provide "a positive enduring." For this reason, Anna had decided to initiate formal lectures in the class, even at the risk of losing the rapport she had established with the teenagers.

Contrary to Anna's fears, the class went very well. Anna believes this was due to the fact that she was able to integrate in a natural and spontaneous way her more structured approach with the earlier less structured one. This integration is illustrated in Anna's description of how she decided to give a test and how the class reacted:

> When I was lecturing it became very important to me to know...that they were going to keep [it] with them, and so I decided that we would have an exam. In the middle of the lecture I said we're having an exam on this material and the reward would be whatever they wanted, and although I don't like the competition of grades, that the highest grades would receive a bonus and they could choose what that would be too. And so that was a very spontaneous kind of happening.... Why I felt good about it

---

[1]Anna was one of the first subjects interviewed, and her account was obtained before the decision had been made to ask for incidents that had occurred at least a year previously. She is therefore the one subject who discussed a recent experience of self-esteem. Some possible consequences for the findings in this case are considered below.

was that I let myself go and they were open to it. I could see it in their body language. They just sat up and took note, and they didn't become hostile or sluggish or anything.... I had some trepidations about being too structured with this particular group, so I was...just a little bit hesitant about this approach of lecturing. And when it hit me that I could make learning fun, then I felt good about myself that I was still open to being flexible and that it was a spontaneous kind of thing and [that] it was well received.

At the time of the interview, Anna was feeling confident that the class would continue to go well and that the students would get the kind of solid knowledge she wanted them to have. Moreover, she felt more certain of the class's involvement with her and with the rest of the church community:

I think basically...the young people I am with right now—I think they trust me. I think they want to learn. Yeah, I felt really good about Sunday, Sunday was a real high day for me.

It is not difficult to find precursors to this experience in Anna's early life history. Anna grew up in a small city in New England during the 1950s. Although she lived in a predominantly white neighborhood and attended integrated schools, the social community in which Anna was raised was all black. Central to this community was the church. Anna remembers the church community as a warm and intimate one, and her own attendance of Sunday school was an important part of this experience:

[My Sunday-school teachers] were always very caring. The good thing about Sunday-school teaching is that it's an intimate kind of relationship. They usually know your family and know a lot about you, even to the point of seeing you come into the world. So it was always a very caring kind of thing that makes you think of an extended family.

Anna remembers Sunday school as a place where she could display her talents and abilities. In particular, she remembers the women who taught Sunday school:

They were extended, in quotes, family. Aunty this and Aunty that, you know. (The teachers?) Yeah, yeah.... And you always had the feeling that the person cared for you.

During the interview, Anna described several Sunday-school teachers who stood out in her memory. Chief among these was her own mother.

Although Anna was never in any of her mother's Sunday-school classes, she has vivid memories of them and of the role her mother played among the young people in the church. One of the groups Anna's mother taught was the teenagers, and Anna recalls her mother's popularity with them:

> She stayed young with them, you know. She'd dress young, she'd talk young, she took time, she remembered their names, she remembered situations they would share with her, and she was for real, you know, she wasn't put on.....
> I had those kind of feelings of "I want to be like my mom," you know.... You always thought of your mother as being so old and I was seeing this woman who was so old with all these young people who thought she was groovy.

Sunday school was not the only activity in which Anna's mother was involved. Both of her parents participated in all the important functions of the church and Anna recalls the meetings that were held at her house:

> I can remember one group meeting there.... They were probably the most-active and the most-liked women's group in the church. They were really fun.... My dad and the other men would be in the other room and then they would meet and we all liked it. But, yeah, there'd be lots of meetings at our house.... (Did you go to [any of] those meetings?) No, you stood on the staircase and you looked down. And if you were real good, then you were given a treat.

But Anna's experience of the church was not entirely positive. The religious orientation was rigidly fundamentalist, and Anna feels that the children in the congregation had God "stuffed down their throat":

> You *learned* scriptures, and you *learned* the Bible, and you *learned* God is good, God is love, which I think kids resist. You know, you find them dropping out by the time they're old enough to stay home by themselves.

Anna did not drop out, but as she got older she felt increasingly dissatisfied. One of the most disconcerting things was the resistance she experienced to the questions she asked:

> No one was there to answer my questions. The kinds of questions that were questioning, the probing kinds of things. They were Bible people and how dare you ask [laughs].

Anna remembers having questions about death and about whether Jesus had ever committed a sin. But when she asked these questions of the pastor and other adults, they reacted uncomfortably or gave her "an adult's answer, no answer."

To a certain extent, Anna experienced this problem as a generational conflict. She recalls, for example, how she felt as a teenager when she taught a group of people in the church just younger than herself;

> I felt as though they could trust me because I too was still growing and I wasn't rigid in my thinking. It's sort of like [pauses]—it's sort of like "I might not have all the answers, but you're better off asking me, a person who can understand you, than asking someone who thinks they have all the answers, but really has no sensitivity to you."...[It was] a protectorate kind of thing. (What do you mean?) That they would be safe with me.

The generational conflict extended to Anna's relations with her parents as well. Anna describes her parents as optimistic people who were "always plugged into happier people and very uplifting sides of people." At times, however, their acceptance of things as they were did not seem right to Anna. An example is her father's conservative attitudes on race relations. Anna describes her father as "the head of the household, a working man, a family man" of few words and strong character. He had been raised in Alabama during an era of absolute discrimination, and when he had come North he had brought with him the attitudes he had needed to survive in that earlier situation. Anna became painfully aware of these attitudes—not only in her father, but in her mother as well—when she encountered discrimination in public school.

Public school was Anna's major contact with the white world as she grew up, and she experienced it as a punitive and rejecting environment which was the locus of a major contradition. On the one hand, Anna was encouraged by her parents and others to regard her teachers with a respect bordering on reverence:

I just never thought of them as human. Somehow or other they were given this divine [laughs] privilege of knowing so much about *everything*—they were automatically given undue respect in the community, you know. You *don't* talk back to your teacher [laughs]. You open doors for your teachers, no matter age, sex, you know [laughs].

On the other hand, the teachers toward whom Anna looked with such respect often showed disrespect and prejudice toward her and other black children. Anna was most aware of this attitude in the attention given to students. In general, the teachers seemed to assume that the black children would not do well, and they invested more time and interest in the white children.

I remember the feeling of not having people expect the best from me, which makes you feel less than what you are. I remember not receiving encouragement when I knew I was worthy of it. And...in the same way, not receiving reward when it was due.

Anna, whose grades were average, recalls one incident in particular:

I can remember a Spanish teacher, tenth grade, telling me that I shouldn't aim so high. That's almost an exact quote. And that hurt. That hurt. I think that...at that age level you should always be encouraging. And if you want to bring a child into a realistic perspective, there are gentler ways to do it instead of killing the spirit. And that's what he did; at least he tried to do it.

When Anna discussed such incidents with her parents, she found no support for her grievances:

Once or twice, maybe more, when my mom and dad would talk about what was making me unhappy at school...I'd just say "Boy, that teacher so-and-so," and they would say "But you respect your teacher." And I would say to them, "Why should I respect someone who doesn't respect me?"...You see, we're talking about this big kind of attitudinal difference between generations. It was still, "No matter what, Anna, you respect your teachers."

Disappointed in her parents' response, Anna formed a strategy of her own:

So respect became, okay, fine, I'll use my manners, I'll be

polite, I'll go in, do my work, and come out. But it does
not mean I have to have any great feelings of admiration.

If we look back on Anna's account at this point, we can see a
recurring theme, one which begins to suggest the outlines of a
central conflict. Anna describes a series of encounters with hostile
forces that necessitate the establishment of enclaves of safety and
security. The importance of staying within these protective
boundaries is repeatedly emphasized in her account. For example,
the warm security of the black community of church and Sunday
school is contrasted with the neglect and rejection of the white
world of public school. Likewise, Anna describes a camaraderie with
other young people in the church and a wish to establish a
"protectorate" against the rigid and insensitive older members of
the community. Even within her own person, Anna describes
establishing a boundary in that she learned to present a respectful
facade while keeping her own thoughts and feelings to herself.

If Anna needed to maintain these boundaries, however, she also
wished to transcend them; and this wish to transcend constitutes
another motif in her story. One of the most important ways in
which Anna worked to transcend boundaries was in her support of
racial integration and rapprochement. During the years she was in
high school, for example, she did what she could to promote this
cause in a personal way. But it was no easy matter:

> I was one who worked hard at keeping things together.
> And there were black students, you know, that you'd have
> to say were racially hostile.... But I certainly was one who
> would relate to them as well as to others and always try
> to integrate things, you know. I had a lot of black friends
> and a lot of white friends, and I would—I would have
> hoped that teachers would have given me some support in
> that. They didn't.

Anna was left on her own, therefore, in her attempts to "keep
things together" between black and white. The discovery that the
school personnel would not help in this effort was a bitter
disappointment to Anna, for there were some who she sensed could
have made a difference. For example, Anna had a counselor whom
she admired a great deal:

> He was everything that [a counselor] should be. He was a
> person that you could trust.... [He] made himself
> available.... He was always there, a friend first.

When Anna talked to her counselor about the discrimination she experienced in some classes, he was concerned and sympathetic. But when it came to doing something of substance to change the discriminatory system, he and the other adults that Anna looked up to were "a lot of talk and no action":

> The soothing of me was fine, but I would have far more appreciated it if he'd confronted that [Spanish] teacher. That's one step better for me.... That's standing for me and with me.

At another point in the interview, Anna expressed regret that none of the people who had seemed concerned had ever gone before the board of education or any public forum to talk about the discrimination in the school. When I asked Anna how such an action would have affected her, she said:

> That would have regained probably my respect for them.... If I have that respect I feel better about me and who I have chosen to...look up to, you know—that that's a person of good character which carries me beyond the walls of the school.

Idealized adults, therefore, failed Anna when it came to confronting the issue of discrimination. They were as helpless as she before the boundaries separating the races. Her mother and her father exhorted her to affirm the discrimatory system, to respect the people who treated her with disrespect. The counselor and the teachers she admired soothed her in private but dared not cross the boundary into the realm of public action "beyond the walls of the school." It was left to Anna to find her own ways of transcending these boundaries and overcoming the corresponding constrictions within her own person.

In the years following high school, Anna pursued a number of new activities and experiences. She worked for a living and got married; she involved herself in civil rights activities and began to think about studying for the ministry; eventually, she entered college and seminary. Anna feels that she grew as a person in many ways during these years. One manifestation of this growth is a decision she made when her first child was born. Remembering her own childhood experiences with fundamentalist religion, she changed denominations to a church that was "much more in step with modern thinking." Anna's present church is "one of the forerunners in social concerns." Moreover: "It's also an interracially mixed church, and its theme is pluralism, not just economic or social but racial too."

This crossing of denominational boundaries was a significant move, and it symbolized a development in Anna's thinking during these years: the clarification and elaboration of a personal ideology of integration and transcendence both on an individual and a social level. Anna sees this ideology as something which she originally acquired in childhood and which she has only recently come to understand. During the interview she discussed her ideology in terms of what she called her "Christian education":

> What I learned I didn't know I learned then.... I learned that we're all human beings and that somehow or other, however you want to term it, we all come from one source and that that alone should be enough to make us more willing to get along with one another and care about one another. I learned about humanity from my Christian education. I learned that somehow or other there's something or someone watching over you. I'm still not crystal clear on this mysterious and omnipotent force, but there is something there, that's been proven out.... I hate to start using the theological terms, but it's something that will be with you, you know, what you are, the essence of you, the eternity, the innermost part that will survive throughout all the ages, you know. Something in me and something in you that would still be in common with Cleopatra [laughs] or any [other] people.

By putting one in touch with one's eternal essence, therefore, Christian education alerts one to the commonality of all people and the need for universal caring.

In contrast, Anna regards public education as "a this-too-will-pass kind of thing," dealing with transient and ephemeral knowledge. However, she also believes that public education has its values: "I can say that public education has helped me in the thinking process, you know, just like an exercise machine will help you in toning up your muscles."

Associated with this belief is a part of Anna's ideology that might be called "the doctrine of the head and the heart." The feeling side of life is important, but it must be supplemented by solid, factual knowledge. The integration of these two produces a more complete person. Anna summarized this idea when she talked to the students in her Sunday-school class on the first day:

I said..."We're going to blend all of our thinking from here, the head, with the thinking that comes from here, the heart. And we're going to come out with what we represent to us, and all of that's acceptable in the eyes of God."

We are now in a position to appreciate more fully the meaning of Anna's incident of self-esteem and to understand how it presents a specific resolution of the central conflict which has been described. Anna's work with her Sunday-school class was an integrative enterprise from the start. Originally, she took on the class in order "to draw the young people into the community," and one of the reasons she felt good about the class session she described was because it seemed to contribute to this process. It is also worth noting that Anna's students are all white males, which makes her presence as teacher integrative in another sense as well. Moreover, Anna's work with her Sunday-school class has been guided by her ideology. This ideology is particularly evident in the unstructured approach she employed at the beginning of the year, an approach which she hoped would open her students up to a more complete experience of their religion and themselves: "The first of the year I said 'All Sunday-school and Christian education doesn't have to go on in the building and we can leave here and go wherever we want.'" Passing beyond the boundaries of the building may be seen as a metaphor for the attempts Anna has made to cross boundaries with her class, attempts such as departing from the ordinary Sunday-school curriculum, visiting places outside the church, and interacting with classes from other religious denominations.

The session which Anna described at the beginning of the interview, however, was a special one because it represented an integration on a higher level. Anna felt that it was time to integrate head with heart, factual knowledge with the feeling side: "I need to know that they're walking out of there with something—something that they can talley, you know." Anna believes that by itself the unstructured approach might have left only a fading impression. The addition of solid knowledge would provide the students with something that would make their experience of the class permanent and essential, and would simultaneously connect them with Anna in a transcendent way:

I guess I could get heavy into, you know, everyone having this wish to be immortal in some way—that whatever I hand them that they take it, use it, and hand it on, but that they somehow always get to say who and...where it was [that it came from]. For me, you know, [for] that part of my ego.

In sum, then, Anna's experience with her Sunday-school class represents an integrative act in which a number of boundaries are transcended: the young people are brought into the community; racial and denominational lines are superseded; the head and the heart are brought together; and Anna achieves a special relationship with her students that transcends time and place, and gives her a kind of immortality. All of these aspects involve the crossing of boundaries that Anna encountered at other times in her life in connection with dangerous, external forces. However, the extent to which this resolution is symbolic or genuine has yet to be investigated.

There are certain respects in which Anna's account resembles Denny's. Like Denny, Anna describes an ideology that is often sweeping and intellectualized. She talks about "essence" and "humanity" and it is sometimes difficult to see just what these terms could mean for ordinary life. Whereas Denny's ideology is historicized, Anna's is *theologized*, as she herself observes.

In this connection, it is interesting to note that Anna's self-esteem incident does not involve anyone in her family. Anna's work with her Sunday-school class is consistent with her interest in integration and community, but we may also wonder whether the work is not somewhat peripheral to the real concerns in her life. In discussing Denny's case, I indicated the peripheral nature of the sunroom incident and cited it as evidence of a symbolic rather than a genuine resolution. The same thing may be true for Anna.

There is a complicating factor which should be mentioned in passing. As was noted above, Anna was the only subject who described a recent experience of self-esteem, and this fact in itself might have some bearing on why she reported a somewhat peripheral event. Nevertheless, there is a deemphasis of family life in Anna's account in general. Anna did not go into much detail in describing family interactions, even when talking about her early life history. In this respect, too, her account resembles Denny's; it seems to be maintained in a relatively safe arena, detached from important aspects of her identity.

There is also a sense in which Anna's account resembles John's. Like John, Anna describes a recurring motif, that of establishing protective enclaves in a hostile world. Within these enclaves, Anna is either protected by idealized figures or takes on the protective role herself. We have seen this theme in Anna's description of the black community of her childhood, the Sunday-school class she taught as a teenager, and the comforting private relationships she had with certain people at public school. We might wonder, therefore, whether Anna's work with her current Sunday-school class is yet another instance of this motif. If the class is a peripheral setting, it is ideally suited to serve as an enclave of mutually supportive and accepting relationships. In fact, evidence that such is the case can be found in a statement Anna made at one point in the interview. She commented that she had been more successful with the Sunday-school class than other teachers had been, and she attributed this success to her own greater understanding and accpetance of the students and their consequent acceptance of her. Moreover, Anna mentioned that the physical location of the class had been changed and that this had helped her to establish a rapport with the students. The new location was a room further from the main corridor of the building and somewhat insulated and protected from external distractions.

These characteristics point to defensive aspects in Anna's experience of self-esteem. The nature of Anna's ideology and the peripheral character of the Sunday-school class suggest a certain division in her field of meaning; and the repetition which is evident in Anna's account suggests that little may have changed, that her work with the Sunday-school class may be one more instance of symbolic solidarity in a hostile world, an undoing rather than a reconciliation of her central conflict.

However, Anna's incident also *differs* from Denny's and John's in certain important ways. These differences demonstrate how the defensive aspects of self-esteem can be counterbalanced by other characteristics which bring greater unity to the field of meaning and render change less symbolic and more comprehensive. The presence of these characteristics does not make Anna's experience of self-esteem completely "genuine" any more than the disruptions in Denny's and John's accounts make their experiences completely "defensive." But Anna's case does seem to illustrate important features of genuine self-esteem, and for this reason I will conclude this chapter with a consideration of some of these features.

It will be recalled that defensive self-esteem was defined in some detail. We will not go into such detail to define nondefensive self-esteem, for the earlier formulation need only be readapted. Defensive and nondefensive self-esteem are not different entities that need to be defined in separate terms. Rather, they are different ends of a continuum. Accordingly, we can characterize the nondefensive end as follows: *An experience of self-esteem can be regarded as nondefensive insofar as it involves a resolution of a central conflict that includes a change in the way one thinks about one's own identity and the world. This change occurs when an individual achieves a broad resolution of a central conflict over a large portion of the field of meaning. While such a resolution may be regarded as symbolic, it is not primarily so.*

Two consequences follow from such a resolution: first, a true reconciliation rather than a mere reversal of the central conflict is usually involved; and second, a real and lasting change in a person's life usually occurs.

We can see how these characteristics are evident in Anna's account. To begin with, Anna's ideology is not detached from ordinary life in the nearly total way that Denny's is. There are certain parts of her ideology that serve a mediating function, connecting abstract conceptions with her actual life history and day-to-day experience. This mediating function is represented in Anna's account in particular statements which combine linguistic and semiotic elements in such a way as to give ideological direction to specific projects and concrete situations. Moreover, the close combination of these linguistic and semiotic elements and their underlying integration with the larger field of meaning seem to make possible—in certain respects, at least—an actual reconciliation of Anna's central conflict as opposed to a mere undoing of it.

An example is a series of comments that Anna made about identity. At several points in the interview, Anna alluded to the importance of finding out who one is. She described periods of self-discovery in her own life, and she talked about trying to encourage this process in her Sunday-school students. As I suggested above, one aspect of this project is represented in Anna's doctrine of the head and the heart. Bringing the two together is very important in establishing one's identity:

> The first thing I did was try to make them feel good about themselves in the sense that they had the capacity to think and to feel and there was nothing wrong with either and there is a balance and some mix in both of them.

This conception, which Anna repeated several times during the interview, brings her abstract formulations of "essence" and "humanity" into a somewhat more specific context. Anna's next words continue the process, connecting her theory of identity to specific activities in the Sunday-school class and to her own early experience:

> I tried to make them feel good about their religiosity, that it was okay to have doubts and it was okay to question, and in fact they should.

It will be recalled that Anna's early experience included a strong sense of a split between the warm and human church community and the rejecting world of public school. At this time in Anna's life, head and heart *were* divided, and Anna was given the message both in church and in school that the two do not go together. Of particular interest is Anna's recollection of the pastor and other adults avoiding her questions about religion. What makes Anna's work with her Sunday-school class a *genuine* resoluton of her central conflict—in some respects at least—is that themes which are presented as incompatible in descriptions of Anna's early life history are brought together here and reconciled both in conception and practice. By expressing one's doubts and asking questions, one's religiosity is promoted, head and heart are reconciled, and one comes closer to finding oneself.

From the standpoint of signification, Anna's doctrine of the head and the heart can be seen as a general linguistic structure which organizes a variety of other linguistic and semiotic elements in her account. In statements relating certain linguistic terms like "thinking" and "questioning" to others like "feeling" and "religiosity," Anna's theological formulations are crystalized into specific strategies which are semiotically grounded in descriptions of the Sunday-school class and its activities. Moreover, this multileveled structure of signification is thematically related to other signification in Anna's account—particularly to memories of early conflicts, and to explanations and insights about these conflicts which Anna subsequently developed. By virtue of this extended organization of signifiers, Anna's activity in the Sunday-school class both embodies and supersedes themes that were formerly contradictory. Furthermore, this resolution is accomplished not by an undoing or reversal, but by a *reconciliation* of conflicting elements.

This point can be emphasized by comparing Anna's account to Denny's. In the semiotic structures of Denny's life history, two themes are also represented as incompatible: receiving the benefits of his father's success and establishing himself as an able individual. This conflict was represented most clearly in Denny's description of his father reminding Denny that his life has been easy and that it has not challenged him with adversity. Denny's ideology presents a solution to this dilemma, but it does so in predominantly abstract terms which lend themselves best to reversals in symbolic actions. Denny does not (for the most part) attempt to *reconcile* the contradictory themes of receiving material benefits and establishing his own worth and abilities. The basic terms of his central conflict therefore remain unaltered. He continues to believe that having material benefits and proving oneself worthy are inherently incompatible, and that only by rejecting the former can one accomplish the latter. The same can be said about John, who attempts to reverse the humiliation he experienced as a child by receiving acclamation from someone like his father. It does not occur to John that self-respect might be achieved in a way that does *not* require the observation and acclamation of some other person.

Anna, however, achieves something closer to a true resolution by bringing themes which were originally thought to be incompatible into a new relationship with each other. It appears that Anna has been able to achieve this integration, in part, because she has been self-reflective. By examining and reconceptualizing specific experiences associated with certain periods of her life, she has transformed important signifying structures; and this transformation, in turn, has promoted other changes associated with other life-historical and conceptual structures.

Anna's attitude toward teaching is a good example. At one point in the interview, Anna described how her ideas about education had changed during the course of her life. As a child, she experienced the public-school system as a "foreign intruder" which "betrayed" students by harrassing them with testing and competition instead of helping them. After studying education herself, however, she became convinced that testing and competition could aid in the educational process *if* it were done with the proper attitude. Again, Anna reconciles the themes of head and heart; but what is more important here is that this linguistic restructuring not only gives new meaning to her previous history, it also becomes an organizing tool by which Anna can restructure other experience.

At the beginning of the interview, Anna described how she had decided in a spontaneous way to give a test to her Sunday school students. The test was like a spot quiz in school, except that Anna had let the students themselves decide what the reward would be. This event seems to be the kernal of Anna's good feelings about the Sunday-school class:

> And when it hit me that I could make learning fun, then I felt good about myself that I was still open to being flexible and that it was a spontaneous kind of thing and [that] it was well received.

In this statement, Anna describes experiencing herself in a new way. Previous to this class session she had been loose and flexible with her students, but had not done much teaching in the usual sense of the word. It is clear from the wording of the above passage that Anna was not sure she could take on the ordinary teaching role without becoming rigid. Her doubts are not surprising in view of the fact that Anna describes a split between looseness and rigidity in her childhood. A number of the idealizations in her account feature people who are warm and accepting, but not particularly strong—for instance, Anna's descriptions of her mother and other adults teaching Sunday school, and her high-school counselor giving her comfort. The opposite theme is evident in Anna's descriptions of certain adults who took on strong and demanding roles but who were not sensitive to her. This theme can be seen in Anna's characterizations of her parents insisting that she respect her teachers and in her memories of the church people forcing God "down her throat." Anna herself seems to have alternated between these two themes, as is illustrataed by her establishing a "protectorate" with her peers and a facade of rigid politeness with her teachers.

In the above passage, however, Anna describes a reconciliation of these themes. She is able to use the ideas she has developed about education to effect a shift in her identity. The reconciliation she has made in the ideological realm is applied in action in the Sunday-school class by appropriating aspects of both kinds of idealized figures. Through the use of different elements from the field of meaning, therefore—by exploiting their semiotic and linguistic features and bringing them together in new ways—Anna resolves her central conflict in the context of the Sunday-school class with a new and successful kind of behavior. This resolution is the kind that has been characterized as nondefensive.

In Anna's case, then, we can see how defensive processes are counterbalanced by a nondefensive tendency toward genuine change. The unity of the field of meaning—the ultimate indivisibility of psychological experience—is turned to the subject's advantage. As I have indicated, this kind of transformation seems to involve the exploitation of the semiotic and linguistic characteristics of meaning. In the next chapter, we will consider this process further and examine some of the ways in which it seems to be effected.

FOUR _____

The Limits of
Self-Esteem

IN THE FOREGOING CHAPTERS self-esteem has been discussed as an experience with personal meaning. In this discussion three constructs have been employed. The first two—ideology and idealization—designate the linguistic and semiotic structures, respectively, which embody an individual's ideals. The third construct—the central conflict—refers to the problem that the individual's ideals are aimed at solving. We have analyzed self-esteem as an experience in which an individual successfully applies ideology and idealizations in order to bring about an actual or symbolic resolution of a central conflict.

At the time these three constructs were introduced, however, certain important issues were left vague. Specifically, it was suggested that these phenomena were present in some form in all the accounts reported in this study, but we left unanswered the question of whether they are *universal* and *essential*. For example, will ideology always be found in an individual's account of self-esteem— and, if not, what would a nonideological account look like? Can a person describe a history without idealizations? Or, again, what is the significance of the central conflict? Is it unique in a person's life, or is it only one of many such conflicts?

In this chapter we will consider these questions in the context of specific case material. However, the strategy that was employed in the previous two chapters will be reversed. Rather than focusing on strong examples of ideology, idealization, and the central conflict, we will turn attention to the *weakest possible instances*—cases in which these three constructs seem to be minimal or problematic in some sense. In the first two cases—those of Charlotte and Lou—we will see accounts in which ideology and idealization, respectively, appear to be missing. We will therefore critically examine these two phenomena and the extent to which they are necessary in the attainment of self-esteem. In the third case—that of Ruth—we will encounter not a deficit but a surplus. Ruth presents not one but *three* separate instances of self-esteem. Since there are no apparent connections between these three incidents, we shall consider whether they all address the same central conflict, and, if so, in what manner.

In addition to exploring the limits of these constructs, we will continue with the larger task of this study—that of examining self-esteem as a meaningful experience. Accordingly, close attention will be given to the characteristics of signification in subject's accounts. In the first two cases, we will consider what ideology and idealization tell us about the roles of linguistic and semiotic systems in the construction of meaning, particularly in such processes as psychotherapy and personal reflection. In the third case, the analysis of the central conflict will be used to make some observations about the organization of meaning in a life-historical account and the way in which this organization can be studied by the interview method. Consideration of these topics will prepare the way for the final chapter, in which we will move from an examination of unitary cases to a more general discussion of self-esteem and meaning in social life.

Let us turn, then, to the first case at hand—that of Charlotte. In this case, we will encounter an experience of self-esteem described in terms that are relatively nonideological. Moreover, there is a general deemphasis of ideology throughout Charlotte's account. This deemphasis seems to be associated with certain difficulties in Charlotte's life, and this fact will suggest some important things about the nature and function of ideology. We will consider the linguistic features of ideology and how these features are exploited in the construction of meaning. This examination, in turn, will help to explain how ideology plays a particular role in processes such as psychotherapy, and, by implication, how ideological change can contribute to the modification and transformation of an individual's self-esteem.

CHARLOTTE: FINDING GUIDELINES

Charlotte is a white thirty-six-year-old mother of four who lives with her children in a small apartment in a middle-sized midwestern city. Charlotte has been a single parent since she and her husband were divorced nine years ago. About two years ago Charlotte's ex-husband lost his job, and since that time she and the children have been living on county aid.

A tall woman with gaunt features, Charlotte speaks in a slow and pensive way that conveys the sense of someone who has carried a large share of life's burdens. During the interview, she seemed to be thoughtful and often emphasized her answers by repeating them. Occasionally, she made herself the butt of a joke, such as when I first called her to set up the interview. After we had briefly discussed the nature of the interview, she laughed and responded, "If you want to interview a real nut, okay."

When asked about a time she had felt good about herself, Charlotte described how, two years previously, she had begun to deal with her teenage daughter Beverly in a new way. Prior to that time, Charlotte and Beverly had been involved in an escalating series of battles. Charlotte attributes these struggles to her attempts to maintain what she now considers excessive control over Beverly. Charlotte did not approve of Beverly's friends and became increasingly concerned about where her daughter was going and what she was doing:

> She was fifteen, I was trying to control her whole life.... As soon as she got that age there was no really controlling [her]. I could *think* I was controlling her, but I [knew] as soon as she walked out the door...she was going to do what she wanted to do.... And then I'd sit here and I'd worry about what she was doing, you know, whether she was doing what she said she was doing or this or that. And I just literally was driving myself nuts about it. And so I'd turn around and take it back out on her.

At times Charlotte would catch Beverly in a lie, which would precipitate a battle. At other times Beverly would act in a challenging way, answering her mother back or acting like a "smart ass." Charlotte describes how such behavior would "trigger" her off:

> I would just go so nuts screaming and yelling.... I would get so mad that the only way I could finally get it out

[was] just by hitting her, pulling her hair...you know, anything nasty I could think of doing.

Eventually Beverly ran away. A friend of the family got involved at this point and arranged for Beverly to see a therapist at a local community agency. Beverly went to the clinic and agreed to return on a regular basis. She did so for about four months, at which time Charlotte was asked to join the sessions. An extended period of joint therapy was begun which included Beverly and Charlotte, and eventually the rest of the family. It was at this time that Charlotte began to learn how to deal with Beverly in a different way:

> Talking about it [I realized] that the things I was doing to Beverly were things I *hated* that my mother did to me....
> I guess I found out it was okay for her to hurt me and, uh, I wasn't going to die, I wasn't going to be shamed from whatever hurt she did to me. And I felt good that I was able to handle it without going nuts....
> Since then I've learned to let go and let her, you know, run her own life. And if she's going to make mistakes, she's going to have to figure them up.... And I guess that's one thing I really feel good about myself—I no longer have that need in me to be physical with her.

Charlotte describes a major change, then, in her behavior toward her daughter; and this change has also affected Charlotte's feelings about herself. During the interview, Charlotte and I talked in some detail about the change and we explored the reasons why she felt good about it. Although there were some ideological elements in Charlotte's explanation—elements that will be discussed below—her reasons for feeling good about herself in this situation seem to have been *non*ideological for the most part. Rather than elaborating her experience of self-esteem in terms of ideals and beliefs about the social world, Charlotte gave her experience meaning in terms of her own past family life. Primarily, Charlotte felt good about learning to deal with Beverly in a new way because Charlotte's behavior was different from the way her own mother dealt with *her*.

> (What was it about [learning to deal with your daughter] that felt the best to you?) I guess just myself looking at maybe I was doing things wrong, I was going about things wrong. And I think I felt good about myself because it was something that my mother had never done with me. I was...making an effort to try and listen to what Bev was saying to me instead of just wanting her to listen to what

I had to say.... I felt like it was something...that my mother was never able to do.

Charlotte's mother had never shown much openness or willingness to look at her own role. Instead, she had tried to exert the kind of control over Charlotte that Charlotte describes trying to exert over Beverly.

My mother was always yelling at me and telling me what to do.... Yeah, she yelled at me a lot....
There's not a night I don't remember—it used to be kind of a joke-type thing with my brother and I. See her car coming down the street, you know, "Well, here comes the old bitch, she'll start in." And she did [laughs] as soon as she walked in the back door she started yelling about this and that.... (What kind of things would she yell about?) Stuff laying around. [Pauses] Dirty dishes in the sink, maybe a couple of bowls.

Like the battles with her own daughter, the battles between Charlotte and her mother became especially intense when Charlotte became a teenager. Because Charlotte's mother was particularly concerned about the possibility of her daughter having sexual relations, she tried to keep track of Charlotte's whereabouts. Charlotte remembers her mother catching her in lies on some occasions; but more than this, Charlotte remembers her mother accusing her falsely and not allowing her to respond:

I never got my side of the story in with my mother. I only got the first three words of a sentence or..."I did not do that," you know? But I never got to explain or say what I *did* do.... [And] when there was things that she accused me of that I didn't do...I just wasn't going to take it. I wasn't going to be accused of something that I hadn't done.

But the battles between Charlotte and her mother seem to have been symptomatic of longer-standing problems which go back almost as far as Charlotte can remember.

Charlotte describes her mother as a self-sufficient and competent woman who put more time into housecleaning and working outside the home than she did into her relationships with her children. Several times during the interview Charlotte marvelled at her mother's abilities, espcially as a worker and an independent person; but Charlotte also feels that her mother's need to work made her somewhat negligent as a parent:

You know, I think back now, I don't know where in the
world she got the energy that she had of working a job,
an eight-to-five job, five days a week, and still kept the
house so goddamned immaculate. You know, I don't know
where she got all the energy from, other than she didn't
put anything into any time with us kids. (You mean that's
where she got the energy from?) Well, I think that...the
time that she should have been with us kids...she was
busy cleaning, cleaning, cleaning. She's a very clean person
[laughs], she cleaned everything every week.

If Charlotte's mother withheld herself from her children, however,
she did so especially with regard to Charlotte. Charlotte feels that
her mother was disappointed with her because she was never able
to match her older sister's high marks in school. For such reasons,
Charlotte believes that her mother liked her least of all four
children.

The only time I ever remember her showing any really
physical-type love towards me is if I was sick, and I mean
really sick.

Charlotte was frequently sick with ear infections as she grew up.
Her mother cared for her during some of these illnesses, but as
Charlotte got older her mother went to work more often, leaving
Charlotte home alone sick and feeling deserted. In other ways, too,
Charlotte remembers feeling her mother's absence. Although her
father was usually available, Charlotte also needed a female:

There was times I wanted to talk to her. I was too
embarrassed about some things to talk to my dad. But she
was never there to talk to.... (What kinds of things were
they?) Female, you know. She never even told me about
menstruating until the day I started.

At another point in the interview Charlotte mentioned that her
mother had never talked to her about sex and that her mother-in-
law had finally told her about such things as contaceptives just
before marriage.

Charlotte feels that the distance between her mother and herself
has continued into the present. She stated that her mother is still
disappointed with her and disapproves of how Charlotte has
managed her life. At the same time, Charlotte believes that her
mother will never change:

It isn't so much for her to love me, just for her to show
it, that she loves me. But I don't—I don't think she's
capable of doing that.... She's capable with my brothers
and my sister, but with me she's not....
   I [have] realized, you know, I just—I can't make her care
about me. Uh, [pauses] I probably will never be what she
wanted me to be and so she just never will.

When we talked about her father Charlotte painted a very different
picture. Her comments about him during the course of the
interview were almost unqualifiedly positive:

I think while he was alive I felt good about myself all the
time.... I guess I never really felt bad during that whole
period of my life....
   He just was always there, um—[pauses]. He did things
with us kids. There was times he wasn't really a parent,
you know, he wasn't thought of as being a parent. (What
do you mean by that?) Um, I guess he just would get
outside and he'd play with us, you know, he'd play football,
baseball, basketball.... He seemed to be the father that
always helped us out....
   He was a very mellow, easy-going person, and he was a
lot of fun. He was the complete opposite of my mother in
a lot of ways. Like I said...she would bitch, but when *he*
came home...he always had something nice to say to you.
Something kidding or something—it was always something
that made you laugh or made you smile....
   All of my girlfriends just, you know, they all liked my
dad.... A lot of it with me was just completely reversed
from what all of my friends had. They had their mothers
and I didn't [but] I had my father, which, you know, it
never bothered me.

When it came to discipline, Charlotte describes her father as calmer
and more rational than her mother:

If it was something my dad was going to deal with...it
was a talk thing, you know, there wasn't any yelling or
screaming....
   He usually stuck to his word. Discipline usually was being
grounded with my dad. There wasn't any, you know, real
hairy scene.

In this connection, Charlotte emphasized several times during the
interview that her father would always ask her for her side of the

story and that he would always listen to what she had to say.

The relationship between Charlotte's parents emerges as somewhat paradoxical in her account. To begin with, Charlotte describes her mother and father as getting along with each other extremely well. She attributes this primarily to her father's influence:

> I think he put more into the relationship than she did, a lot more, and that's probably why it worked out....
> If he was home she never came in yelling. She never did.... (Why not?) I don't know. I guess I always figured it was because she didn't want Dad to see what she could really be like [laughs] when he wasn't there.... She was a lot of fun at times. But she wasn't yelling and screaming at us. (When he was there.) Um-hm.

At the same time, however, Charlotte describes a certain tension between her parents. Charlotte believes that her mother was jealous of Charlotte's close relationship with her father and that this jealousy affected not only her mother's feelings about her, but other family interactions as well. These relationships and Charlotte's feelings about them were clarified near the end of the interview when I asked Charlotte whether her mother had ever gotten physical with her in the same way that Charlotte had gotten physical with Beverly:

> No. Not really.... You see, she had my dad to provoke into that.... (What do you mean?) Well, she would get him so mad, you know, and yelling at me, and then I would yell back at her...[and] she'd yell and scream... "John, she's lying, I know she's lying." (and then what would happen?) And then...the conflict or the verbal argument between her and I would just get him—same type of thing that would get me so mad, the verbal argument between Beverly and I.

When things reached this point Charlotte's father would "use a belt" on her.

This information is somewhat surprising in light of the idyllic relationship with her father that Charlotte describes above. Just as the conflicts with Beverly would "trigger" Charlotte, so the conflicts between Charlotte and her mother would "provoke" Charlotte's father, who would then punish Charlotte physically. Charlotte, however, never held this against her father:

I blamed it on my mother. (Why?) Because I felt she was
the one that was at fault. Because she was the one that
was making the accusations, and a lot of the time...they
were accusations that I just couldn't let her make.... (And
your father would believe her accusations?) I think he had
to. (Why?) Because I think he felt the same jealousy that I
felt too, that my mother had about my dad and I being so
close. [Pauses] I think he had—I think he had to in front
of her.

In these interactions, then, Charlotte seems to be scapegoated in
order to preserve the family equilibrium. Her punishment protects
the mutuality between her parents without changing her
relationship to either one of them. At one point this idea was
suggested to Charlotte:

(As you describe it, it's as though you were—you had to be
sacrificed so that things could be okay between your mother
and your father. That's what it sounds like.) I guess—uh,
yeah, I guess so. I guess so. I never thought about it that
way.

To this affirmation, however, Charlotte added two qualifications.
First, her father had not gotten physical very often; usually he had
just sent her to her room. Second, no matter what happened
between Charlotte and her parents, her father would always sit
down with her the next day and listen to what she had to say about
it. This second qualification seems to be especially important, and
Charlotte repeated it several times during the interview: "Always,
always, always, the next day he talked to me and listened to my side
of the story. I never got my side of the story in with my mother."
Her father's willingness to listen to her side of the story, therefore,
seems to have carried a great deal of significance for Charlotte; and
this willingness appears to be the one thing that most sharply
differentiates Charlotte's experience of her mother and her father
as parental figures. Let us consider this difference in more detail,
for it will bring us to a formulation of the central conflict in
Charlotte's account.

Charlotte describes a poor relationship with her mother, going
back almost as far as she can remember. Her mother is
characterized as distant, critical, and always disappointed with
Charlotte. It is significant that Charlotte describes her mother as
"cleaning, cleaning, cleaning" rather than spending time with her
children. Throughout the interview, Charlotte employed imagery

portraying herself as a possibly dirty or unseemly person who might receive attention from her mother only as someone or something to be cleaned up. One example is Charlotte's embarrassment and wish for her mother when she began menstruating. When Charlotte describes battles with her mother they are usually over messing the house or sexuality, a topic that seems to have been regarded within the family as dirty. In this light, it is worth noting that the only time Charlotte ever recalls her mother giving her positive attention, "physical-type love," is when she was suffering from infections.

Charlotte seems to have experienced her mother as a perfectionistic person who regarded her as an object to be straightened up or put in order, almost like a part of the house. The one thing that Charlotte seems never to have experienced from her mother was recognition of herself as a person with needs and feelings of her own. At one point in the interview, Charlotte emphasized this point by correcting one of my questions:

(Do you think [your mother] dealt with you poorly before you became a teenager?) [Pauses] I don't think she dealt poorly with me. I don't think she—she didn't show *me* enough love, for *me*.

The point seems to be that Charlotte's mother did not do a poor job of "dealing with" her daughter; rather, she was *always* "dealing with" Charlotte—trying to control her and put her life in order. The thing that Charlotte wanted from her mother but never received was love for *herself* as a worthwhile person in her own right.

Charlotte seems to have turned to her father partly as a substitute. Charlotte presents her father as an ideal parent: he is mellow; he is kind; he is "always there." Most important of all, though, is the fact that Charlotte's father is described as someone who listens to what she has to say and regards her as a person with her own point of view. Charlotte frequently emphasized this point by contrasting her father with her mother:

He was the complete opposite of my mother in a lot of ways. . . .
A lot of it with me was just completely reversed from what all of my friends had. They had their mothers and I didn't [but] I had my father, which, you know, it never bothered me.

But it *did* bother Charlotte. Again and again in the course of the interview, Charlotte returned to the subject of her mother and to the disappointment and rejection that her mother has conveyed to her. Charlotte's bond with her father seems never to have made up for the problems with her mother. One reason for this is suggested in Charlotte's comment that her father "wasn't really a parent, ...wasn't thought of as being a parent."

Charlotte's tie to her father is close and gratifying, but it is not entirely parental. In certain respects he is more like a peer than a father, and she is more like a companion than a daughter, which seems to be the reason why Charlotte's mother is described as jealous of Charlotte and her father. Another consequence, however, is that Charlotte's father does not provide a fully adequate model of parenting. While he does demonstrate the ideal of loving attention, there is another parental function which Charlotte represents, not in descriptions of her father, but in a *latent* idealization with respect to her mother. This function is that of parental guidance and control.

At several points in the interview, Charlotte described her mother as capable, strong, and competent. At times, in fact, Charlotte expressed a kind of awe at her mother's abilities. For example, Charlotte indicated that she compares herself to her mother a great deal; and on one occasion she commented, "I guess I just always have had a real inferiority complex about my mom." That this inferiority complex includes the issue of responsible parenting is clear from the following passage in which Charlotte talked about her struggle to control Beverly:

> I guess I really wasn't so worried about [Beverly] as I was about her doing something that was going to make me look bad.... (To whom?) Probably to my mother.... (What kinds of judgments...were you concerned about your mother making about you?) I guess that I wasn't capable of raising kids, you know, that I wasn't capable of doing a good job of it.

Despite her mother's shortcomings as a parent, therefore, Charlotte seems to have retained her as a model of parental capability, especially with regard to controlling children. And this idealization seems to have become particularly problematic for Charlotte when her own daughter reached her teenage years.

Charlotte's original experience of self-esteem now becomes a comprehensible as a specific solution to a central conflict. In Charlotte's account, the themes of parental love and parental control are presented as contradictory and incompatible. The former is concretely represented in Charlotte's idealized descriptions of her father and the latter in the latent idealization of her mother as a demanding and capable person. The split between these two themes caused a number of problems for Charlotte when she was growing up, but of greater relevance to the present discussion is the difficulty it caused for Charlotte in her own parenting. Charlotte wanted to be a loving parent to her daughter, but when Beverly began to rebel Charlotte had to assume the role of parental authority and responsibility. Given her mother's example, this task meant trying to exert an extreme and unyielding control over Beverly. The joint therapy sessions were helpful to Charlotte because they enabled her to see that she was repeating her mother's behavior and that this strategy was doomed to fail with Beverly, just as it had failed with Charlotte. Knowing she would have to regard her daughter in a different way, Charlotte began to ease up and to listen to her daughter's point of view, a strategy which was reminiscent of idealized interactions in which Charlotte's father would listen to *her*. Charlotte felt good about this change because it meant avoiding her mother's mistakes and balancing parental control with the kind of loving attention shown to her by her father.

There is a danger here, however, and it is a danger of which Charlotte is well aware. The possibility remains that Charlotte's move from uncompromising parental control to openness and parental love will be a shift from one extreme to the other. To use the terms that were developed in the last chapter, the resolution of Charlotte's central conflict might take the form of a reversal rather than a true reconciliation. Charlotte herself expressed this fear during the interview:

> I do handle it differently with Lisa [Beverly's younger sister], but sometimes I think I've gone completely the opposite. Sometimes I think I let Lisa walk all over top of me. But you see I don't know for sure 'cause I've not done it this way. Although I do realize there's a few, you know, guidelines that you do have to go along with.

Charlotte's fear of going to the opposite extreme is understandable in light of her experience in her family origin. Her mother and father presented models of parenting that were extreme and incompatible. Moreover, Charlotte herself is a single parent; she does not have a partner who can share the burden and make it easier for her to define her own role. As she herself indicates in the above passage, she must find a way of performing *both* parental functions, of providing a mixture of both love and guidance. And, while it is one thing to understand this as a general principle, it is quite another to know the specifics—the particular "guidelines" which a parent needs to present to a child.

Here we encounter, once again, the question of ideology. As has already been noted, Charlotte's account is relatively nonideological, and from the beginning she elaborated the meaning of her self-esteem in terms of past events rather than ideals and beliefs. We can now see a problem in Charlotte's life associated with this conceptual style. Charlotte's uncertainty and her wish to find a set of guidelines can both be understood as an ideological *insufficiency*, a sense that she is adrift admist the complexities of choices open to her. In the following passage Charlotte expresses some of her confusion about being a parent and her sense of operating in a vacuum:

> I worry a lot about it, I worry a lot about my
> responsibilities. What are they, you know? And I've never
> been a parent before so this is all—every age and every
> stage is something new for me to go through. I'm hoping
> with the other three it's going to be easier for me.

At other points in the interview, too, Charlotte expressed feelings of uncertainty and bewilderment. On one occasion she joked about being confused, and on another she summarized her adult life as a rather chaotic series of disconnected changes. Moreover, her account itself is sometimes difficult to follow. She often had trouble responding to questions and expressing herself in clear and specific ways. All of these characteristics betoken a lack of clear ideology, of an organizing framework in Charlotte's life; and all of them underscore the importance of such a framework in orienting oneself in the social world.[1]

It should be emphasized, however, that ideology is not completely *absent* in Charlotte's account. If we recall the characterization given in chapter 2, we can see that there are reasons for expecting to find a minimum of ideology in *any* account, as long as the subject uses some degree of linguistic abstraction to discuss social beliefs and

---

[1]Once again, it should be noted that we are talking about the structure of meaning in a life-historical account, not a causal or developmental process. Charlotte's confusion is not *caused by* a lack of ideology; it *is* a lack of ideology.

aspirations. The particular way a subject uses socially relevant general concepts will define the major terms and ideas of an ideology; and Charlotte's account is no exception in this sense. For example, when asked about good parenting, Charlotte sketched the broad outlines of an ideology corresponding to the ideal of loving attention that we have already seen exemplified in the descriptions of her father:

> (What do you think makes a good parent?) Oh, God. [Pauses]...I think a good parent has got to be there for the kids. I think there's a lot of times you have to give up some stuff of your own.

At another point, Charlotte revealed elements of a social theory related to her other ideal, parental responsibility and control:

> "Society holds—I don't care what they say, society holds parents responsible for what their children do.

Ideological elements *are* present in Charlotte's account, therefore; but as the above passages illustrate, they are sketchy and somewhat overarching. They present vague imperatives like "being there" and being "responsible" for one's children, but there is nothing in the way of actual guidelines for carrying out these imperatives. Moreover, the above two passages are the *only* statements in Charlotte's account that are formed in purely ideological terms— that is, as generalizations about social life detached from reference to specific individuals and events. Charlotte's ideology, then, stands in marked contrast to others we have seen which lay out elaborate and detailed rules of conduct for specific social situations (e.g. Ed's case); and her uncertainty does not seem to reflect an *absence* of ideology as much as it does a vague and undifferentiated one that is difficult to apply in practice.

The joint therapy sessions Charlotte described at the beginning of the interview seem to have been helpful, in part, because they assisted her in making small but important additions, modifications, and distinctions in her ideology. In these sessions, Charlotte realized she was attempting to carry out the same program of excessive parental control her mother had tried to enforce; and through discussion and practice Charlotte found that her parental (social) responsibilities were not as absolute as she had believed: "I found out it was okay for her to hurt me and, uh, I wasn't going to die, I wasn't going to be shamed from whatever hurt she did to me."

Accordingly, Charlotte learned to combine some of the elements of her father's loving attention with the ideal of parental responsibility she had learned from her mother:

> [I learned to] swallow a few things and shut my mouth and listen to Bev...because maybe she *does* know better than what I do....
> I've learned to let go and let her, you know, run her own life. And if she's going to make mistakes she's going to have to figure them up.

These statements represent ideological modifications; and by virtue of such modifications Charlotte was able to make compromises with her daughter and to undercut the vicious circle of rebellion and overcontrol that was tearing their relationship apart. In so doing, she demonstrated parenting that was both responsible and loving— a reconciliation of the terms of her central conflict and the heart of Charlotte's experience of self-esteem.

IDEOLOGY AND CHANGE: LINGUISTIC TRANSFORMATION

It is interesting to note that this case, which is probably the least ideological, is also the one case in which psychotherapy plays a crucial role. The modification and extension of Charlotte's ideology seems to have been extremely important, and psychotherapy seems to have been particularly effective in promoting this kind of change. The affinity between psychotherapy and ideological change has been noted and discussed by a number of authors in recent years. Let us consider what some of these authors have had to say and what their statements imply about the relationship between ideology and self-esteem.

We may begin by recalling that "ideology" refers not only to political and philosophical beliefs, but to the whole range of ideas that an individual has about the social world and his or her place in it. As noted in chapter 2, such a set of ideas provides a context in which important terms define each other; that is, ideology involves a set of relations among terms that define an individual's field of linguistic (conceptual) meaning. This field of linguistic meaning has been given increasing attention by clinicians attempting to reformulate psychoanalytic principles in nonmechanistic terms. For example, Lacan (1953, 1966) has written about psychopathology as a disturbance of language, and Lorentzer (1976) has analyzed psychological symptoms in terms of "desymbolization" and the "privatization" of language. Other authors have focussed on processes of linguistic transformation. For example, Cheshire (1975) has suggested that the therapeutic effect of psychoanalytic interpretation can be understood as a structural transformation analogous to the kinds of grammatical transformations Chomsky (1957, 1966) has described between the "deep structures" and "surface structures" underlying linguistic behavior. This theory has been elaborated in some detail by Edelson (1975), who has also tied it much more closely to the specifics of Chomsky's work.[1]

Eckstein (1978) has suggested an alternative framework for thinking about linguistic transformation and psychotherapeutic cure. Drawing upon Wittgenstein's (1953) philosophical investigations of language, Eckstein proposes that the psychoanalytic process involves an interplay between the "language games" of the analyst and the patient. According to Eckstein, every analysis is "multi-lingual," that is, involves the articulation of a number of different regions of linguistic meaning in the patient's life. These so-called "language games" are accompanied by the analyst's own special language game—the application of his or her interpretive framework to the patient's linguistic productions. By virtue of this interaction, the patient's language games are gradually transformed

---

[1]Chomsky's theory has had a significant impact on Anglo-American writers interested in reformulating psychoanalytic principles, but the application of Chomsky's system to psychoanalysis raises some very difficult problems. For example, Chomsky's conception of "deep structure" is completely discontinuous from the psychoanalytic conception of a dynamic unconscious in a number of important ways. Chomsky has repeatedly emphasized (e.g., 1966, 1969) that this term refers to innate structure at the biological level, a conception that differs radically from the psychodynamic conception of a repressed unconscious. Moreover, the deep structures of Chomsky's theory are alleged to be both inaccessible to consciousness and invariant, characteristics that pose severe obstacles to any attempt to relate them to psychotherapeutic change. If these problems were not bad enough, however, a worse difficulty remains. Chomsky's deep structures are *syntactical* structures, and, as such, they determine grammatical forms which are devoid of meaning in the ordinary sense. In fact, in his original discussion of these structures, Chomsky pointedly drew a distinction between meaning and grammatical form (Chomsky, 1957). Once again, the difference between these structures and those of the dynamic unconscious is a radical one.

into a more realistic "problem-solving language" in which the emotional difficulties associated with the structural insufficiencies of the patient's former language games "vanish" (pp. 340, 344). This account is closely modeled after Wittgenstein's conception of philosophy as a kind of "therapy" that transforms linguistic obscurities into unambiguous constructions in which philosophical problems "completely disappear" (Wittgenstein, 1953, p. 51).[1]

Let us further consider this theory of *linguistic transformation* by elaborating Wittgenstein's conception of the language game in more detail.

A language game, as Wittgenstein uses the term, is any social practice in which words are systematically used. Language games are played in all aspects of human life, and every social situation generates its own particular language game with its own particular rules and vocabulary. For example, a builder and assistant play a language game when the former gives instructions to the latter. The words which they exchange—"block," "pillar," "bring," etc.— are tokens in the game; and each of these words is meaningful because each refers to the objects and activities that contribute to and are defined by the overall project. The sum total of ordinary language can be regarded as a vast system of overlapping language games; and since any particular word is usually employed in a variety of different language games, the shades and nuances of its possible meanings form "a complicated network of similarities overlapping and crisscrossing" (1953, p. 32). While this system gives language both its flexibility and its power for representing the practical demands of everyday life, it also makes meaning impossible to conceptualize in any single or definitive way.

---

[1]Just as Cheshire's and Edelson's theories are tied closely to Chomsky's linguistics, so Eckstein's theory is tied closely to Wittgenstein's philosophy, suggesting that Eckstein's theory may suffer from similar limitations. For example, important psychodynamic concepts like repression and ambivalence have no counterparts in Wittgenstein's philosophy, and Eckstein's analysis seems to be in danger of neglecting these aspects of the psychotherapeutic process. A simple equation of emotional disturbance with philosophical confusion is not tenable. Nevertheless, the analogy between psychoanalysis and Wittgenstein's philosophy seems to go further than the one involving Chomsky's generative-transformational grammer, particularly when we consider the question of ideology and self-esteem. This follows from Wittgenstein's emphasis on *meaning and social processes*, an emphasis embodied in his concept of the language game.

For this reason, Wittgenstein holds that the meaning of a word can be established only in relation to particular activities—that is, in relation to the particular language games in which it is ordinarily used. To understand the meaning of a word like "being," for example, we must know how people use the word in ordinary discourse. If in the context of abstract discussion such a word becomes detached from its ordinary usage, it tends to lead us into confusing philosophical entanglements; the job of the philosopher is to resolve such entanglements by retracing the paths of linguistic practice, the various language games from which the word originally became detached. The philosopher thus transforms linguistic misconstructions into comprehensible structures by reconnecting them with ordinary language and the practical activities of everyday life. By virtue of this process, philosophical problems (like questions about the nature of being) are dissolved and replaced by the ordinary problems of day-to-day living.

Let us return now to the question of ideology.

Any set of goal-directed activities that characterizes the life of a family may be thought of as a language game. In Esther's family, for example, the pattern of activities associated with outings, holidays, and other events constituted a language game oriented around the goal of family closeness. In chapter 2 we considered the ideology Esther has developed in connection with these experiences—her ideology of closeness and community. We also noted in that chapter that ideology is abstract, not concrete; it is a *linguistic* structure, that is, a system of concepts with *general* application. This conception is consistent with Wittgenstein's analysis of the language game. Because they are generated in a normative or customary social practice, the terms of a language game are *rule-governed* and so refer to *classes* of instances rather than single events. For this reason, linguistic terms define *general concepts* capable of elaboration into systems of belief. In Esther's case, the concepts associated with the language game of family closeness are "nurturing," "teamwork," "family," and so forth. We saw that Esther had developed these concepts into a highly organized linguistic structure defining the ideals and beliefs of her ideology. But these were not the only concepts around which Esther's ideology was organized. We saw another ideological constellation articulated in concepts like "respect," "education," "potential," and "individuality." These terms were associated with a different language game in Esther's past, the interactions in which she and her father had talked about labor, politics, education, and self-improvement.

It is significant that Esther's ideology is an organization of concepts associated with *two* different language games from her past—a pattern we have seen in other cases as well. In Ed's account, for example, concepts associated with interactions with his mother—"salesmanship," "reputation," "success"—were integrated with another set of terms relevant to Ed's relationship with father— "bucking the system," "doing it without a degree," "being an individual." These cases illustrate that ideology is a realm in which the concepts associated with different patterns of family interaction can be brought together into a single system of meaning. This possibility follows from the linguistic character of ideology, the abstract nature of the concepts that are generated in relation to language games. Because such concepts refer to *classes* of events, they can be redefined by redrawing their boundaries, which amounts to reclassifying and reconstructing the interactions that constitute a particular language game, past or present. The concepts associated with various language games can therefore be altered with respect to each other to form new sets of relations. Accordingly, we can see that ideology is an arena in which the meanings associated with different life-historical experiences can be *integrated and reconciled with each other*. Moreover, the concepts of an ideology can be broken down, reorganized, and resynthesized in a variety of ways if the individual is willing to reflect upon and reclassify his or her experience. An example is Esther's attempt to reconceptualize her relationships with other people by making a distinction between "dominating" and "nurturing" behavior. Because the conceptual process allows for such reorganization, ideology makes possible the reclassification and reconstruction of experience in such a way as to generate *new meanings and new behavior*.

The construction of an ideology can be seen as the process by which a variety of fragmented and heterogeneous language games associated with an individual's life history are transformed into a more integrated and flexible linguistic structure. The major function of ideology is to present solutions to the central conflict. The concepts that define these solutions are the individual's ideals, and a successful ideology is one that embeds these ideals in a conceptual matrix sufficiently abstract and general to apply to a wide range of new situations, but sufficiently concrete to recommend specific courses of action for solving specific problems. Thus, there is a strong analogy between the activity of the philosopher as characterized by Wittgenstein and that of the individual striving to realize his or her ideals. Like the former, the latter is troubled by problems in meaning. As opposed to the abstract problems of the philosopher, however, these are problems of life-historical meaning, defined in the fragmented and contradictory language games associated with early family interactions. A successful ideology will transform these language games into a rich and consistent linguistic structure that guides the individual to solutions of his or her central conflict in the present. The conceptual entanglements associated with early life history are therefore superseded and replaced by specific problem-solving strategies in the real world.

In Charlotte's account, the importance of ideology is evident in the consequences that follow from its absence. Charlotte seldom discusses parenting in abstract, conceptual terms. Occasionally, she alludes to vague ideals like "being there" for the child or "providing guidelines," but much more frequently she tells what it means to be a parent by recounting concrete experiences from her own past. In this light, it is not surprising that the conflicts between Charlotte and her daughter took the form of entanglements that seemed to repeat Charlotte's interactions with her own mother. It appears that Charlotte and her daughter were reenacting—with virtually no modification—the same language game that Charlotte had learned from her own mother. Charlotte's experience in therapy helped her to change this situation, partly by modifying this language game. With the help of her therapist, Charlotte was able to redefine the meanings of certain important terms (e.g., a parent's "responsibilities"), to develop new concepts for new interactions with her daughter (e.g., letting Beverly "figure up" her own mistakes), and to integrate these concepts with elements of another language game, the one associated with her father (e.g., "being there"). All of these modifications were important in changing Charlotte's relationship with her daughter, and they all represent steps in the development of a viable ideology, the transformation of a constellation of fragmentary and heterogeneous language games into a richer and more consistent linguistic structure.

This is not to say that the development of ideology is *all* that is required to free an individual from the entanglements of early life-history. There is also reason to believe that psychological growth requires the transformation of the more concrete structures of life-historical meaning as well, something which has already been implied in previous comments about idealization and the necessary role of semiotic structures. We have identified these structures as elements of an *object* language that grounds and supplements the abstract formulations of ideology. It would be reasonable to assume, then, that like ideology, these structures also require modification if an individual is to make important changes in his or her life. In the next case we will consider this question critically. Lou's account presents an incident of self-esteem that is tied to early life history through the usual structures of ideology and a central conflict. At the level of idealization, however, there is a break in the pattern we have seen in other cases, for Lou presents no obvious idealized descriptions in his early family history. We will have to determine, then, how Lou applies the abstract formulations of his ideology to the real world. This determination will lead us to a closer look at some important elements of Lou's life history and to the general role of idealization and other semiotic structures in the process of psychological growth and the attainment of self-esteem.

LOU: AN ORGANIZATION TO BELONG TO

Lou is a white thirty-nine-year-old hydraulics inspector who is currently employed by a large aerospace corporation in the midwestern United States. He lives with his wife and four children in a pleasant house in the suburb of a large city. During the interview, three of Lou's four children were home, and their excitement and activity provided a chaotic background to our conversation. In contrast, Lou spoke in an unbroken, almost mesmerizing style, answering my questions with a relentless stream of details, repetitions, examples, and related ideas.

The experience of self-esteem that Lou chose to talk about was an ongoing one which had begun a year and a half earlier. At that time, Lou had agreed to become an adult leader in his son's Boy Scout troop. At first, Lou had taken on this role out of a sense of obligation "because somebody had to do it." As time passed, however, he discovered that he enjoyed the role and found it highly rewarding:

> You take a bunch of boys out like I did on a winter event and give them an opportunity to compete against each other in winter games like sliding down a hill or sledding races, and seeing the looks on their faces and the excitement they get doing it I think makes you feel good.... I think that's the biggest satisfaction out of scouting itself.

Scouting was not available in Lou's town when he was growing up, and he feels good that he has been able to bring this kind of enjoyment to his own son. But Lou believes there is more to scouting than having fun. At certain points in the interview, he explained how scouting can help to shape a boy's life in a positive direction. One way is by providing organized activities:

[Scouting provides] something for the kids to do.... [It] gives them something to strive for.... Maybe it builds a little ambition....
They say, supposedly, [there's] not supposed to be any convicts in prison that's ever been a Boy Scout. I don't know about that, but...the turnout must be pretty good.

Another positive function of scouting is to give the boys recognition:

My policy is that if they achieve something they get a badge of recognition or something.... It gives them a chance to show off what they've done, what they've accomplished and stuff like that.

More than this, though, scouting gives the boys a sense of belonging and an experience of equality:

I think it gives them...an organization to belong to, you know, the ideals of scouting—you've got one uniform and you all look the same, no matter if your parents are well off or not well off.... It doesn't matter what Mom and Daddy look like, Junior looks just like the other kids. You know, his hair might be different, the complexion might be different, color might be different, but they're all identical in that uniform.

Repeatedly, however, Lou returned to the activities that scouting provides and the enjoyment these activities bring to the boys—the aspect of scouting which Lou has found to be the most rewarding as an adult leader:

You see them boys really work hard and enjoy it, and when they get done with it they can say "Hey, I did this."...And their face really beams and you do enjoy it, you know, I do, anyway. When I see that kid break out in a smile, that just gets to you....
Of anything I've ever done so far, that's what I enjoy the most.

In Lou's description of his own boyhood, scouting and other organized activities emerge as important factors, not by their presence but by their absence. Lou grew up in a small agricultural community in the 1940s, and he recalls the community as an uneventful place where people were occupied full time with farm work:

> The majority of the people were farmers, and farm work, it's long hours. You're farming big farms and...you just didn't have time for extra stuff.... Everybody worked hard, was busy, you know, and there just wasn't much activity.

There was little in the way of organized activities for Lou and his peers:

> We didn't have any adults to help us do anything, lead us.... Had to do everything on our own, and it gets awfully boring doing the same thing day in and day out.

At one time there had been a scout troop in town, but Lou's hope that he might join was dispelled:

> Just prior to me getting old enough to be a scout, they disbanded the troop.... The scoutmaster, his son got up in age and got out, so he quit and there was no replacement. So all the time I was a young kid coming up he had had the scout troop and all of a sudden there wasn't one.

Against this backdrop of social monotony and adult non-involvement, Lou describes his boyhood as a restless search for things to do; and this situation seems to have been exacerbated by Lou's experience in his family.

Lou was the oldest of four children and the only boy. Many relatives from both sides of the family lived and worked in the area, and Lou states that more than half the population of the town were his relatives. Lou remembers his female relatives—his mother, his grandmother, his aunts, and his sisters—as being nearby and available during the day whenever he wanted them. For example, he states that his mother was "readily available" as someone to talk to. But Lou also conveys the sense that his male relatives were more important to him. When asked about adult influences in his childhood, he talked about males most of the time, making only brief and qualified allusions to females. At the same time, Lou also conveyed the sense that these male relatives were generally busy and unavailable to him—a state of affairs which seems to have been particularly true with regard to Lou's father.

Lou describes his father as a distant and uncommunicative man who worked long hours that left little time for family life:

> My dad worked in a grain elevator. He run that and that was a six-day operation. In the summertime during harvest it was seven days—long hours, as long as the farmers were bringing in the grain.

Lou recalls visiting his father at work, but his description of these visits gives the impression of a father-son relationship that was more hoped for than real:

> I used to go over there and spend a lot of time. (How did he feel about you [doing that]?) Oh, he didn't never say nothing against it. I don't know if he enjoyed me being over there or what, he never really said.... He might give me heck if I climbed in the wrong places.... Anytime I wanted to go over there I could go there no problem. (Um-hm.) There ain't but so much time you can spend there, you know. (Um-hm. Sounds like he didn't communicate a lot to you one way or the other when you would go over and see him at work.) Not really. I talked more to my uncles when I was over there....
> That was about the extent of being around my dad.

Work, however, was not the only thing which came between Lou and his father:

> He drank a lot, too, so I didn't see much of him. (You mean he'd be gone in the evenings?) Right.... We didn't do that much together, you know, as a family....
> As far as I can remember he always drank. But it just got worse as he got older, I mean it bothered me more.... I was quite a bit bothered and might have been resentful for it or something, like I say, because he did work long hours and stuff and at night he wasn't home 'cause he'd go up drinking.

Lou recalls his parents arguing about his father's drinking:

> They used to argue all the time, my mother used to holler at him all the time....
> (What kind of things did your mother get angry about?)...I think it was mostly my dad's drinking and his spending all the money on booze, and not having money

for stuff for the house and stuff like that. She knew he
was making the money but he was throwing it away in the
bar.

More than these arguments, though, Lou remembers his father's
absence from the home. In Lou's descriptions of his childhood, it is
the *lack* of family life and the *emptiness* of the home that stand out
above all, particularly as Lou got older and his mother went to work.
In the following passage, Lou describes the atmosphere in which he
and his sisters grew up:

> We didn't go [out] that much, didn't get to go any place
> because the old man was either soused out or spent all the
> money.... So it wasn't that much of a family life I don't
> think. And even after TV came in, we got a TV, there
> wasn't nobody else around the house. Mother went to work
> and Dad was never home.

In both the community and the family, therefore, Lou describes a
lonely and monotonous existence in which his father and other
adults left him to his own devices. Lou characterizes himself during
these years as a "hot-tempered" and "ornery" boy with "a lot of idle
time, a lot of time to get into trouble." This remark was amply
illustrated in the details of Lou's life-historical account. Time and
again throughout the interview, Lou recounted stories of minor
misdeeds and unruly behavior that had gotten him into trouble with
adults:

> We used to break the streetlights every once in a while.
> That was the big thing, or throw rocks at each other....
> In the wintertime throw snowballs. I remember one
> incident, uh, we were throwing them off the roof of the
> house.... We threw the snowball [at a car] and it
> happened to be a state trooper.... I remember the rock
> throwing because I hit one of my cousins in the head with
> a rock and cut his head open. I got creamed over that.

But in Lou's account of his boyhood almost *everything* seems to end in
adult annoyance.

> [You would] get in trouble whatever you did, you know.
> Go there, throw rocks, whatever; go down to the creek and
> somebody'd fall in, you'd go home and get heck for getting
> all wet [laughs]....

[We] used to go hauling [boxes] home, make big
clubhouses out of that. Then Dad would holler about all
the cardboard all over the yard....
(You didn't have very much opportunity to...feel that
you were doing things that were worthwhile or good or—)
No, none that I can ever recall doing. When we thought
that we was doing something like going down to the creek
fishing...I remember all I did was catch hell for going
home with wet shoes.

In his life-historical account, then, Lou is portrayed as a boy with
nothing to do, who has no role in the community and little family
life, who is invisible to adults except when engaged in something
troublesome or annoying, who is bored, restless, testy, and
chronically searching for something to do, something to relieve the
dreariness of it all:

There was no one to organize things, there was no place to
go to play basketball 'cause the schools were locked up....
Nobody to play volleyball with unless you got enough guys
together.... You couldn't ever play football and whatever....
    I know a few times [I] would stand on the street corner
with my cousin and just fight for something to do [laughs].
Get in a fight, go home, the old man would whoop you for
getting blood all over yourself....
    I got into fights as a kid, you know, neighbor kids and
cousins and whatever. I didn't care who they were, I'd fight
them.... Just one way to get rid of the anger.

It should be added at this point that Lou did recall one exception
to the dreary vista described above—his membership in the Ground
Observer Corps, an organization that existed for a short period of
time at the end of the Second World War. Although the experience
was an ephemeral one, it does seem to suggest the kind of
involvement that Lou wanted but never really experienced in other
situations.

The Ground Observer Corps was an organization of volunteers
who watched the sky and reported any aircraft that were
observed. Lou and the other boys in his town were recruited as
daytime observers, given books of information about different kinds
of airplanes, and assigned specific hours for observation. Lou recalls
the experience as an enjoyable one which brought everyone
together for a single purpose:

[We] had one cause. Everybody was part of it. A lot of it was kids in it, plus there was some grown-ups running it. You had your hours.... It was something to do. You didn't just have a lot of spare time. You belonged to something, the rest of the guys belonged to it. You weren't the only one, you know, you was the same as they were. I don't know if that—that meant something to me or what. Maybe that's why today I belong to organizations.

For Lou, then, the Ground Observer Corps seems to have presented a kind of social involvement and purpose that was utterly lacking in the rest of his experience. But this organization did not last long. After about six months it was dismantled and replaced by the more sophisticated techniques of radar and computers. As in the case of the Boy Scout troop, an organization which had promised to be meaningful was dissolved and Lou was left with nothing to do once again.

Let us take stock at this point and attempt to articulate the central conflict in Lou's story. If we consider Lou's descriptions of family and community life we can discern a recurring conflict in his account, a conflict between the themes of social responsibility and personal gratification. The interplay between these two themes is presented most clearly and concretely in Lou's characterization of his father. Lou describes his father as a man who works long hours and whose only gratification in life is indulging in alcohol. The incompatibility of these two spheres of activity—the responsible world of work and the gratifying world of drink—is heightened in Lou's description of his father's keeping them rigidly apart by confining his drinking to off-hours. With regard to the family, however, no such split is possible, and Lou's father chooses alcohol over the solidarity of the family.

In Lou's situation, too, this conflict is evident. Lou describes a boyhood of restless alienation in a dreary and rejecting social world. The adults in his life—and indeed the very community itself—are occupied with dull and endless labor, and they seem to respond to Lou only to rebuke and curtail his efforts to find stimulation and amusement. In Lou's construction of his boyhood there does not seem to be any socially acceptable way to enjoy oneself. Lou's attempts to do so seem to be defined as troublesome and destructive no matter what they involve. Moreover, Lou himself appears to have adopted this view of things, and he describes himself as becoming ornery and unruly. The experience which Lou describes in the Ground Observer Corps is an interesting one because it seems to represent a reconciliation of this central conflict. In this organization Lou is able to do something that is simultaneously enjoyable *and* socially meaningful. It seems likely that this experience is also what Lou had hoped to attain in Boy Scouts before the troop was disbanded. In order to fully appreciate Lou's attitude toward Boy Scouts, however, let us consider some further life-historical material.

At the age of twenty Lou joined the navy, and for the next eight years he remained in the service and traveled around the world. Lou enjoyed his time in the navy, and at one point in the interview he discussed his travels with some fondness. Besides providing some of the adventure he had long wished for, this period seems to have constituted a kind of moratorium in Lou's life during which he consolidated certain important elements of his adult identity. One of these elements was Lou's commitment to the military and its ideology.

Lou describes himself as "military minded" and he currently belongs to the naval reserve and the American Legion. During the interview he explained how the military had become important to him, and he related its meaning to his childhood experience:

> I like a uniform, like dressing up, you know. I think part
> of it too is the discipline. (Um-hm.) Didn't really have that
> much when I was growing up as a kid, you know, just
> Mom hollering. Dad was never around to say much, and
> you did pretty much what you pleased.... But, uh, you got
> in [the navy], you got discipline.... Something was
> expected of you, you had to do it. You know, when you
> did your job other people were depending on you and you
> depended on other people 'cause it was more like team-
> work.... You go to sea, if you don't do your job there's
> a whole lot of other people going to pay.... Every man's
> got a job at a certain time. [If] he doesn't do his job
> then the whole thing is in jeopardy.

In this passage Lou emphasizes the importance of teamwork and discipline in achieving the goals of the military. As Lou points out, "discipline" means much more than simply being "hollered" at; it means setting aside one's immediate interests in order to join with other people in doing something worthwhile and important. Teamwork and discipline, therefore, are key elements of a linguistic framework that reconciles personal and social interests; and in this manner Lou's military ideology provides a set of guidelines for resolving his central conflict.

This ideological constellation, however, is not the only one Lou developed while he was in the navy. Lou seems also to have used the moratorium time of the service to clarify his thoughts about family life, and he developed some ideas about what had been missing in his own childhood. He remembered other families in which people had done things together, and he recalled that the children in such families had seemed to grow up happier:

Their family life seemed—seemed more *family* than mine, more closeness, and as they grew up and had families [of their own] they never had any problems....
I don't know when it was but I had it in my mind that if I got married and had kids I was going to spend some time with them and be available to do things with the kids.

At this time Lou developed an ideology of parental involvement aimed at creating the kind of family life he had never had—a family life that would be both responsible and gratifying, bringing parents and children together in a context of shared activities. This ideological constellation represents a second set of guidelines for resolving Lou's central conflict—one that has retained importance in his current life. At many points throughout the interview Lou articulated this ideology, enumerating things that he does with his children and expressing the belief that sharing these activities will have a positive effect on his children's lives:

I spend a lot of time with the kids and the family, and anything we do for the kids or around the house we discuss before we do, you know.... I say [marriage is] a fifty-fifty proposition, and the kids are part of that fifty-fifty proposition.... We do stuff, we take the kids with us. Have them around and they learn what life's about—maybe some of the better stuff, 'cause it's going to be a rough road ahead, you know, as they grow up....
They'll have a good experience as kids and hopefully it'll make an impression on them and they'll be halfway decent adults when they grow up.

Both of the above ideological constellations—the military ideology of teamwork and discipline and the family ideology of parental involvement—are important in Lou's current life. Both are evident in his attitudes toward scouting and both can be seen in his experience of self-esteem. For Lou, scouting is an "organization to belong to" in which the boys are "all identical in that uniform." Scouting provides the social structure necessary to make enjoyable activities possible, and it teaches boys the importance of teamwork and organization so that they can be better adults. At the same time scouting allows Lou to share in activities with his son and to provide him with the kind of close and enjoyable father-son relationship that Lou never had. Working as a scout leader, therefore, enables Lou to put both aspects of his ideology into effect and to bring about a specific resolution of the themes of his central conflict.

Like most of the other cases we have considered, this one shows a close connection between ideology and self-esteem. Ideology defines the social meaning of self-esteem and simultaneously presents the guiding principles by which it might be attained. However, there is a sense in which Lou's account is different from all the others reported in this study: his case is the only one in which a subject described an early family history with no clear instances of idealization.

This is not to say that Lou reported no positive relationships with people in his family. On the contrary, he describes a close and comfortable tie to his mother:

> I got along with her real good, you know, no problem with her.... She was always at home. If you had any problems, anything, [you could] go see Mother.

But Lou's characterization of his mother does not extend much beyond this statement, nor does it seem to offer any specific solutions to his central conflict. Moreover, when Lou talks about the dilemmas of his childhood—the boredom, anger, monotony, and rejection—the roles of females seem to be peripheral. It is to males that Lou looked for adult leadership and guidance, and these males, while more important to him, were consistently less available. At several points during the interview, Lou talked about his male relatives—and the story was always the same. He describes liking them and looking up to them, but somehow they never seem to have been very close to him or influential in his life. Lou's contacts with these relatives do not seem to have extended much beyond shared work and routine activities. In the following passage, for example, Lou talks about the uncle with whom he was the closest:

> (Was he a favorite uncle or anything like that?) Well, maybe a little bit because I had more contact [with him]. But I don't really consider any of them a favorite more than some of the others. I knew them all well, and I just had more contact with him 'cause I did work with him.... (What was he like?) I don't know—just an easy-going guy,

could explain things to you, any job, anything.... And like I say, more so that I worked with him...and so I had more contact with him. That's about the only thing I could say about him.

The above two passages illustrate a point made in chapter 2 when idealization was initially discussed. Idealization does not simply mean regarding a person in a predominantly or entirely positive light; rather, it is the carrier of a specific and differentiated *meaning*. Idealization is defined by a particular theme, that is, an ideal which points the way to a better life. Moreover, not just any theme will do. The themes of talking to his mother about his problems or learning about work from his uncle would qualify as ideals in Lou's account only if they presented elements of a specific strategy for resolving his central conflict. The conceptual aspects of this strategy would be represented in Lou's ideology, and the concrete illustrations of such a general strategy would be provided in these and other memories and images. But such does not appear to be the case. While the interactions with his mother and uncle are represented as positive ones, neither relationship seems to offer elements of a potential *solution* to Lou's central conflict, nor does either of them seem to represent in action the abstract terms of Lou's ideology. For this reason, they cannot be considered idealizations as the term was defined in chapter 2.

Another point made in chapter 2 is that idealization involves a semiotic employment of imagery, that is, the use of images to represent objects (people) in the context of the individual's history. It was suggested that this characteristic makes it possible for idealizations to serve a unique function, namely, the representation of ideals in an "object language" which adds experiential substance and specific behavioral guidelines to the abstract formulations of ideology. Idealization differs from ideology, then, in that idealization expresses the meaning of an ideal in a different *mode*, one that is much more pragmatic and immediately useful. A question can be raised, therefore, about Lou's case: Since there is no clear evidence of idealization in his account, how does Lou make use of the abstract formulation of his ideology? Is it possible that he skips the level of concrete imagery and applies them directly? The answer to the question appears to be no. Lou *does* seem to have certain sources of concrete imagery in which his ideals are semiotically represented. To see what these sources are, let us consider his experience in the navy once again.

We have already seen that Lou calls himself "military minded" and adheres to a military ideology. The major tenets of this ideology concern the importance of teamwork and discipline in achieving valued and meaningful goals. But Lou does not articulate this ideology in purely abstract terms—he supplements it with images from his experience in the navy:

> I like a uniform, like dressing up, you know....
> It was more like teamwork.... You get out there with five thousand men on a ship, every man's got a job at a certain time. [If] he doesn't do his job then the whole thing is in jeopardy....
> I had one colored boy that worked for me that, uh, when he made petty officer he says "Well, they might not take orders from me." I said, "Hey, you're a petty officer. I don't care what color you are. When you give an order it's just like me giving an order."

In Lou's account, then, the ideals associated with military ideology are concretely illustrated, not with reference to any one person, but with reference to the military itself. That is, Lou finds experiential substance for his ideals of teamwork, discipline, and equality in an *idealization of the navy* (a phenomenon familiar to clinicians under the rubric of "institutional transference"). Such is the idealization that appears to underlie the first ideological constellation in Lou's account. But what about the second ideological constellation, Lou's ideology of family involvement?

It will be recalled that Lou did a lot of thinking while he was in the navy, and that family life was one of the things he thought about. He remembered families he had known in which the fathers had been present and people had done things together:

> Their family life seemed—seemed more *family* than mine, more closeness, and as [the children] grew up and had families [of their own] they never had any problems.

At one point, Lou was asked to elaborate:

> (I was wondering if you could tell me more about who you were thinking of). Well, I had one—one close friend I grew up with.... Him and his dad were—seemed a lot closer than me and my dad. Him and his dad did things together, went places more often. In fact, I went with them quite a few times. But, uh, it seems like, you know, he grew up [to be] a pretty nice guy. Got a family and everything, no problems. Uh, that's one of them I was thinking of, the main one.

From this passage we can see that there *is* at least one idealized figure in Lou's early history, though not in his family. The interactions Lou recalls between his friend and his friend's father demonstrate an ideal of family closeness that represents a specific solution to Lou's central conflict. Of course, we have no way of knowing how accurate Lou's memory is in this particular case. It may be that Lou has reconstructed, on the basis of his own need, a mythical version of an idealized relationship between this father and his son. In fact, we can assume that some such activity *has* taken place, that Lou *has* reconstructed this father-son relationship. As Lou himself explains, not until he was in the navy, years after observing the interactions between his friend and his friend's father, did he think back on these interactions and their significance. This consideration, however, does not vitiate the main point. What is important here is that Lou *did* need an example of family participation, a concrete image of this ideal in action. It matters little whether or not Lou's version is an accurate representation of the original relationship as long as his description provides a meaningful pattern for Lou in the present.

We can see, then, that there are idealized images in Lou's account after all. The images are somewhat different from the ones we have seen in other cases, but their presence supports the contention that some kind of idealization is an indispensible prerequisite to self-esteem in every case. This point has not received much attention in the clinical literature; clinicians have tended to focus on either the latent idealizations associated with conflicted family interactions (the "punitive superego") or the extreme and wholesale idealizations associated with narcissistic pathology (e.g., Kohut, 1966, 1972). It seem likely, however, that there is a normal and adaptive way in which idealizations guide an individual to conflict resolution and love of the self.

THE RECONSTRUCTION OF HISTORY:
SEMIOTIC TRANSFORMATION

In the previous case, we saw how Charlotte used the process of psychotherapy to extend and modify her ideology, and ultimately to bolster her sense of self-esteem. This process was discussed as a form of linguistic transformation, and recent work in psychotherapy and language was drawn upon to clarify this idea. Lou's account provides additional insights. Like Charlotte, Lou went through a period of reexamining and clarifying his ideals, not in psychotherapy but in the moratorium period of his tour in the navy. Like Charlotte, Lou seems to have developed important aspects of his ideology during this period. But Lou's account suggests that a parallel process was also taking place, namely, that Lou was identifying and reconstructing images from his past and present experience to give concrete meaning to his new ideological formations. Accordingly, we can extend what was said about psychotherapy in the last section.

The psychotherapeutic process, and indeed any form of psychological growth, would seem to involve not only linguistic transformation but some kind of *semiotic transformation* as well. The literature on psychotherapy and language has suffered from neglecting this principle. Eckstein's (1978) emphasis on the language game and Cheshire's (1975) and Edelson's (1975) allusions to generative-transformational grammar have implied that psychotherapy is an essentially cognitive process. But the concrete power of imagery—of memories, fantasies, and other modes of nonverbal signification—can hardly be understated. The role of these concrete signifiers was deemphasized, to a certain extent, in the discussion of Charlotte's case because we were concerned then with the problems and functions of ideology. We can assume, however, that the modification and reconstruction of semiotic elements, particularly the idealizations of her mother and her father, were—and will continue to be—an important aspect of Charlotte's psychological growth.

A closely related question is that of modeling and identification. What we have referred to in this study as idealized figures could also be called role models, and the process of idealization could be regarded as identification with these models. Lou's account seems to point to the importance of modeling and identification in the resolution of the central conflict and the attainment of self-esteem. There is, however, a mixed attitude toward this phenomenon in the psychotherapy literature. On the one hand, psychodynamically oriented clinicians have played down the importance of modeling and identification in the psychotherapeutic process and have laid more stress on the attainment of insight. On the other hand, some clinicians, notably those associated with behavior modification and social-learning theory, have laid great stress on modeling and identification. For example, Bandura (1969) has criticized insight therapies for encouraging patients to dwell upon past negative experiences, and he has produced a number of studies indicating the therapeutic efficacy of positive modeling and identification. Let us assess this controversy by considering, once again, the characteristics of idealization.

Idealization and other forms of life-historical imagery have been discussed in this book as semiotically organized structures representing objects rather than concepts. This definiton is correct as far as it goes, but it will be useful at this point to make another distinction. There are various kinds of semiotic systems, of which imagery is only one. Imagery, however, has a major feature which distinguishes it from other semiotic forms. This feature is its function of *copying* or *reproducing* the object that it represents. The importance of this function was first recognized by Peirce (1932) in his discussion of what he called the "iconic" function of language. According to Peirce, one of the things language must do is to represent objects as identifiable, consistent entities with certain characteristic sets of properties. This task is fulfilled by certain linguistic and semiotic structures—called icons—which represent the properties of objects by reproducing them. A mental image is one kind of icon.

A number of authors since Peirce have recognized the importance of mental imagery in carrying out the iconic function of language. In general, these authors have stressed the dynamic aspects of the process; that is, a mental image is not merely a passive imprint of an object, like a photograph. Rather, the image is a transformational schema by which the structure of the object becomes an organizing principle for the individual's own action. Langer (1960) thus identifies the "sensory sign" as the vehicle that stimulates practical action appropriate to a given object (p. 267). Likewise, Piaget and Inhelder (1966) argue that mental images develop only in conjunction with the capacity to imitate (p. 69), and Wittgenstein (1953) and Ryle (1949) analyze imagery as the ability to reproduce that which the image represents. These characterizations differ to some extent, but they all share the conception of the image as a kind of internal schema by which the individual recapitulates the structure of the object world in his or her own actions.

In this connection, we may recall once again Freud's (1914b) formulation of the repetition compulsion as the reenactment of repressed infantile scenes. It is interesting to note that Freud regards such repetitive behavior as a form of *remembering*. One could easily argue that the patient's behavior is merely an empty automatism, since it replays itself again and again outside of the patient's comprehension. Freud is quite clear, however, in interpreting such repetition as a form of remembering, and he lays considerable stress on this point. What Freud seems to be emphasizing—and what all of the above authors seem to be implying in one way or another—is that the iconic organization of behavior is a form of *signification* and that unreflective behaviors—stereotypic movements, reflexive acts, and imitation—*express meaning in an embryonic form.*

This gives us a rather different perspective on the phenomena of modeling and identification. We can agree with Bandura that modeling and identification are extremely important in the attainment of self-esteem. They are meaningful behaviors of a very basic kind, namely, the reflexive and imitative acts which, through the transformational schemata of life-historical imagery, mediate and structure our relationship with the real world. We could hardly survive without imitative learning, let alone construct a meaningful social order. The importance of such learning, however, does not mean that imitation is sufficient for the construction of meaning in the *full* psychological and social sense. The stereotypic behaviors associated with imitation are meaningful only insofar as they guide and direct action in a variety of specific situations. These behaviors cannot contribute to the resolution of a central conflict in any systematic or consistent way unless the individual actively *appropriates* them—that is, brings them together with other elements of his or her life history and ideology in an act of self-reflective understanding. Anything less threatens to leave the individual acting out identifications as blind gestures in a divided and disrupted field of meaning. The role if identification, therefore, must be viewed as complementary to that of self-reflection or insight. Neither of these processes can be productively employed without the other, and both of them represent necessary phases in the construction of meaning.

So far we have considered cases in which the theoretical constructs of ideology and idealization are pushed to their limits by an apparent absence or alteration of their form. We will now consider a case in which the third construct—that of the central conflict—is also pushed to its conceptual limit, but in a completely different way. In Ruth's account—the last case to be reported in this study—we will encounter three separate and apparently unrelated incidents of self-esteem. We will examine all three incidents in the context of Ruth's life history and will see the extent to which they can all be considered resolutions of a single central conflict. In this connection we will consider the question of what constitutes a unitary central conflict; and the answer to this question will illuminate certain characteristics of meaning and the study of meaning by the interview method.

RUTH: CARRYING THE BURDEN

Ruth is a forty-six-year-old black woman who works as a financial counselor in a large metropolitan hospital. A mother of four, Ruth is currently separated from her second husband and lives with two of her children in a large city in the western United States. Her other two children live on their own. Ruth was sleeping when I arrived at her house for the first interview, and she answered the door buttoning herself up in a robe. In addition to presenting herself in this somewhat seductive manner, Ruth seemed to be very relaxed about the prospect of being interviewed. Her friendly manner and comfort with the situation made her one of the easiest subjects to talk with. She seemed grateful for the opportunity to discuss her early experiences and to clarify some of her feelings about them; and at the end of both sessions she expressed positive feelings about the interview process itself.

Ruth initially chose to talk about an experience of self-esteem which had occurred four months prior to the interview. At that time it had become necessary for Ruth to undergo a hysterectomy, and the thought of surgery had "totally frightened" her:

> I went into that very frightened and I think I just really
> overdid it.... I knew that I wouldn't be having my
> relatives come out to visit me, it's too far.... So bearing
> all this in mind, I was really almost petrified.

When the day of the operation came, however, Ruth surprised herself by handling it much better than she had thought she would:

> All of a sudden the day I went in I wasn't scared anymore.
> (And you were brave through the operation?) Right. I
> was—I was amazed. (Why did that amaze you?) Because I—I
> just knew I was going to be afraid.

As it turned out, the operation did involve some complications. The doctors were unable to bring Ruth's blood pressure up to normal for several hours after the surgery. Nevertheless, Ruth remained calm the entire time.

> I really went through it...much better [than] I thought I'd
> be.... I wasn't afraid of anything. It went beautifully.... I
> was happy with myself for that.

After Ruth had summarized this incident, I pointed out that it had occurred within the last year and asked her if she could think of any other incidents that might have happened more than a year previously. Ruth replied that she had not really done or accomplished very much. I suggested that she did not necessarily have to think of an accomplishment, just a time when she had felt good about herself, and this suggestion immediately brought another incident to mind.

Three years previously, Ruth's oldest daughter Valerie had been promoted to the position of buyer for a large chain of clothing stores on the East Coast. This position carried with it considerable responsibility and power and represented the culmination of eleven years of hard work, not only on Valerie's part, but on Ruth's as well. Ruth had helped Valerie in a number of ways: she had stood behind Valerie's wish to make it in the fashion business; she had given her consolation and encouragement when things had gone wrong; she had taken care of Valerie's son for extended periods when Valerie was in merchandising school and when she had to change cities. For these reasons Ruth feels she had "quite a bit" to do with Valerie's eventual success. In fact, when Valerie received the letter promoting her to buyer, she sent it to Ruth along with the comment, "This could not have been done without you."

> Oh, I was elated. I was just so happy I took it to work and put it on the bulletin board.... I was really proud, very proud because...it was such a struggle to get there. I think that makes it bigger.

During the course of the interview, Ruth spontaneously reported a third time when she had felt good about herself. This incident occurred on Ruth's job, and she described it as an illustration of the fact that she has an unusual ability to work with people. Ruth's job as financial counselor involves helping people who are hospitalized to find ways of paying their bills. This task can be extremely trying for both the counselor and the patient since it involves dealing with money in a time of crisis. Ruth feels she is especially good at this work, and she commented that, of all the counselors, she is the only one who regularly gets gifts from her patients. For example, one man she had worked with gave her forty dollars, telling her to take her husband out to dinner. Ruth describes her reaction to this incident:

> I wasn't sure I could [take the money], so I went to my supervisor and asked him...was there any reason that I shouldn't take it, and he said "No, you earned it." I was

elated about that; I didn't tell you about that. See? Something else peeked out.

These three incidents are described by Ruth as times when she felt good about herself, and any one of them might have served as a single experience around which to orient the interview. We might even expect them to represent resolutions of three different central conflicts in Ruth's life. On the other hand, some kind of underlying unity cannot be ruled out. For example, all three incidents seem to involve, in some way, the general issue of carrying a burden in time of stress. If, however, a single central conflict is indicated, the way in which three such heterogeneous experiences of self-esteem are related to this conflict and to each other would seem to be an important question.

In the pages that follow, we will explore these issues by considering the three incidents in the context of Ruth's life history. We will examine the ways in which the incidents are more closely related than they might at first appear to be, and how they can all be viewed as solutions to a common central conflict. At the same time, however, we will consider the extent to which they are independent of each other and essentially autonomous as life events. Let us begin by examining Ruth's early family experience.

Ruth was born and raised in a large city during the later years of the Great Depression and the Second World War. Her parents were divorced when she was three years old and her father went to another city where he studied to become a dentist. Ruth and her younger brother grew up with their mother, who did not remarry. Ruth remembers her mother working very hard during those years, first as an assembly-line worker, then as a nurse's aid, and later as an assistant baker. Although times were not easy, Ruth reports that her mother sent money to help her father in school whenever she could.

Ruth describes her mother as a strong and reliable person who never failed in her duties as a provider and caretaker:

Mother was—well, naturally she was the backbone, she was everything to us.... She worked and took care of my brother and myself.... I can't ever remember not *having*, you know. For quite some time until my father—at least until he went in the service, she wasn't getting anything from him.... Times weren't easy. Although the Depression was over, they weren't easy then...and I just think she must have been an awfully strong person, you know?

Besides working full time and supporting the family, Ruth remembers her mother visiting school, helping Ruth and her brother with their homework, and aiding in scouts and other activities:

> We used to go on [Girl Scout] winter trips, and they had plays and things.... She'd come over and bring cookies whenever we had any kind of, you know, programs [laughs] and whatever. She was right there when we needed her. All the time, she was there. (She was very available to you.) Mm, she was there. And sometimes I know she must have been so tired 'cause she looked tired. She looked tired all her life [laughs].

Before she died, Ruth's mother became ill and was partially disabled by a stroke:

> She always looked after herself until she got *so* sick and she couldn't. And I've never seen a person with more stamina than she had. After she lost the use of her left side...she always thought she'd have that again.... She never gave up, never.

During this period, Ruth looked after her mother and talked to her a great deal:

> A lot of times she was a lot of help and inspiration to me, because when things were bad between my husband and I and when [my youngest daughter] was running into...problems, I could sit and talk to her...and vent my feelings to her.... That was very helpful, *very* helpful. I miss that an awful lot.

The bond Ruth describes with her mother is a stong one, and it is reminiscent of the bond Ruth described at the beginning of the interview when talking about her oldest daughter and herself. Something is suggested here about Ruth's conception of the family, and especially of the roles of mothers and daughters. We will return to this issue again, but for the present let us consider Ruth's relationship to her father.

It has already been noted that Ruth's father left the family and went to another city to attend dental school when Ruth was very young. Ruth did not see much of her father while she was growing up, but she did have some contact with him. For example, she remembers getting letters from him in which he urged her to think about her future and the possibility of going to college. Occasionally, Ruth's father also visited the family. Although these visits were short and very infrequent, they seem to have had great significance for Ruth. Throughout the interview, Ruth described her father as an elusive and enigmatic figure who intermittently appeared on the scene and seemed to offer the promise of love only to withhold it or disappear from the picture once again.

> He'd come and take us shopping or to the movies, and then sometimes we'd go over to his brother's.... No zoo's or good things [laughs].... He wasn't there for my graduation.... Not on my birthday or Christmas Eve.... So he wasn't there for those days, those are the important days to me....
>   He was in school in my primary years and then he went in the service.... Whenever he came on furlough or whatever to visit, you know, I was proud, but that didn't make up for not being there a lot of other times that I missed.

At times Ruth recalled generous things her father had done, such as helping the family financially and buying a house for her mother. At other times, however, she described the aloofness that characterizes her father's personality even at present:

> I call him, you know, he's just really busy.... It makes me mad when I call him. I know he's busy but he projects this...urgency, you know, like, "Oh well, yes, I'm talking to you but you know how precious my time is."

In response to this behavior Ruth expresses anger, sadness, confusion, and, above all, a penetrating sense of loss and longing for the father she never quite had:

> I hear my friends talking about their fathers and how much they care for them.... I always wished that I could have had that kind of relationship. I never did....
>   I can't say that I care about him like most children would care about their fathers, 'cause I don't know him that well.... I don't *know* this man that well (um-hm)...though he's done so very much for me.... I can't figure him out. We think different and he's just—he's just the word "father."

Even at the very end of the interview, Ruth continued to try to clarify her feelings about her father:

And yet I can not say he doesn't love me. I believe he really and truly loves me. It's just the way he displays it that sort of shakes you up a little [laughs].

Ruth's father, then, is a very problematic figure in her life. For as long as she can remember, her interactions with him have entailed a sense of rejection, a sense concretely represented in the fact of his leaving the family when Ruth was young. But there is another theme in Ruth's history that renders this rejection even more potent, a theme which seems to carry the message that the rejection was justified and that Ruth's father had a good reason for leaving the family. This theme is the emphasis throughout Ruth's account on the importance of advancing oneself professionally.

When Ruth describes her father's absence and aloofness, she often does so in terms of his professional career. For example, Ruth characterizes her father as a "busy" man who projects a sense of "urgency" about his time. Ruth also remembers letters from her father in which he encouraged her to think about her future and to plan for college—a major topic of concern between Ruth and her father:

He wanted me to do what he did, to go on to school.... (To go on to college?) Right, uh-huh. (How do you know that?) 'Cause that's all he ever talked about.

Ruth's mother, too, emphasized the special importance to blacks of education and hard work:

She always said, "You're going to have to try even harder 'cause it's harder for us to get ahead.... You've got to [do] better, you've got to [do] the best."

Of particular significance is the way Ruth's mother described the struggle Ruth's father went through in dental school:

She told me that when he first went to school...she tried to send him a little [money] to help him along 'cause he didn't have anything. And he was really struggling, trying to make it. She told me about all those things....
    She said..."I wasn't making that much, but whenever I had a dollar or two to spare, I would send it to him." I

said, "Do you think he appreciated it?" She'd think. "Yeah, I think he appreciated it, but I just couldn't continue to do it because things were rough for me, too."

There is something poignant about this loyalty. Even after their divorce, Ruth's mother does the little that she can to help Ruth's father with his career. There is another sense, however, in which this loyalty seems to countenance—and even to validate—the disruption of the marriage and family. Ruth's mother helps her ex-husband in his struggle even though it is a struggle effected at the expense of herself and the children. By the mother's own actions, the father's decision to leave the family is mythologized and affirmed.

This situation seems to be connected to a central conflict in Ruth's account, a conflict defined by her contradictory relationship to her father. Throughout her account Ruth expresses a terrible sense of rejection by her father; and yet this rejection is only a partial one. What seems to make the rejection so painful to Ruth is the fact that it *is* only partial, that her father *does* seem to care in some way. He appears on the scene and looks as though he wants to give; and then he disappears or withdraws into aloof preoccupation with his career. The impression is given that Ruth and her mother *might* be important to Ruth's father, but not as important as professional success. At the same time, Ruth's mother seems to have affirmed that such is the case, both in her advice to her daughter about getting ahead and in her validation of her ex-husband's struggle to succeed. Accordingly, the existential question for Ruth seems to have become how to establish a sense of worth after being defined as less important than her father's career. The solution Ruth proposes to this problem has two major aspects.

The first of these aspects grows out of the special relationship between Ruth and her mother. We have already observed Ruth's idealization of her mother as a strong, providing person who was always available to her children. Not only did Ruth's mother fulfill her parental obligations, but she did so alone, without help from Ruth's father. Ruth was very aware of the extent to which her mother was the sole provider: "Mother was—well, naturally she was the backbone, she was everything to us." As she grew up, Ruth came to feel that it was her duty to help her mother:

[We] had responsibility.... When I came in from
school...she'd tell me what we were going to have for
dinner and I'd prepare the things that I could; and on the

weekends if she had to work...I knew I had to get up and clean the house.... I took care of it, you know, and it made me feel good that she could come home and relax.

Throughout the interview, Ruth talked about obligations in the family, and she described many ways in which she has cared for her mother, her husband, and her children. But more than this, Ruth's characterization of family life is structured in a particular way, and it reveals an important constellation of ideology in her account. As the above passage illustrates, Ruth regards the family as a mutual system in which people must cooperate with each other and work together; and first and foremost in this mutual system is the special bond between women in the family—that is, the bond of loyalty between mothers and daughters.

In Ruth's account of her life, it is not only her father who stays aloof from the family. Males in all generations are portrayed as distant or unreliable when it comes to supporting the family. For example, Ruth describes her current husband as an alcoholic who is unable to fulfill his familial obligations; her first husband was "never any asset" to his children; her brother no longer maintains "close" or "intimate" ties with the family; her son does not appear to be "close to anybody"; her paternal grandfather was unable to manage the family's money; and her maternal grandfather—whose wife was institutionalized—was unable to provide appropriate parenting for his daughters. It is only women who can keep the family together, and women must carry the full load. Just like her mother who had to be the "backbone" of the family, Ruth states that she had to be "both parents" to her children. This is the reason for the special relationship between mothers and daughters, and it also defines a meaningful place for Ruth in the social world, given her existential dilemma. In a world where men let the family down and withdraw into their careers, it is the special role of women to carry the burdens in the family and to help and support each other:

She took care of us and she was always there.... I guess that's why I was that way with my kids. I wouldn't leave them, you know, and she never left us.

A second aspect of Ruth's ideology complements the above, but also contradicts it to a certain extent. This aspect concerns the importance of professional advancement in a woman's life. We have already seen that Ruth was encouraged by both her father and her mother to educate herself and to improve her lot. An interesting note, however, is that when Ruth describes her own potential advancement, it is ultimately justified in terms of marriage and family. For example, at one point, Ruth described how her father had urged her to finish high school after she had dropped out:

Maybe he was talking about jobs and the problem that we [blacks] have, you know. "You won't be able to make a good living and raise your children.... You won't be able to help them when they're going to school."

At another point, Ruth described how her mother had encouraged her to go on to college:

She always wanted me to finish school...[to] get as much education as I [could]. She wanted me to have nice things...and we'd talk about how I would get them. (What did she say?) Well, she told me [to] go on to school and go on to college, perhaps—maybe meet someone who could help me or we could help each other, and I could have a family. The regular; nothing unusual, I think.

At still another point, Ruth talked about what she had wanted for her own daughter:

Most of the time anyone raising girls would try and get them married [laughs]...into good families and this sort of thing. But my thing was that you should really always have something to do of your own and...that makes you more attractive to someone of the opposite sex.

To a woman, therefore, professional competence is important not only for improving one's lot but for attracting a man and having a family. It is not difficult to guess how this notion is related to Ruth's central conflict. Given that her father chose professional success over family, it would make sense that a professionally competent woman might be the kind of person who could win a man like Ruth's father. Advancing herself professionally, therefore, offers a woman the possibility of attracting a competent male back into the scene, someone who can validate her as a woman, ease her burden, and reestablish a full-fledged family life.

At this point, let us return to a consideration of Ruth's three self-esteem incidents. At the beginning of this case, we considered the question of how these three incidents might be related. We noted that all of them seemed to involve the general theme of carrying a burden in a time of stress, and we hypothesized that this theme might relate to a single central conflict in Ruth's account. We have now identified what appears to be a central conflict in Ruth's early history growing out of her contradictory relationship with her father. Moreover, we have seen that one of the ideological solutions Ruth proposes to this conflict does involve the theme of carrying a burden—the special burden shared by women in the context of the family. Ruth's other ideological constellation—the one concerned with professional success and winning a competent male like her father—may also figure in these incidents, though how it might do so is not immediately evident. Keeping these ideas in mind, let us consider Ruth's incidents more closely to see how they relate to the central conflict and the ideological clusters which have been identified. We shall begin with the buyership incident.

It is clear that Ruth played an important part in Valerie's promotion to buyer; as noted above, she gave her daughter support and encouragement in a number of ways. We also noted that Ruth's relationship with Valerie, reminiscent of Ruth's relationship with her own mother, seemed to reflect Ruth's ideology of women's obligations in the family. This linkage was particularly evident at the beginning of the interview when I asked Ruth which of the first two self-esteem incidents she had reported—the operation or her daughter's promotion—had been the most important to her:

Her buyership, I think, meant the most to me. Um, I guess that's because it—it meant so much to her, and we both— we worked together on that. Uh, [the operation] was just something that I did on my own. That's a rather selfish one I think.

At one point in the interview, Ruth talked about helping her daughter and related this activity to her own mother's role:

Ooh, there were low times, you know, when she needed someone to say, "Listen, it's rough now but it's going to be better, you just can't give up."...I'm sure my mother would have done the same thing if I had been struggling and trying to—trying to do something, she would have been right there.

At the same time, it is clear that Ruth's support for her daughter is an application of her ideology of professional advancement. In the following passage, Ruth describes how she encouraged her daughter to acquire a professional role:

[I told her] you should have something to do
yourself...something that you enjoy doing.... It's kind of
bland, you know, if you don't know anything, [if] you don't
have any intelligence, no education at all.... But if you do,
then you can hold your own. You certainly would be more
attractive to someone of the opposite sex.

Both aspects of Ruth's ideology, then, are expressed in the
buyership incident. Likewise, they lead back to the central conflict in
Ruth's account, for they present solutions to the existential
question which it poses—the question of a woman's place in a world
oriented around men's careers and men's absence from the family. It
seems reasonable, therefore, to interpret the buyership incident as a
specific application of Ruth's ideology and a specific and limited
resolution of her central conflict in the real world. Let us now see
whether a similar state of affairs exists with regard to the other
self-esteem incidents Ruth reported: the gift she received on the job
and the operation she faced with courage.

It is not difficult to see how the gift incident concerns the issue of
professional success. Ruth reported the incident as an example of
her excellent performance on the job and her exceptional ability to
work well with people under trying circumstances. As noted above,
Ruth's job can be unusually stressful and requires a special kind of
interpersonal sensitivity. This point is worth considering in more
detail, for it will lead us back to the component of Ruth's ideology
which is not as obvious in this incident—the ideology of familial
obligation.

Ruth likes her job as financial counselor because it enables her to
help people. At one point in the interview, she compared her job to
social work. There is, however, a more difficult and diplomatic
aspect to the job, for Ruth has to get the patients' cooperation in
paying their bills. This task requires all of her interpersonal skills:

You've got to know how to work with those people.
They're sick and they don't need that money talk, [laughs]
but you've got to talk money.... You've got to know how
to do it without hurting them.

This kind of problem is not new to Ruth. Before her present
position, she worked in a number of situations requiring
interpersonal sensitivity, including two jobs as a collection agent. At
one point in the interview, Ruth commented on her professional
life: "[It's] always the same type of thing, I'm always solving

problems." Nor is professional life the only arena in which Ruth has found herself solving problems. In her personal life, as well, Ruth reports attending to one family crisis after another most of her adult life. For example, she describes caring for her mother during periods of illness, looking after her husband when he was drunk and suicidal, aiding her father in troubles with his business, taking care of her youngest daughter who is physically disabled, and helping her oldest daughter after a divorce, in school, and during a period of hospitalization. At one point, these demands became too much for Ruth: "I would just go from one situation to the next to the next...[until] I found out that I had [an] ulcer."

Ruth entered therapy at this time. We need not go into the details of the experience, but one of the things Ruth learned about herself is the extent to which she had oriented her life around carrying the burdens for others in her family: "It seemed like I had been doing this all my life, even as a child." We have already seen this aspect of Ruth's identity in her ideology of family responsibility. What is important to emphasize here is that the role associated with this ideology is a central one and not limited to the family. The role is used to structure other situations as well, as Ruth herself observed:

> I think I do [enjoy carrying the burden].... I've always had
> stressful jobs. (Um-hm.) I can't stand anything that's
> mediocre.

Ruth's role on her job, then, seems to be an expression of her ideology of family responsibility, although an indirect and symbolic one. In the financial counselor job Ruth can take a stance that is protective and maternal, but also involves carrying the burden in crisis situations. In this manner, not only do Ruth's accomplishments on the job represent the successful application of her second ideological cluster—the ideology of professional advancement—but they also signify an adherence to the first cluster—the ideology of family involvement—in the symbolic realm defined by her job in the hospital.[1]

---

[1]This kind of symbolic resolution we have already seen in chapter 3; however, a qualification is in order here. Ruth's ideology of familial obligation is probably already best understood as a limited and symbolic solution to her central conflict (which seems to concern her worth in relation to her father and in general). For this reason, the structuring of her role at work along the same lines might be considered a *second order* symbolic resolution. The same thing applies to the other symbolic constellation described below.

There is another way in which the incident on Ruth's job seems to have been symbolic. The gift which Ruth received attested to her ability as a financial counselor, but there is also reason to believe that it represented, on another level, a symbolic confirmation of Ruth as a woman capable of winning a man. The evidence for this statement is Ruth's description of the incident, which seems to carry with it overtones of a secret seduction. The following passage contains Ruth's account of the incident:

> This guy came into...my office and he said—he closed my door. I said, "You don't have to close the door." And he said, "I'm going to give you something. I want you to take your husband out to dinner." And he just gave me forty dollars. I said, "I'm not with my husband."...He says, "Take it anyway."

In this connection, we can remember that Ruth relates professional competence to sexual attractiveness and that professional life seems to represent, in part, the possibility of winning the kind of attention she never received from her father. Again, in a highly symbolic mode, Ruth's central conflict seems to be represented and resolved.

Let us turn now to Ruth's final incident of self-esteem, the operation. Initially, Ruth described feeling good about herself because she was brave in this situation. But as we discussed the meaning of this bravery, it became clear that—once again—Ruth was talking about *managing obligations* in a crisis situation:

> I wasn't jittery. I thought I'd be nervous and everything, but I wasn't. (Well, suppose that you *had* been nervous and jittery and afraid...what would be so terrible about that?)...Oh, I—I always have to be super brave when I know I'm really not. All my life...I guess that's because, again, you know, Mother was working, everything was left in my charge. [She talks about having to manage things in the family.] (You always had to be the brave one.) Kind of. (It sounds like in the case of the operation you were concerned that you [would not be the brave one].) Right. [Laughs] I thought I was going to be a [pauses] pain. (A pain?) Uh-huh. Well, you know, I didn't want to be crying and carrying on and acting stupid.... (Who would you have been a pain to?) The staff.... I have to work with these people. [Laughs]...I didn't want them saying, "Oh, don't let her ever come in here...again. We don't want to take care of her as a patient, she's horrible!" (Um-hm.) You know, I

didn't want that. I didn't get any, I was good.... They
never had to do nothing. I did everything. I would have
changed my bed if they had let me.

Once again, Ruth carries the burden in a stressful situation. Her
family role is projected into the hospital, even though she is a
patient this time instead of a worker. Of particular interest is Ruth's
concern that her co-workers might experience her as a "pain." A
major component of Ruth's ideology is the camaraderie among
women oriented around the special duties and obligations in the
family. Here we can see it in the symbolic arena of the hospital,
expressed in Ruth's consideration toward the (predominantly
female) staff.

Ruth's other ideological constellation, that of professional
advancement, is indirectly represented in this incident, for the
hospital is also Ruth's place of employment. More important,
however, is a symbolic victory of another kind. It will be recalled
that Ruth was not expecting visits in the hospital from any of her
relatives since they live many miles away. After the operation she
was surprised to find that her father had come to see her:

When they finally let him in the recovery room, he came
up and kissed me. I almost fainted.... I said, "God, I
wonder if he's sick or something."... I can't remember the
last time he kissed me.... I don't even know if he ever *has*
if you want to know the whole honest to goodness truth
about it!

For Ruth, then, who has longed for her father's love all of her life,
the operation had a significant ending. Not only was she able to
manage the situation, to bear the burden without complaint, but
she also received a response—and even a show of affection—from
her father. At this particular time, in the symbolic arena defined by
the operation, the lifelong conflict Ruth has experienced in relation
to her father seems to have achieved a specific resolution, if only for
a moment.

This completes our survey of the meaning of Ruth's three
incidents of self-esteem. In each of these incidents, we have found
some kind of resolution of Ruth's central conflict. In all three
situations Ruth affirms, in one way or another, the roles associated
with parental idealizations and the ideologies of family responsibility and/or professional advancement. In all of them she seems to
suggest, overtly or covertly, that adhering to these principles will

ultimately bring the kind of attention and affection she wanted but never got from her father. For these reasons, Ruth's three incidents of self-esteem seem to be founded on a common principle: the resolution of a single and overarching conflict in her life.

At the same time, however, these three incidents suggest something of the variety of forms that such a resolution can take. Not only is there a variety of situations in which a resolution can be effected, but there is also a variety of strategies employed (self-directed versus altruistic), modes of resolution (actual versus symbolic), degrees of defensiveness (extent of displacement from the original conflict), etc. Moreover, the particular aspects of Ruth's identity implicated in the resolution vary from one situation to another. For example, one of Ruth's incidents directly involves her relationship with her father; the other two do not. One incident involves her role as a mother, another her role as a worker, and another a temporary role as a patient. Two of Ruth's incidents directly concern her ideology of professional advancement; the third one does not. And so forth.

THE PARADOX OF MEANING: UNITY IN DIVERSITY

It is remarkable that human beings tend to organize so much of their experience in relation to specific and recurring life-historical themes. Psychoanalytic authors have occasionally noted this phenomenon and discussed it in one context or another. We have already considered, for example, Lichtenstein's (1977) concept of the identity theme and Freud's (1914b, 1920) conception of the repetition compulsion. Another author who has discussed this issue is Brenner (1973, 1976), who has laid more stress on the ways in which "normal" behavior is structured by life-historical conflict.

Brenner has collected a variety of clinical anecdotes illustrating how ordinary behavior can follow the same psychodynamic lines as neurotic symptoms. For example, he reports the case of a male patient whose behavior was predominantly pleasant and cooperative. Although this behavior was not in itself problematic, Brenner suggests that it reflected an unconscious conflict stemming from a childhood experience in which the patient had been threatened with the loss of an important adult. According to Brenner, the patient had developed an idea that he would be abandoned by important others if he did not act in a pleasant and cooperative way. On the basis of this case and a number of others, Brenner concludes that "psychic conflict...[is] as important a part of normal mental life as it is of what we label pathological mental functioning" (1976, p. 174). By the same token, Brenner denies that there is any clear dividing line betwen normal and neurotic behavior, and he notes that the therapeutic altering of a significant psychic conflict can have far-reaching consequences, affecting areas of a patient's life that neither the patient nor the analyst had expected to change:

> It's like what happens when one cuts the main stem of a vine that has grown so that for years it's leaves have mingled with those of the tree that supports it. Only as it's leaves wither and turn brown can one see how widely the vine has spread among the branches of it's host and to what unsuspected places it has grown. (1976, p. 171)

There is, however, a flaw in this analogy. The various manifestations of a psychic conflict which we find throughout a person's life are not merely products or derivatives of that conflict; these manifestations are also used by the individual to understand and reconstruct the conflict itself. As was emphasized in chapter 3, meaning is indivisible, and the semiotic and linguistic systems which constitute an individual's field of meaning serve as both the blueprints and the objects of a constant process of intrapsychic reorganization and reconstruction. For this reason, the causality between a central conflict and its derivatives is best understood not as one-way, or even as two-way, but rather as *multidimensional*—as though each of the leaves in the above analogy were shaping the characteristics of the stem, and of each other.

Moreover, this causality is mediated through the irreducible activity of the human subject. Signification is not a system of objects or of causal interactions among such objects. Rather, it is a form of human conduct by which the object world is confronted and transformed. Systems of semiotic and linguistic signifiers are the patterns of behavior that contribute to this project. By virtue of these patterns, experience is organized in certain characteristic and recurring ways, which are the themes we see repeated at various points in a life-historical account. Yet every instance of such repetition is also an instance of *reorganization*, a compromise formation in which the individual applies existing understanding to a new situation. The recurrence of the central conflict, therefore, is accompanied by constant modification as the patterns of signification making up its particulars are systematically varied and applied in new ways.

Closely related to this idea is another point. The experiences that constitute a life history are so numerous and the interrelationships between them so complex, it is doubtful that any well-defined psychological structure could be identified as the core of a particular conflict. In fact, the concept of a single central conflict is, in a certain sense, a fiction. This fiction has been employed liberally in the foregoing pages to make it possible to talk about the relationship between conflict and self-esteem without having to add constant qualifications. But the central conflict is probably best understood as a *family* of conflicts—a group of interrelated patterns of conflicting themes existing at all levels of semiotic and linguistic organization and united by a shared "family resemblance"—that is, "a complicated network of similarities overlapping and criss-crossing" (Wittgenstein, 1953, p. 32). The unity of the central conflict resides in this family resemblance, this overriding pattern of thematic similarities; and the multiplicity of its derivatives is a reflection of the many and varied situations in which the conflict is manifested. It was because of these features that Freud, Breuer, and other early writers referred to psychodynamic conflicts as "complexes."

Let us clarify this abstract formulation with a concrete example. The central conflict in Ruth's account has been indentified as residing in her contradictory relationship with her father, a relationship in which he seemed both to recognize her worth and to deny it; but this is a general formulation which actually covers a variety of closely related conflicts in Ruth's account. For example, there is the conflict between Ruth's wish to have a father and the reality of her father's absence as she was growing up; there is the conflict between her father's gestures of caring and his accompanying manner of aloofness; there is the conflict between Ruth's mother giving her full support for the family and simultaneously affirming her husband's decision to leave; and there is the conflict between Ruth's sense of responsibility to the family and her wish to advance herself professionally. Each of these conflicts represents a unique aspect of Ruth's dilemma and each provides a vantage point for understanding the others. They are all different but they share certain formal similarities, partly because they have been used to structure each other. Taken together they constitute what may meaningfully be called a single conflict, the central conflict in Ruth's account. However, they also represent themes that are genuinely independent in some sense, both conceptually and situationally.

In light of this analysis, it is clear that there is a certain degree of arbitrariness when it comes to designating the central conflict in a particular account. In Ruth's case, for example, I have identified the central conflict in terms of her father's ambivalent behavior; but the conflicting themes growing out of this situation could have been designated as "family versus profession," "self-sacrifice versus achievement," or "carrying the burden versus being cared for." Each of these formulations emphasizes something different, while indicating, in a general way, the complex of themes that constitutes the central conflict. Any one of them might be used for bringing coherence to Ruth's account, depending on what the interpreter wished to accomplish. For example, we could have employed the first designation ("family versus profession") for understanding the buyership incident, the second ("self-sacrifice versus achievement") for understanding the gift incident, or the third ("carrying the burden versus being cared for") for understanding the operation incident. Any of these designations would be valid as long as it gave meaning to the self-esteem incident by connecting it to the life-historically relevant material of Ruth's conflicted family interactions.

Something similar is also true for ideology and idealization. A subject's ideology, for example, is only a limited region of a broader field in each case, as illustrated by the three incidents in the present account. If we had considered only the gift incident, we might have emphasized Ruth's ideology of professional advancement, alluding to her ideology of family responsibility mainly to illuminate certain aspects of her central conflict. On the other hand, if we had focused only on the operation incident, we might have emphasized these two ideological components in reverse. (The buyership incident would probably have required an equal consideration of both components.) The same can be said for idealization. Certain of Ruth's idealized descriptions of her mother and father would probably figure in a consideration of any of the three self-esteem incidents, but certain other ones would probably appear only in connection with specific incidents.

These considerations also suggest something about the investigation of a particular phenomenon like self-esteem. Each incident in Ruth's account presents a different perspective on what self-esteem means to her. Each shows a unique face, but each is related to the others through the mediating connections of life history and personal meaning. If we elicited a number of such incidents in any subject's account and if we inquired diligently into the meaning of each one, we could not help but converge on the fundamental structure of self-esteem in the subject's life. By the same token, any experience of self-esteem is a potential route to the underlying structure of the phenomenon, for meaning is indivisible and patterns of life-historical conflict repeat themselves throughout a subject's account at all levels of psychological organization.

A closely related issue concerns the amount of interviewing necessary to establish the meaning of an event in a subject's life. This question is occasionally raised in connection not only with interview research, but also with biographical study, clinical practice, and other disciplines concerned with life-historical investigation. The present analysis suggests that the permissible limits of such investigations are rather broad, for life-historical conflict and meaning are recapitulated, in one form or another, at virtually every moment of an individual's life. Meaning is always immanent in a subject's words and actions if only the investigator knows how to extract it. To give an example, all of the essential elements of Ruth's central conflict and its resolution were present in the first five minutes of the interview. Even at the moment of our initial contact, Ruth presented herself in a manner that was simultaneously seductive, amiable, and comfortable, as though to set me at ease and begin winning me over. She had agreed to be interviewed for purely altruistic reasons, and she conveyed a sense of willingness to carry this burden without complaint. When questioned about incidents of self-esteem, she revealed another concern—that she had not really accomplished very much—and it was not difficult to sense that Ruth did not wish to appear to be a "bland" person who "could not hold her own." Both sides of Ruth's ideology were present, therefore, as was the attempt to employ them in the project of winning me over and achieving a symbolic resolution of the terms of her central conflict.

If meaning abounds from moment to moment, however, it is the job of the investigator to determine just what it is, and this determination requires much more than a few minutes of contact. One can never be certain when one has located the truly important elements in a subject's life-historical account, and the possibility always remains that something crucial will emerge if the interview is continued. In fact, it would be extreme hubris to think that a few hours of interviewing could fully illuminate the depths of an individual's life—depths of which even the individual may know little. Most of the memories reported by subjects in this study probably constitute what the psychoanalyst would call "screen memories." They are relatively accessible semiotic structures, residing in the domain of the subject's self-reflection and standing in the way of earlier, less syntonic life-historical images. But if screen memories conceal, they also reveal; and the present investigation suggests that specific structures of conflict and meaning present themselves again and again in an individual's life, providing the forms in which his or her language is cast, defining the range of his or her possibilities and concerns, and equipping the individual with ways of understanding the endless variations of unfolding reality.

_____

FIVE

Self and
Other

IN THIS BOOK we have focused upon self-esteem as a meaningful phenomenon. We have examined the life-historical and conceptual themes that subjects describe in relation to self-esteem and the semiotic and linguistic systems of signification that constitute the underlying structure of this phenomenon. In discussing these psychological constellations, however, little has been said about their relationship to the *self*. This is no small question since the self is the focus and organizing principle of self-esteem. In this final chapter, therefore, it seems appropriate to give some consideration to the topic. We will review certain features of the foregoing cases, summarizing the major points which have been made. At the same time, the phenomena under investigation will be related to the activity and structure of the self.

But what exactly *is* a self? In the existing psychological literature the self is usually regarded as a set of attitudes and beliefs about one's behavior, appearance, skills, and so forth. More specifically, this characterization defines a person's "self-concept," a socially determined constellation of ideas which endures over time and is reasonably identifiable as a discrete entity. Yet this simple and appealing notion of the self can lead to extraordinary difficulties and complications, particularly with regard to questions about identity formation and social influence. For such reasons, theoreticians who have dealt in depth with the nature of the self have often been forced to abandon this rather static notion and to develop conceptions which emphasize the dynamic characteristics of the self and its essential continuity with the larger processes of social interaction and personal transformation. How might we think about the self, then, in a way that gives recognition to this dynamic dimension?

Before considering an answer to this question, some comments are in order about the nature of meaning. In chapter 2 it was emphasized that meaning is both complex and irreducible, that it must be understood as both a complicated system of signifying elements and an integrated gestalt of sense and coherence. In order to deal with this twofold nature, a pair of conceptual tools was proposed—one of them predominantly analytic and the other predominantly synthetic. The former was the analysis of language, particularly as defined and conceptualized by Saussure (1916); and the latter was Schafer's (1976) "action" perspective, which regards meaning as integrated behavior by a human agent. Although both of these tools have been employed in the foregoing chapters, the former has been used rather more explicitly. We have examined the fine structure of semiotic and linguistic systems, but have left their dynamic context somewhat implicit. At this point, therefore, it should be emphasized once again that although semiotic and linguistic systems are enormously complex networks of signification, they are also ongoing, irreducible *actions by people*.

Methodologically, it is very important that we keep this "action" perspective in mind, for it helps us avoid certain conceptual problems. For example, self-esteem has been characterized as a three-tiered structure of personal meaning—a complex organization of ideology, idealization, and a central conflict. But it would be a mistake to regard this three-tiered structure in a literal and concrete way, as though it were actually a real object. A person does not "have" structures and organizations of meaning as much as he or she *enacts* them and *lives* them. When we discuss Esther's ideology, for example, as an integration of the themes of nurturance and respect, we do not mean that she has erected an edifice of interlocking themes of nurturance and respect that now stands between her and the world. We mean, rather, that she has learned how to think, talk, and act toward other people in a way that she believes to be both nurturant and respectful.

Meaning, then, is a dynamic form, not a static thing. It resides in the ongoing conduct of people and it cannot be understood in a concrete way. And yet, there is a problem here; for there is a particular and very important sense in which any meaningful activity *can* be regarded as an object. Specifically, when we talk or think about an action that someone has performed—make it the focus of our attention or interest—we constitute that action as the "object" or our concern. In the following discussion it will be useful to refer to an object of this kind as an *objectification* in order to distinguish it from the kind of static entity usually designated by the word "object."

We have been dealing with objectifications all along in this book. Every time we have considered a "structure," an "organization," or a "system" of meaning, for example, we have objectified some aspect of a subject's meaningful activity. Such objectification is unavoidable if we wish to talk about meaning in any kind of extended way; but the process carries with it the danger of reification. An objectified activity can easily be regarded in much too fixed and concrete a manner. As noted above, for example, we may slip into thinking of the structure of self-esteem as a kind of static "edifice"—or worse, as some sort of mechanical interplay between ideology, idealization, and the central conflict considered as "components." In chapter 1 it was suggested that this kind of reification can be very destructive to the investigation of meaning and has generally led to reductionistic approaches that have failed to illuminate the nature of self-esteem. At this point, therefore, it is worthwhile to emphasize the principle which underlies the "action" perspective: an *objectification* of a subject's behavior must not be regarded as a real *object*.

Let us consider now a special case of objectification, the case in which an individual objectifies his or her own activity. This process occurs when someone observes, remembers, describes, or reflects upon his or her own behavior—past, present, or future. The situation is a very important one for it involves a reflexive move: human activity turns upon and objectifies itself. Certain authors have noted that such a reflexive move is the essence of the *self-process*, the activity by which an individual comprehends his or her own person and place in the world. The result of this self-objectifying activity is the system of images and ideas that collectively constitutes the *self-image* or *self-concept*. These two aspects of mental life—the objectifying activity that turns upon itself (the self-process), and the system of objectifications that results from this activity (the self-image or self-concept)—are the two phases of the self which Mead (1934) has designated as the "I" and the "me."

Mead's theory is a complex and subtle one, but certain aspects of it can be stated briefly. In Mead's terminology, the "I" refers to the activity of the individual reflecting upon his or her experience and reorganizing and expressing it in new ways. The "me" refers to the product of this activity, the ever-changing objectifications of personal and social life that make up the individual's conception of self-in-the-world. These two aspects of the self are in constant interaction. The "I" generates new constellations of the "me" by objectifying itself and then responding to these objectifications with further activity and further objectifications. Mead calls this process the "conversation of gestures" between the "I" and the "me"; and he characterizes it as an internalized version of the social interaction by virtue of which one's identity is defined and understood.

From this point of view, it is clear that self and meaning are constructed together. The self is objectified in a context of meaningful interaction; and meaning is progressively organized in relation to an individual's self. This interdependence is particularly true with regard to an individual's experience and conceptualization of his or her self-esteem. To know how and why one feels good about oneself, one must assess and evaluate one's own activity, particularly as it contributes to a meaningful social order. Comprehending the meaning of one's self-esteem, therefore, necessarily involves an act of self-reflection and the systematic objectification and organization of one's experiences into a representation of self.

In the following pages we will consider this process in detail. We will review certain features of the foregoing cases, using them to explore some of the intricacies by virtue of which the self is reflected upon, objectified, and conceptualized. We will examine this process in both its active aspects (the "I") and its passive aspects (the "me"), and in the reflexive interplay by which these elements contribute to a complex sense of self-in-the-world. Let us begin with the activity by which the self is constructed, the self-reflection of the "I."

THE WORK OF THE "I":
SELF-REFLECTION AND SELF-TRANSFORMATION

The process of self-reflection has been evident in all the cases in this study. In fact, the mere recounting of life history is essentially and unavoidably self-reflective. But self-reflection can take a wide variety of forms, and it can vary a great deal from one person to another. In chapter 3, for example, it was noted that some accounts were less self-reflective than others and that this lack seemed to be related to defensive self-esteem. Behavior that is minimally self-reflective can be characterized as objectifying only limited or superficial aspects of one's activity. This behavior appears to be a way of isolating aspects of the self from each other and defending oneself from a potentially painful conflict. For example, Denny freely expressed his ideas about society and history, but he steered away from talking about his family and emotional life; and John recalled a series of incidents which had happened to him, but he made no connection between these events and his own most personal wants and needs. When we examined the fields of meaning associated with these two cases (i.e., the full range of activities objectified by these subjects, or the overall structure of the "me" in each case), we found them to be disrupted and divided at certain crucial points.

Contrasting with these accounts were cases in which subjects were more fully self-reflective. In these latter cases subjects objectified a broader and richer variety of their own thoughts and feelings, bringing life history, present relationships, and self-conception all together. Moreover, because they were able to draw upon their experience more freely, these subjects seemed to comprehend their lives in a fuller way and to be capable of changing in the direction of greater integration. An example is Anna, who described an incident of self-esteem which was consciously associated with past experiences of discrimination, family conflict, and self-discovery, and which involved an integration of activities that had previously been regarded as incompatible. When self-reflection was discussed in the context of Anna's case, it was suggest that this process can lead to a self-esteem that is comprehensive rather than symbolic, involving a reconciliation of the themes of the central conflict rather than a mere reversal of them.

In chapter 4 some suggestions were made about how this process occurs. We considered the accounts of two subjects who described periods of self-reflection in connection with the experience of self-esteem. Charlotte told about a time in therapy when she had clarified and reconceptualized some of her ideas about how to handle her daughter, and Lou described a moratorium period in the service during which he had remembered and reevaluated certain family experiences. These processes were designated linguistic and semiotic transformations, respectively. Linguistic transformation refers to the process of redrawing conceptual boundaries in order to generate a new linguistic structure—in this case, a richer and more useful ideology. Semiotic transformation refers to the selection or rearrangement of particular memories and images to form new patterns of life-historical experience—in this case, more relevant paradigms of idealization. It was suggested that both of these processes are essential components of self-reflection and that they presuppose and supplement each other. Linguistic transformation involves the examination and reconstruction of personal meaning at the level of generalities—the level concerned with classes of events; and semiotic transformation involves the examination and reconstruction of personal meaning at the level of particulars—the level of concrete images of specific life situations.

Self-reflection, then, is a complex process which transforms and reorganizes personal meaning at both the general and the particular levels. This process is what Mead seems to have had in mind when he described the "I" as an integrative principle which is the "source of unity" of our actions (1934, p. 279). This process is also what psychoanalytic theorists seem to have intended in the concept of the "synthetic function of the ego" (Nunberg, 1931). We must be careful, however, for the organizing activity of self-reflection is not a mere "unification" or "synthesis" of experience. If we examine the case material carefully, we can see that this activity is something much more subtle. At the level of life-historical imagery, for example, self-reflection seems to involve a *particularization* of experience. Thus, Lou had to identify a variety of specific interactions in the navy and in his friend's family to serve as paradigms for action in his current life. It is only at the conceptual level that such heterogeneous elements are brought together into an integrated system. Even here, however, the "I" is not a mere "synthetic function." For example, Charlotte could not create a viable ideology by simply combining the conceptions of parental availability and parental control. Instead, it was necessary for her to *redefine* these concepts and to begin developing a new linguistic system based on new concrete experiences. The process of integration, therefore, involves a full *reorganization* of conceptual boundaries in order to create new systems of relations among selected semiotic elements.

The self-reflection of the "I," then, is an extremely complex activity which reorganizes personal meaning in a dialectic of semiotic and linguistic transformation. This process leads an individual to greater integration and more comprehensive self-esteem, but not by indiscriminate synthesis or bland unification. Instead, self-reflection develops structures on all levels simultaneously, gradually producing conceptual systems which thematically reconcile wide varieties of reconstructed images and other particulars into a richer and more heterogeneous field of meaning.

This field of meaning is the reality in which the individual lives, the system of objecifications that guides his or her actions. We come, therefore, to the other phase of the self, the representational schema that Mead calls the "me."

THE STRUCTURE OF THE "ME":
THE DIALECTIC OF SELF AND OTHER

Every individual's field of meaning is oriented around his or her own person, for the events which the individual objectifies are primarily his or her own interactions with the environment. In objectifying these interactions the individual objectifies himself or herself in a variety of situations and modes; and in this manner, "self-representations" are constructed at all levels of semiotic and linguistic organization. Esther, for example, describes herself in a number of different ways, and each of these descriptions can be said to establish a different kind of self-representation. At the level of ideology she represents herself as a person who believes in fair labor practices and who tries to promote a sense of community; at the level of idealization she portrays herself as a girl admiring her father's humanity and an adult attempting to exercise it more consistently than he did; and at the level of the central conflict she paints the picture of a person who was enmeshed in her family of origin and is now trying to find a balance between nurturance and respect in her current life. All of these representations can be said to contribute to Esther's "self-system." The semiotic elements of this system constitute Esther's self-image and the linguistic elements constitute her self-concept.

But a crucial point needs to be made here. The activities which are objectified to represent the self never occur in isolation. As suggested above, they are *interactions* between subject and world; and in objectifying these interactions, the subject objectifies not only himself or herself, but other people as well. Moreoever, objectifications of other people are not simply additions to or embellishments of the self. Rather, they are essential to the very nature of the self, for they provide the system of meaning in terms of which the self is defined. Without a context of social interaction, the individual's objectification of his or her own activity might represent the individual as a physical organism, but could not represent the individual as a *self*. We can see this statement to be true when we look at a life-historical account. In Esther's case, for example, all of the elements which have been cited as components of the self presuppose interactions with other people. In fact, *most* of the descriptive material in Esther's account is about other people— her family, her co-workers, her friends, her "expanded family." She is always defined in relation to them, and it is only through them that we learn about her. Esther's account is not anomalous in this respect; the same is true for all the other subjects in this study. In every case, *the self is defined only in the context of social interaction.*

The existing psychological literature has not been clear about this self/other dialectic. As noted above, for example, academic psychologists have tended to treat the self as a relatively fixed object, a focal point of certain attitudes and behaviors. The social world is introduced only at the last moment, so to speak, when self-ratings or traits are correlated with social events. The result is that the dynamic context of the self is bypassed and replaced with a set of highly abstract, mechanistic relationships. Psychoanalytic authors have tended to err in the opposite direction. Rather than introducing the social world at the last moment, they have tended to drop it prematurely. The interactional context of personality is recognized in the "fused" self-object representations of early childhood; but the conceptual separation which the child later makes between self and other is regarded by many psychoanalytic theorists in a literal and concrete way, as though the mature self could *actually* be separated from the context of social experience in terms of which the self is, in reality, continuously redefined.

Only a few writers have given full recognition to the dynamic and interactional nature of the self, and these writers have encountered problems of their own. For example, Sullivan (1950, 1953) emphasizes interpersonal processes, but he falls into a mechanistic account when he analyzes the self as a functional "dynamism." Mead, on the other hand, preserves the active individual and the social construction of meaning, but he does so at a highly abstract level in rather philosophical terms. What is lacking in all these characterizations is a consideration of *actual case material,* for it is only in the context of such case material that the self/other dialectic can be fully specified.

In the present study, we have considered a great deal of such case material and we have traced its structure of meaning, particularly in terms of ideology, idealization, and the central conflict. Each of these three constructs can be regarded as a specific aspect of the individual's "me"—that is, a specific kind of individual activity that is objectified in relation to other people and that locates the individual in a world of social meaning. Ideology, idealization, and the central conflict, therefore, designate regions of the self/other dialectic where particular aspects of personal identity are defined and elaborated. In the following pages this idea will be extended and illustrated with specific case material. Each of these constructs will be examined as it actually appears in Esther's account, and we will consider how each one contributes to the structure of the self and to the larger structure of the self/other dialectic in which human identity is always embedded. Let us begin with the construct of ideology.

Ideology and the Self/Other Dialectic

In chapter 2, ideology was defined as a set of ideas about human nature and the social world and was analyzed as a linguistically organized system—that is, a system of concepts representing meaning at an abstract, general level. In chapter 4 we considered the nature of the concepts that make up such a system. It was suggested that these concepts designate rule-governed classes of events and that they can be defined and altered with respect to each other in a number of complex ways. In every ideology, however, there are certain concepts that designate certain particularly important classes of events. Chief among these concepts are those which refer to situation-specific normative social behaviors—that is, concepts which define particular *social roles*.

To give an example, Esther relates some of her ideas about family life as follows:

> I think that the family that really works well is the family
> where the parents recognize that each member of that
> family is an individual with separate kinds of talents [and]
> different kinds of drives.... You must always recognize
> that these are individuals who [you] should not be
> dominating. Dominating and nurturing are two different
> things.

In this passage Esther lays out an aspect of her ideology; but more than this, she outlines a system of roles within the family. For example, Esther states that parents should recognize their children's individuality and nurture it in a nondominating way. At the same time, Esther implies something about the role of children in the family. They should let their parents know about their individual drives and talents and should accept their parents' nurturance as long as it does not become a dominating force. While not stated explicitly, we can infer this role conception from the fact that the parental role Esther envisions could not be effected without a corresponding acceptance on the part of the children. This inference illustrates an important characteristic of ideologically constituted social roles: they exist in a context of shared goals and obligations, and they are always reciprocal or complementary in some way.

Closely related is another point: the concept of a social role presupposes certain ideas about human nature—that is, every role concept postulates that people want certain things and respond in certain ways to specific kinds of treatment. Esther assumes, for example, that parents and children share a wish for family life and that a family "works well" if the parents nurture their children and respect their individuality. Concepts of roles, therefore, are supported—implicitly or explicitly—by auxiliary concepts designating expectable patterns of human behavior in specific social situations. More simply stated, role constructs transcend the modalities of "ought" and "is." Not only are such constructs aimed at prescribing what people *should* do, but they are also aimed at describing what people *actually* do.

Let us now address the question of how ideology might be related to the self-concept. Ideology is an abstract system which applies to social life in general, but we have seen that the subject connects this abstract system to his or her own specific situation through the semiotic structures of life history and current perceptions. Even if the subject did not do so explicitly, we could still assume some such mediating process, for an ideology is a set of ideas about human beings in the social world, and the subject knows himself or herself as a member of this world, a specific human being. When Esther says "you must always recognize that these are individuals who [you] should not be dominating," she is, of course, talking about herself. Esther believes that *she* must recognize children as individuals, that *she* should nurture them without dominating them, that *she* can make the family work well. Within the complex of social roles outlined by her ideology, therfore, Esther locates herself in the role of parent with all its attendant obligations and possibilities; and her concept of this role is, in part, her concept of herself.

As we have just seen, however, Esther's idea of parenting is complementary to her idea of being a child; and both of these conceptions assume certain things about family life and human nature in general. Esther can only be a parent if other people play the roles of children and other members of the family. This statement returns us to the point made above, namely, that representations of self and other are constructed together in an interactional context, and that it is impossible to represent the self without representing the world of other people. If we trace the full system of roles and obligations outlined in all the sectors of Esther's ideology, we will find a rich and complicated network of role conceptions which encompasses not only Esther and her family, but *all* of the people in Esther's world.

Moreover, this system of roles is not connected to specific individuals in any simple way. For roles are reversible, and it is always possible for someone to assume a role that was formerly occupied by someone else. To put it another way, not only do roles transcend the modalities of "ought" and "is," they also transcend those of time and person. For example, we have noted that Esther's ideology provides her concept of herself as a parent, but the above passage also tells us something about Esther's concept of herself as a child. Through the conceptual framework of her current ideology Esther understands what she experienced growing up; she knows herself as a girl who had needs as an individual, who wanted parental attention, but also wanted privacy and respect—in short, who wanted to be nurtured but not dominated.

Ideology, then, makes a variety of contributions to an individual's self-concept. It establishes the role constructs by which the self is known, coresponding constructs by which others are known, and an overarching framework of natural relationships and obligations in which self and other can be understood in a process of social interaction. In addition, ideology supplies a way of understanding oneself as one used to be, or could be, or will be, given a shift in social roles. In general, ideology is an elaborate representation of meaning in the social world, and the concepts of ideology provide the individual with the basic terms for constructing a social self in a wide variety of forms and possibilities. The power of ideology to constitute the self in so many of its different modes and aspects—in all of the roles an individual plays, as well as the corresponding roles he or she has played in the past or might play in the future—this power follows from the fact that ideology is a system of meaning constructed in a context of social interaction. Out of this infinitely rich field of social meaning, certain patterns are identified by the reflective process and woven into a shifting and multidimensional conception of one's own person. It is not meaning which is derived from the self, but the self which is derived from meaning.

Researchers of the self-concept have generally shied away from these complications. Instead of regarding the self as a changing product of the individual's reflective activity, they have tended to treat it as a fixed and concrete structure. For example, Coopersmith

(1967) defines self-esteem as the evaluative attitude which one holds toward oneself "as an object" (p. 21); and Rosenberg (1965) begins his investigation of self-esteem by postulating "that people have attitudes toward objects, and that the self is one of the objects toward which one has attitudes" (p. 5). The insufficiency of this perspective is evident in the fact that it has compelled researchers to generate an increasing variety of different "self" constructs in an attempt to account for the richness of social experience and the shifting modalities of human thought. For example, Rosenberg alludes to the "ideal self," the "committed self," the "fantasy self," the "inferred self," and the "presenting self," among others, and suggests that researchers will need to determine the inter-relationships among all of these constructs (1965, pp. 273-75). But such an enterprise can lead only to greater confusion, for reflective individuals in a changing field of meaning will continue to encounter new varieties of social experience, which, in turn, will necessitate still more theoretical constructs and more interrela-tionships. The various aspects of the experience of self cannot simply be pulled out of their interactional context like the basic components of a complicated machine. To treat them this way is to reify the self-concept—to confuse an objectification with an object.

We can examine these problems in a microcosm if we consider a construct that has been popular in both the experimental and the clinical literature—the so-called *ideal self*. A number of authors have suggested that self-esteem can be understood in relation to this entity and the extent to which an individual approximates it in his or her own mind. In chapter 2 we briefly considered a technique for measuring the "self-ideal discrepancy" and some of the problems associated with this technique. Chief among these problems was the meaningfulness of the fundamental construct assumed by this procedure, that of the ideal self.

There can be little doubt that people have ideals and that they try to live by these ideals, in some respects at least. There can also be little doubt that people are capable of reporting their ideals in a wide variety of formats, including the ideal-self inventories which psychological investigators sometimes ask them to fill out. But this fact in itself does not demonstrate that ideals are *actually* structured in terms of an ideal self. We have already seen that inner life unfolds in extremely complex and fluid ways, so it would seem worthwhile to make careful inquiries into the relationship between ideals and the self before drawing any conclusions of this kind. Let us, then, consider the phenomenon of idealization as we have observed it in life-historical accounts and see how the phenomenon is related, through the process of social interaction, to the conception and image of the self.

Idealization and the Self/Other Dialectic

We may begin by noting that none of the subjects in the present study described an ideal-self image in any strict sense of the term. To be sure, they often talked about their ideals and standards, and the ways in which they have tried to live up to these ideals and standards in various situations. For example, Esther talked about how she has tried to promote a "sense of community" and a "nurturing" environment at work that would allow the people she supervises to develop their own special talents and abilities. The image which Esther describes might be considered that of an ideal self, but she does not present it as such; and there is as much reason to regard it as an *actual*-self image, since Esther describes it in the context of her current activities.

Much more vivid in Esther's account—and in all of the accounts in the present study (possibly excepting Lou's)—are the idealized descriptions of important figures from the past, especially parents. For example, Esther describes her mother as follows:

> My mom is a loving lady, and she's not only loved by her children, but also by her peers. She's outgoing, she's big-hearted and sensitive to people.

Likewise, Esther describes her aunt:

> She was an enormously talented woman. She was a fantastic seamstress.... She was the decision maker in the business.... And she was a magnificent cook.... There wasn't a thing that she couldn't do.

And her father:

> He never went to school.... [He] learned how to read and write, but he never attended formal school.... My father read a newspaper in Yiddish and an English newspaper every day of his life, and he wouldn't let things like the *New York Daily Mirror* or the *New York News* in the house...He had standards.

These images seem to be idealized in a much deeper and more significant way. This depth is evident both in the tone of the language and the thematic detail of the descriptions, which emphasize the admirable qualities and exceptional abilities of the persons described.

We might infer from these observations that it is not the ideal self that is important for self-esteem, but the idealized images of other people. However, things are not quite this simple. When we examine the idealizations of life-historical figures in the current investigation we find that they lead us, inevitably, back to the self and its idealization. This conclusion follows from the analysis of ideals originally presented in chapter 2. It was suggested that ideals are best understood in *thematic* terms—that is, as specific activities which offer a potential solution to the subject's life-historical central conflict. Esther's idealizations of her mother, her aunt, and her father, for example, center on the themes of nurturance and respect, themes Esther tries to put into effect in her own life in solving her own existential dilemma. Esther's ideals are defined, therefore, in terms of specific activities which *she herself* performs or might potentially perform. And when Esther describes herself carrying out these activities—such as in her account of herself at work—this description can be understood as a form of self-idealization, for it represents Esther as demonstrating her own ideals in action. An image of this kind—one that portrays a person as applying his or her ideals in a real (or imaginary) situation—is probably the closest thing we can find in ordinary experience to an "ideal self."

Idealizations of self and other, therefore, are tied to one another in a deep and instrinsic way. In order to identify one's own actions as conforming to one's ideals, one must know these actions as instances of paradigms demonstrated by idealized figures from past personal history. By the same token, idealized images of life-historical figures presuppose an idealization of the self, for these figures must demonstrate paradigms of action which are relevant to one's own central conflict. Furthermore, idealizations of self and other are complementary in current relationships as well. When one objectifies oneself as carrying out one's ideals, this process necessarily entails the objectification of others. In order to play the role of ideal worker, for example, Esther must do so in relation to other people who are willing, in some sense, to play the roles of ideal co-workers. Once again, self and other are inherently interactional.

If we keep these complications in mind, we can assess the sense and usefulness of the construct of the ideal self. This construct is not without meaning, as it is certainly possible for one to objectify oneself as the demonstrator of one's own ideals. But such a self-objectification can occur in a multiplicity of ways that goes far beyond the abstract, hypothetical mode usually associated with the concept of the ideal self. For example, a subject can talk about applying ideals in his or her current life—as Esther does when describing herself at work—and thus collapse the ideal self and the actual self into a single image. Likewise, a subject can describe applying ideals in a past situation, a future situation, an imaginary situation, a typical situation, or a desired situation—thus cutting across most of the "self" constructs enumerated by Rosenberg, and certain other ones as well. In addition, the subject's characterization of his or her ideal self has meaning only insofar as it simulatneously presupposes, makes possible, and brings into focus a corresponding set of images of ideal others, not only from the subject's past history but in his or her current life as well. The ideal self is probably best understood, therefore, not as a monolithic structure, but as an array of self-objectifications in a variety of modes, all of which involve interactions with other people and all of which are defined in terms of idealizations of life-historical figures.

The existing psychological literature, however, has greatly oversimplified this picture. The ideal self has been presented as a discrete and unitary entity, and this construction has led researchers into a number of conceptual and methodological errors. Experimental psychologists have badly misrepresented the facts of experience by suggesting that self-esteem results from a mechanical comparison between the ideal self and the actual self. At a minimum, this assumption has generated a great deal of inconsistent and conceptually discontinuous research. In clinicial theory, too, the ideal self has been a source of confusion, as is particularly evident in a cluster of problems associated with the psychodynamic construct of the "ego ideal." For example, it has never been clear whether the ego ideal refers to an idealization of self or other. Freud's (1914a) original terminology vacillates between "ego ideal" and "ideal ego," and subsequent authors have located this structure in a variety of positions between the superego and the ego. This ambiguity is one reason why there seem to be *two* theories of self-esteem in psychoanalysis (Jacobson, 1965; Brissett, 1972), one dealing with "moral" self-esteem and the other with narcissism. Moreover, it has never been clear how the ego ideal stands in relation to the "punitive" objects of the superego—nor, for that matter, how any of these constructs is related to the self through the processes of introjection and identification.

It is much more coherent to regard idealization in terms of *interactional paradigms* or *themes*. This perspective eliminates the need for multiple "self" constructs and other theoretical entities, and most of the above problems quickly melt away. In the social act, subject and object coexist thematically, and it is only subsequent to the subject's reflective activity that we can talk about conceptions and images of the self. All constructs that refer to the self must refer to the subject's interpretation of his or her own interactions in the living social world. To recognize this fact is merely to recognize the preeminance of meaning in psychological life.

The Central Conflict and the Self/Other Dialectic

Let us turn now to the third construct—the central conflict. In chapter 2, the central conflict was defined as a set of conflicting themes that cuts across all levels of semiotic and linguistic organization. It was suggested that this pattern of conflicts manifests itself in a subject's account in two rather different ways. In descriptions of early experience, the central conflict tends to be represented as an actual encounter with other people in the subject's family of origin; in discussions of more recent and contemporary experience, it tends to appear as a pattern of meaning by which a subject organizes and understands important events in his or her life. Let us examine these two modes of representation using material from Esther's account.

Esther recalls a childhood in which she was "too well loved." Her parents' affection and concern was so intense that it often became a kind of intrusive control. In the following passage, for example, she describes how her father's attentiveness could be an oppressive burden that stiffled her individuality:

> My two sisters and I would start towards the library, and my father would come with the car and pick us up and take us there. And we really, really resented it. We'd say "we wanted to walk, it's a beautiful day...the trees are beautiful.... Why do you have to do this all the time?" And he thought he was being good to us. (What did you resent about it?) That we weren't allowed to do it on our own.

Even more problematic, however, was Esther's relationship with her mother—a woman who, at times, seemed to ignore Esther's existence as a separate person:

> My mother would call her sister ritualistically every single day on the telephone, and she told my aunt everything about

the three of us. I used to say to my mother hostilely, "are you going to tell her how many times I went to the bathroom today?" There was a kind of indecency about it, you know? If I told my aunt about myself it was one thing, but if my mother did it it was like denying me my privacy as an individual.

In these passages, Esther describes her central conflict in terms of specific interactions with other people in her family. She wishes to establish herself as a separate person, but she encounters direct opposition in her parents' attempts to maintain a close and intense family life. In previous chapters, we have considered this dilemma in some detail; what needs to be emphasized here is that in descriptions of early life history, Esther presents it as an actual conflict with other people.

Esther describes the same central conflict in connection with recent and current experience, but she seldom does so in such an external way. In discussing her own marriage and parenting, for example, she talks about how she has tried to find a balance between closeness and individuality; but she describes this attempt less as a series of confrontations with others than as a struggle to define her own role in the family. At work, too, Esther describes her central conflict not as an external battle but as an attempt to clarify the relationship between community and respect in her own mind and actions. The following passage conveys some of Esther's ideas about closeness and respect, and how these themes might be balanced in both the family and the work place:

> You must always recognize that these are individuals who [you] should not be dominating. Dominating and nurturing are two different things.... And I feel that way about my co-workers at work, most of whom are younger than I am.... If you recognize where everybody is at, what their ambitions in life are, you get to know them.... That doesn't mean that you invade their daily lives, [but]...they [need to] get the feeling that you're helping them to build their skills so that they can help themselves. And the inevitability, you know, is that they're going to leave you. You have to face that too.... (Just like your children.) Yeah.

Esther's account, therefore, shows the central conflict represented both externally and internally. In descriptions of early life history, particularly, the conflict is manifested in disrupted relations between Esther and her parents; in recent and current experience the conflict is more evident in Esther's descriptions of problematic elements within her own identity. In this light, we might say that the central conflict has a developmental history, that it began in Esther's relations with her parents, and that it was subsequently taken up into her self. As a matter of fact, such inferences are frequently made in the clinical literature, and it is generally assumed that conflicts with other people are internalized over the course of development. While this proposition is an interesting one and is supported by a great deal of evidence, it is also conceptually problematic in certain important ways.

Schafer (1968, 1976) has pointed out a number of difficulties with the concept of internalization—particularly, the fact that it seems to involve a concretization of ongoing psychological processes. To use the terminology developed in this chapter, an internally experienced psychological structure is an objectification, not an object. It is an act by a person, not a literal thing which can be moved back and forth across a "self-boundary." If we ignore this important consideration and regard internalized structure in a literal way, we are likely to misunderstand the significance of the central conflict in an individual's life. We might regard the conflict, for example, as an autonomous psychological constellation that is essentially discontinuous from one's current social situation or that runs along side the external world in some kind of parallel process. At best, we will presume that conflict involving the self is somehow connected with conflict involving the other; but we will have little idea of how this connection is effected or what its consequences are for self-esteem. How, then, can we reinterpret the central conflict in terms more appropriate to a self/other dialectic?

To begin with, let us reexamine the instances in which the central conflict seems to be external or internal. I have suggested that externality is associated with early life history and internality is associated with recent and contemporary experience, but this rule is only approximately true. In some descriptions of early history the central conflict is represented internally, and in some descriptions of present experience the conflict is represented externally. Esther's characterizations of her mother and aunt, for example, express some of her own mixed feelings about the roles which they played in the family; and her discussion of her current role at work includes certain allusions to problematic interactions with other people. We should be cautious, therefore, about linking external conflict and internal conflict in simple one-to-one relationships with past and present experience.

This question can be approached more coherently in terms of semiotic and linguistic systems. When a subject describes a central conflict externally—as Esther does in the above descriptions of her interactions with her parents—he or she usually does so by means of a semiotic construction. If we consider the nature of semiotic systems we can see why this is so. Semiotic constructions refer to specific objects and concrete interactions, aspects of the material world that an individual usually regards as external to the self. The confrontations which Esther describes with her parents, for example, are specific events involving specific people, part of the concrete reality in which she grew up. Descriptions of early life history typically take this form, and they therefore present conflict in terms that are primarily external. Recent and contemporary experience, however, may also present conflict as an external phenomenon, insofar as the subject describes such conflict in terms of concrete particulars—the unfolding of actual events in his or her life.

On the other hand, when a subject describes a central conflict as an internal experience he or she usually does so by means of a linguistic construction, as exemplified in Esther's comments about the kinds of roles that are appropriate at home and work. Such linguistic constructions deal with rule-governed classes of social events—that is, general concepts like "dominating" and "nurturing." These general concepts are the tools by which an individual understand his or her experience; but more than this, they are the defining terms of the conception of self which orders the individual's experience and gives it personal meaning. Thus, when the individual reflects upon the central conflict as a personal, "internal" experience of the self, he or she tends to construe the conflict in abstract, linguistic terms. Such reflection usually occurs in connection with recent and current experience, the arena in which the individual encounters issues of present concern in the organization of self; but self-reflection can also take place in relation to the events of early life history.

In chapter 3 it was noted that semiotic and linguistic systems are not entirely separable. Object languages and concept languages seem to presuppose each other in the field of meaning. Let us briefly consider the nature of this interdependence, and what it suggests for the central conflict as an organizing principle of self.

Both semiotic and linguistic constructions are objectifications of the individual's encounter with the social world, but each of these constructions is a different *kind* of objectification associated with a different objectifying (as opposed to objectified) activity. Semiotic systems are generated by activities that objectify *specific* interactions—activities such as identifying, imagining, and describing. Linguistic systems are generated by activities that objectify *classes* of interactions—activities such as distinguishing, classifying, and conceptualizing. There is no clear dividing line between these two types of activity because there is no clear distinction between attending to a single interaction and attending to a class of interactions. A single interaction can only be comprehended as such by locating it in reference to classes of similar and different instances; and a class of interactions necessarily encompasses single instances.

When an individual encounters other people in the real world, he or she must employ both of these processes. The encounter must be objectified in its concrete specifics, and also in terms of similar and different instances in the individual's experience. The former generates a semiotic construction and the latter a linguistic construction; both of these are essential in comprehending the significance of the event. If the encounter is a *conflicted* one for the individual, he or she will objectify it as such both at the semiotic and linguistic levels. However, the individual will probably favor one of these modes over the other, depending upon the situation and upon the individual's personality and current concerns. If the situation is a difficult or threatening one, or if the individual needs to protect an already vulnerable self, he or she will probably construe the conflict in terms of semiotically organized externals toward which he or she can act; and if the situation is a relatively innocuous one, or if the individual is motivated toward self-understanding, he or she will tend to reflect upon the conflict and to objectify it in terms of the linguistically organized categories of inner life.

This perspective eliminates the dichotomy of inner and outer conflict and postulates instead *an unbroken continuum of signification*. We can regard conflict as a pattern of disrupted experience which is interpreted in primarily internal or primarily external terms, according to the balance of the individual's semiotic and linguistic interaction with the environment. This interaction is a response to the events that confront the individual in the real world; but the interaction is also carried out in the ways that protect or challenge the concept of self, according to the individual's capacity and need for self-reflection. To put it another way, conflict in the world and conflict in the self organize each other through the medium of the individual's semiotic and linguistic activities. Disturbances in the field of social experience are directly objectified in the semiotic structures of perception, memory, and imagination, and indirectly objectified in the linguistic structures of conceptual and reflective thought, manifesting themselves, ultimately, as disruptions in the meaning and the organization of the self. Conversely, confusions and contradictions in the life of the self play themselves out through the signals and gestures of concept and object languages in the concrete actions of the individual in the real world. The relationship between inner and outer conflict, therefore, is not a dichotomy, a correspondence, or a simple movement across "self-boundaries"; rather, this relationship is a continuous dialectic between the individual and the world, mediated and buffered in the complex particulars of semiotic and linguistic behavior.

All of the above suggests that the central conflict must be addressed both internally and externally at any stage of development. The individual must resolve disruptions of the self and disruptions of social life in a transformative movement which encompasses both and plays them off against each other. This task is exceptionally difficult, for it requires a systematic integration of self-reflection and social action. Furthermore, other people are not passive respondents who readily accommodate themselves to the demands of one's individuation and conflict resolution. Each person has conflicts of his or her own, and each is struggling to bring about a pattern of resolutions in his or her own particular way. This is the real dilemma of the central conflict and it poses the deepest problem for the individual who tries to achieve self-esteem. It is not enough to bring conflicting themes into a harmonious relationship, even if one manages to do so at all levels of signification and action. Equally important is that the resolution be a viable one in the world of other people, that it allow, ultimately, for a satisfying and fulfilling social existence. Not only does the central conflict involve a disonance in one's social identity, therefore, it also involves a dissonance between society and identity themselves. It is a conflict between self-definition and the need for others, between the forces of individuation and the forces of collective life.

We can see this polarity reflected in each of the central conflicts we have considered in this study. Although we have encountered a variety of issues defining the meaning of subjects' self-esteem, every central conflict in the foregoing cases seems to involve an opposition between individual and social needs. This opposition is readily apparent in Esther's account, for example, where the conflicting themes are individual dignity and familial closeness. In other cases, too, the central conflict invariably involves an attempt to reconcile personal and interpersonal demands: Ed tries to establish himself as a successful businessman, but always in a way that his mother and other people can appreciate; Paul talks about the struggle for survival, and weighs the possibility of trusting others to help in this effort; Denny strives to prove himself, but in relation to his father and other powerful individuals; John wishes to be an exemplary individual, but always in the eyes of his family and colleagues; Anna establishes self-protective boundaries and seeks to transcend them; Charlotte wants to be strong and competent like her mother, but available and giving like her father; Lou recounts a struggle between personal gratification and social solidarity; and Ruth aspires to professional accomplishment, but feels a powerful obligation to her family.

In order to resolve the central conflict, the individual must effect a compromise between his or her own needs and the requirements of social life. But this difficult project can easily miscarry in either direction. The individual may become entrenched in personal concerns and attempt to define a self at the price of his or her connection with other people; or he or she may live a life that revolves around other people, satisfying personal needs and aspirations only indirectly. Both of these strategies represent symbolic resolutions, attempts to solve the central conflict in a limited portion of the field of meaning. In chapter 3 we considered such resolutions as forms of defensive self-esteem, but we did not distinguish at that time between the "self-directed" and "other directed" cases. We can make some observations about them now, however.

The self-directed resolution fits the popular image of defensive self-esteem and involves a preoccupation with the self to the exclusion of one's relationship with other human beings. The obvious case is the narcissistic or grandiose person who seems to feel like the center of the world. However, a self-directed resolution need not involve grandiosity. Such a resolution can center on an impoverished and constricted self, as exemplified by Johann Kremer, the Auschwitz doctor who drably and mechanically recorded his crimes against humanity in a monotonous daily journal (Zimbardo and Ruch, 1975). What makes such self-esteem defensive is not the magnitude of the self, but the ruptures of meaning that isolate the individual from the surrounding environment of common humanity.

The second kind of defensive self-esteem also isolates the individual, but in a somewhat different manner. The central conflict is resolved in relation to someone else and does not involve the self in any direct or obvious way. An example is the mother who dedicates so much of her life to her children that she has no real identity of her own. Such a resolution may not look like *self*-esteem at all, since it centers upon other people. In the living reality of social interaction, however, self and other are inextricably related, and the altruistic behavior which governs this kind of resolution is always, in some manner, an expression of the needs and aspirations of the self. The self is esteemed *through* other people, and they can ever be reduced, in extreme cases, to mere objects or instruments in an elaborate program of generosity and self-sacrifice. In this manner, altruism and selfishness, grandiosity and self-abasement, can all be regarded as variations on a common theme—the theme of disrupted meaning in social interaction and the location of self in a protected symbolic arena.

In this light, it is not surprising that defensive self-esteem usually involves some combination of the above two strategies. In Denny's case, for example, self is emphasized in ideological formulations but devalued in relation to Denny's father; and in John's account, other males are respected, but partly because they respect and admire John. All of this suggests something about the relationship between defensive and nondefensive self-esteem. It is not a mere balance, an equal regard for self and other, that makes a resolution of a central conflict nondefensive. If this were so, "genuine" self-esteem would be much easier to achieve than it actually is. What is required instead is a *qualitative transformation* of self and other, a different kind of relationship. Just as the themes of the central conflict must be truly reconciled rather than undone or reversed, so self and other must be reconciled in a new relationship based on a different and better vision of social reality.

But what constitutes such a vision? We can hardly answer this question in the abstract, for it is primarily a question about meaning; and, as I have emphasized throughout this book, human meaning refuses to be encapsulated in simple generalities and abstract formulations. We can employ a metaphor, however. Ernst Kris (1956) has described the construction of life history as the creation of a "personal myth." The individual weaves memory, fantasy, and current reality together to produce an autobiographical story extending from the past into the present and future. Different people are assigned to play different roles, but always in relation to the self, which is the main character, protagonist, and hero of the story. Unlike the hero in an ordinary myth, however, the hero of the personal myth is the author as well as the central figure. He or she writes and rewrites the story at every moment of his or her life.

Becoming genuinely self-esteeming is probably something like becoming a good author. Interesting roles must be written for the characters, and certain literary forms must be observed. The self must not be given an easy dominance and a string of facile victories, for such a story is shallow and predictable. Nor can the self be accommodated to the roles of others, nor located in a system of trivial relations, for a confused and directionless plot will result. Instead, all of the players must be developed as unique characters, particularly in relation to the self; and the self must be treated with depth and insight so that its heroism can assume full and subtle proportions. The central conflict can be resolved in certain respects, but never decisively so. It must continue to guide the plot, to shape the relations between self and other, and to structure the particular dilemmas of human existence that are to be addressed by the myth.

Self-esteem develops, then, as the personal myth is written and rewritten across the span of the individual's life. The story is refined, the characters are developed, the plot takes on new unity and meaning. And as the author and product of its own transformation, the self moves toward reconciliation in the world of other people.

APPENDIX _____

The Question of Validity

THE INTERVIEW AS DIALECTIC

The use of the interview to study psychological phenomena is not a new idea. There is a long tradition of interview research in social science, and even in the present experimental era a number of investigators still employ this device. However, as a research technique in American social science the interview has fallen into disrepute. Most investigators seem never to consider the possibility of interviewing subjects; and even more revealing is the *apologetic* tone that frequently accompanies the work of those who do. For example, Maslow (1950, 1970) begins an account of such a study with a preface depreciating the work as "technically questionable," and other naturalistic researchers indicate that their work is useful mainly for lending "plausibility" to theory or "generating hypotheses" which still remain to be tested by experimental techniques (for example, see McCall and Simmons, 1969). These attitudes are curious in light of the crucial role that the interview has played in the history of psychology.

The disparagement of the interview seems to concern, above all, its open and relatively unstructured format. Because it lacks the controls of laboratory research, the interview cannot generate consistent or predictable results. Moreover, there is no way of knowing how much the interviewer influences the responses of the subject or interprets them in terms of his or her own ideas. These are serious deficits from the experimental point of view. However, an important point needs to be made here—namely, that *it is methodologically incoherent to evaluate the interview from the experimental point of view.* The interview is a particular kind of research technique, one that is very different from the experiment. It has its own characteristics and its own assumptions; and it cannot be evaluated by the criteria and standards of experimental research any more than an experiment can be evaluated in terms of, say, psychoanalytic technique or architectural design.

Of course, there are legimate questions about the *validity* of the interview as a research technique; and these are questions which must be considered. In the last part of this section, these questions will be addressed. What needs to be emphasized at this point, however, is that the interview is a specific kind of research with specific characteristics that make it very different from other kinds of research. Let us consider some of these characteristics and see how they might best be conceptualized.

To begin with, there can be little doubt that the interviewer does influence the interview process. What may not be as obvious, however, is the *depth* of this influence. Sullivan (1954) has pointed out that both the interviewer and the interviewee cue each other at every moment in a multitude of ways, conscious and unconscious. Moreover, the interviewer expresses, in some sense, his or her entire background and experience every time he or she interprets even the simplest statement by the interviewee and uses the interpretation as the basis for a subsequent question.

> [The interviewer] has an inescapable, inextricable involvement in all that goes on in the interview; and to the extent that he is unconscious or unwitting of his participation in the interview, to that extent he does not know what is happening (p. 19).

The interview researcher, then, can hardly be deluded with the idea that he or she can take a detached or neutral position in relation to the subject. His or her life history, education, and values can all be expected to infiltrate the interview and contribute to the final product. How can we conceptualize this research technique in which the investigator interacts so thoroughly with the object of investigation?

If we turn to the literature of American social science, there is little to help us with this problem. With few exceptions, methodological discussions in this literature are guided by positivism and logical empiricism, philosophical traditions heavily influenced by the paradigm of natural scientific experimentation—the very paradigm we wish to avoid. There is another philosophical tradition, however, that has focused much more directly on epistemological questions about meaning in human life. This tradition is the one developed by European writers on phenomenology, critical sociology, and hermeneutics (interpretation theory). Writers in these fields have addressed a wide variety of issues, and they have developed a number of concepts that seem to be relevant to social science. One of the most relevant of these concepts with respect to interview research is that of *the dialectic*.[1]

The word "dialectic" is closely related to the Greek word for dialogue. Originally, dialectic referred to the process of philosophical debate, but gradually the word has come to denote any interaction in which complex processes are brought together and transformed into a qualitatively new organization at a higher level. Many different kinds of processes can be involved in such an interaction, but the concept of the dialectic is most often applied to human activity and signification. Within the dialectical perspective, social relations and psychological processes are understood to be inherently interactive and synergistic; and phenomena which are

---

[1]The European literature on dialectics is probably as large as the British and American literature on the philosophy of science. For this reason, it is not discussed in any formal or comprehensive way. Worth keeping in mind, however, is the fact that there is an immense body of literature providing an epistemological foundation for the dialectical perspective (and thus for interview research). This philosophical tradition extends all the way back to Kant and Hegel, and is currently being applied by Continental philosophers to a variety of specific disciplines and projects. As noted above, three lines of development seem to be especially important for the development of a dialectical social science. The first of these is the literature of phenomenology and existentialism, which has explored the dialectical roots of human experience and intersubjectivity (e.g. Husserl, 1937; Heidegger, 1927; Sartre, 1943). The second is the literature of contemporary Marxism and critical sociology, which has analyzed the interplay between social ideology and various material influences (e.g. Horkheimer, 1968; Habermas, 1968; Adorno, 1966; Sartre, 1960). The third is the literature of hermeneutics, which has addressed interpretation as a dialectical process that transcends the dichotomy of subject and object (e.g. Heidegger, 1971; Gadamer, 1960, 1976; Rocoeur, 1976; Lacan, 1953, 1966). All of the works cited in this footnote are now available in English-language translations. Moreover, there is an increasing number of good introductions for readers who are not yet comfortable with the style and vocabulary of this sometimes obscure literature (e.g. Palmer, 1969).

ordinarily considered to be dichotomous are viewed as codefining counterparts in a dialectical movement—a movement that transforms them over time, through continuous alteration and qualitative shifts, into a progressively subtler and more highly organized constellation of interacting particulars.

From the perspective of the dialectic, it does not make sense to regard researcher and subject as occupying self-contained and mutually exclusive roles. It is much more coherent to think of the two as interactive participants who shape and change each other as time passes. Likewise, observation and theorizing must be seen as inherently interactive, as must analysis and sythesis, and other aspects of the research process. Interaction is the primary fact of social and psychological life, and it characterizes the research act just as it characterizes other meaningful events. Moreoever, interaction is a dynamic process which tends to lead to higher levels of organization and understanding. This statement suggests that research should be designed not to neutralize or control interaction, but rather to *foster* it in a clear and self-conscious way.

The following pages will lay out a conception of interview research based on the perspective of the dialectic. The multiple case study will be described as a dialectical process which develops through several overlapping phases, each one itself a dialectic. These are the phases of preunderstanding, dialogue, interpretation, generalization, and presentation of the findings. In the discussion below, each of these phases will be briefly characterized and related to each other and to the overall movement of the research dialectic.

Preunderstanding

The dialectic of the multiple case study begins long before the first interview ever takes place when the investigator becomes interested in a particular phenomenon. The phenomenon makes an appearance in the investigator's life, and he or she develops certain ideas about it. As time goes on, the investigator's ideas are gradually modified by his or her experience; but this experience is also transformed as the investigator's ideas influence his or her perceptions. Eventually, the investigator makes some kind of commitment. He or she decides to study the phenomenon on the basis of the preliminary conception that has been developed and the kind of information that might be obtained through a formal process of interview research.

The interaction between experience and conception that leads to the initiation of the research project can be called the dialectic of *preunderstanding.* This stage of the research dialectic is the most primitive because it proceeds informally—perhaps even unconsciously—and culminates only in a preliminary impression. Without this impression, however, research would be impossible, for the investigator would have no orienting framework. Moreover, the dialectic of preunderstanding continues to play an important role even after the research is under way. The investigator uses hunches and impressions to formulate questions in the interview. Likewise, the investigator's preunderstanding contributes to his or her interpretations and generalizations, and it continues to transform and be transformed by the investigator's subsequent experience of the phenomenon. Preunderstanding, then, remains in effect and is taken up *into* the later stages of the dialectic; these later stages can be seen, in part, as a formalization of the dialectic of preunderstanding, for each involves a developing interaction between the investigator's conceptions and the phenomenon being studied.

Dialogue

Once the investigation has been formally initiated, the dialectic goes into a new stage as subjects are interviewed. This dialectic is a complex one and it proceeds on a number of levels simultaneously. We have already observed that interviewer and subject cue each other in many different ways, which include verbal cues (e.g. questions and answers), nonverbal cues (e.g. gestures and intonations), implicit cues (e.g. suggestive ambiguities and unusual locutions), and situational cues (e.g. the way the interviewer contacts the subject, and the environment the subject chooses for the interview). All of these cues serve as symbolic messages that are exchanged between the participants in the interview; but the most important of these cues is probably the actual verbal content of the *dialogue.*

As interviewer and subject jointly explore the avenues by which a phenomenon can be articulated, the interview becomes a moving and self-transforming force with a certain life of its own. It penetrates into regions of meaning that neither the subject nor the interviewer had planned or anticipated. Unlike the experiment, the interview does not have to stop when it reaches a predetermined point or topic, but can proceed on, past previous understanding, to new information and new insight. Moreover, the interview need not stop when it comes to a problem or an obstacle. For example, if the subject cannot answer a question, the inquiry can move into a different mode. The subject and interviewer can discuss the problem and work together on a resolution: Has the subject misunderstood the question? Has the interviewer asked the wrong quesiton? Has the subject forgotten the relevant information, and, if so, what *does* he or she remember? In this manner, both the subject and the interviewer participate in a collaborative dialectic. Each brings a unique perspective to the interview and works to reconcile it with that of the other. Both participants are changed by the movement of this dialectic as each approaches an understanding of other—a place where different perspectives coincide in a mutual articulation of a particular experience.

Interpretation

It is attractive to think that the interview process can lead to a full and complete understanding; in reality, however, the dialectic of the interview eventually reaches certain practical limits. It is seldom possible to conduct a dialogue that covers every important aspect of a phenomenon. Moreover, there are limits to what most people can admit to, discuss, and modify in a process of dialogue. Such limits may always be surpassable in principle, but beyond a certain point the interview becomes psychotherapy—a process neither sought nor agreed to by the subjects of the research project. These limitations require the investigator to supplement the interview with some inferential work. Some educated guesses must be made as to what lies beyond the subject's words—that is, the investigator must venture *interpretations* of the undisclosed meanings of the interview material.

At first glance, the process of interpretation may seem to be far removed from that of dialogue; but Continental philosophers have discussed interpretation as an extension of the dialectic of human interaction. The interpretation represents a "fusion of horizons" of the different perspectives involved in this dialectic—that is, one perspective is the world view embodied in the material to be interpreted, and the other perspective is the external point of view which the interpreter brings to understanding the material. These two perspectives are combined in the interpretive act, which both reconciles and supersedes them. Interpretation, therefore, is not an instrumental task in which the researcher "operates" on the subject's verbal productions, but an extension and continuation of the dialectical process by which discrepant perspectives are brought together and resolved.

Generalization

So far we have considered the research dialectic in relation to the individual subject. However, if the investigator wishes to address the universal characteristics of a phenomenon, he or she must interview a *variety* of subjects. The accounts of these subjects must be compared, the commonalities and differences among them must be identified, and theoretical implications must be developed and systematically applied across cases. To put it another way, the individual cases must interrogate each other in the mind of the investigator; and the themes associated with this *meta*dialogue must be organized by the *meta*interpretations of a theory. This process constitutes another phase of the research dialectic in which individual experience moves toward theoretical *generalization*.

This phase is something like the phase of experimental research in which results are studied and implications are considered; but this similarity is superficial and can be very misleading. In interview research, the phase of generalization overlaps the other phases of the research dialectic and affects them as they unfold: the investigator's preunderstanding is deepened and clarified as he or she begins to see new patterns in subjects' responses; dialogue is transformed as the investigator learns what to listen for and begins to ask the subjects a variety of new questions; interpretations are modified and come to be seen as concrete instances of theoretical metainterpretations. Generalization, therefore, shapes the other phases of the research dialectic and is likewise shaped by them. It is a dynamic process in which a variety of accounts provide the elements of a developing conceptual framework which systematically organizes their heterogeneous perspectives into a differentiated picture of a single phenomenon.

Presentation of the Findings

Eventually, the investigator presents his or her findings to other members of the research community. It may seem odd to talk about *presentation of the findings* as another phase of the research process, but the dialectical perspective recognizes this phase as a continuation of the interaction of the investigative process. All the phases of the research dialectic are repeated in the minds of those who read and think about an interview study. Each reader confronts the phenomenon with a particular preunderstanding, surmises how subjects might have responded to other questions, interprets undisclosed meanings in the material, and forms ideas about the phenomenon in general. Moreover, the dialectical process continues at a new level when readers critique the investigation, and the researcher, in turn, responds to their critiques.

The dialogue among researcher and critics extends and multiplies the research dialectic which previously unfolded only in the mind of the investigator or in the interactions between the investigator and subjects. Ideally, this critical dialogue should function like that of a competent clinical team whose interpretations of a particular case modify, supplement, and enrich each other. Through the understanding that gradually emerges, a three-dimensional picture of the phenomenon is formed. At the same time, specific facets of this picture will catch the attention of particular investigators and make contributions to their own preunderstandings and to the new investigations they undertake. The research dialectic is therefore renewed in further cycles of investigation and in a continuing accumulation and reformulation of knowledge about the phenomenon and about human experience in general.

Some general comments are in order about the dialectical conception that has been laid out. To begin with, no claim has been made about neutrality. The interview researcher is not a detached observer who stands apart from the phenomenon being investigated. He or she is in a constant process of interaction with it, from the beginning of the research to the very end. But this involvement does not mean that the researcher "contaminates" the data or "manipulates" the subjects. The research dialectic is a *mutual* process of collaboration and interaction, one that transforms the agent as well as the object of investigation. Researcher and subjects, theory and data, are all changed by the investigative process. They are brought together in a "fusion of horizons" to produce a particular integration of lived experience and theoretical understanding that other forms of research cannot attain.

Moreover, the dialectical perspective recognizes subtleties of the research process that are often ignored in American social science. In the realm of social interaction and meaning, there is no room for simple and reified dichotomies. Investigator and subject cannot be contained, in reality, by their socially defined mutually exclusive roles; they are human beings in a dynamic field who change and transform each other by their very presence. Likewise, theory and observation are not discrete entities which can be dealt with exhaustively one at a time; they are interpenetrating activities which necessitate and presuppose each other, and they function inseparably in the operation of consciousness. The research dialectic of the multiple case study recognizes these elements as interdependent and allows them to interact in a full and open way in a self-conscious investigation and construction of social reality.[1]

THE QUESTION OF VALIDITY

Now that a conception of the multiple case study has been presented, let us consider the question of validity. As noted above, the interview has fallen into disrepute in American social science, and this state of affairs seems to concern, above all, the validity of the interview as a research instrument. It is important, therefore, that we consider this question with some care.

Let us begin by observing that validity cannot be established in the abstract. Wells and Marwell (1976) note that discussions of validity always presume, implicitly or explicitly, a goal on the part of the researcher. That is, if we want to know whether a research technique is valid, we have to ask: *valid for what?* In the present study, the answer to this question has already been indicated in a number of places. We would like to understand self-esteem as it is given in people's lives—as a meaningful personal experience. It has been repeatedly suggested throughout this book that previous approaches to self-esteem have failed to accomplish this task. Let us consider why this failure has occurred.

Experimental investigation is based on the criteria of prediction and replication. When something can be repeated, demonstrated at will, the experimenter has achieved his or her goal. But this is only

---

[1]To talk about "constructing" reality as part of the research process may sound like heresy, but it is only taking responsibility for what happens covertly in other forms of research. The allegedly "neutral" techniques of experimentation turn out to be not so neutral when examined closely. There is a substantial body of literature in epistemology and philosophy of science indicating that even the simplest observations of experimental research are inextricably and unavoidably shaped by theoretical frameworks, unacknowledged presuppositions, and value orientations (Husserl, 1937; Sartre, 1948; Winch, 1958; Kuhn, 1962; Habermas, 1968; Maxwell, 1974, 1975; Feyerabend, 1975). Accordingly, logical empiricists in the twentieth century have systematically retreated from the belief in a completely neutral science (Carnap, 1936, 1956; Russell, 1948; Wittgenstein, 1953). Evidently, some psychologists have not yet learned about these developments.

one *kind* of criterion, and it establishes only one kind of knowledge. There are other kinds of knowledge that elude the criteria of prediction and replication; and a specific example is knowledge about self-esteem as a meaningful experience in a person's life. This kind of knowledge resides in a system of relations that is unique and irreducible in each separate instance. Such knowledge cannot be captured by a method that breaks it down into standard components. The experiment, however, is designed to perform exactly this kind of reduction. *It is aimed at washing out the very information which we seek—namely, information about unique and specific constellations of personal meaning.* As Wells and Marwell observe:

> Measurement assumes or asserts certain communalities among respondents so that it does not have to consider separately the individual meanings of each case (1976, p. 145).

If we are interested in self-esteem as a *meaningful experience*, therefore, it is the experiment and not the interview which is invalid.

Naturalistic and clinical studies fare better, for they do attempt to recognize the irreducible constellations of meaning in people's lives. These studies, however, have also suffered from conceptual and methodological problems—particularly, mechanistic assumptions and lack of reported case material. In order to achieve full validity, an investigation of this kind must enter totally into the phenomenon. The investigation must be self-consciously dialectical, bringing together conception and practice in a process of mutual interaction and construction of meaning. The multiple-case technique which has been described above is designed to meet precisely these criteria.

There is a potential objection that should be considered, however. I have characterized the multiple case study as a dialectical method that converges upon greater understanding by a process of mutual interaction and construction of meaning. But a critic might raise the question of how we *know* that any convergence toward greater understanding will take place. Each researcher and each critic could very well construct a different interpretation of the phenomenon. In fact, we *expect* them to do so, to some extent, since each starts with his or her own particular preunderstanding. In considering this book, for example, the reader will have his or her own reactions to the case material. He or she will make interpretations of the material, and some of these will undoubtedly differ from those of the author. Moreover, the reader may question some of the author's interpretations and generalizations, suspecting that they do not do justice to the case material. How can it be argued, therefore, that the findings of the present study are valid?

In one respect, this question has already been answered. The research dialectic does not stop with the publication of the findings, but continues in the dialogue among researcher and critics. That different people see different things in case material is not in itself invalidating—and it is even likely to lead to greater understanding in the long run. Each person approaches the phenomenon from a different perspective, and together they construct a multifaceted picture that transcends the point of view of any one person. At the same time, however, we know that some interpretations are better than others, and this fact suggests that there must be some criteria for evaluating a good interpretation or ruling out a poor one. What might these criteria be?

The question of canons of interpretation is a classic one in the literature of hermeneutics. Many authors have suggested canons for various kinds of interpretations (e.g. biblical exegesis, literary criticism, psychoanalysis). While none of these suggestions can be regarded as standard or definitive, the following canons are fairly representative and seem to hold potential for multiple-case research. They are adapted from a set of general interpretive principles suggested by Betti (from Palmer, 1969).

1. The interpretation should affirm the autonomy of the case—that is, it should give us a sense of what it is like to be the person we are talking about;
2. It should bring coherence to the material—that is, it should recognize the totality of meaning in a particular case and the meaningful location of specific elements within this overall context;
3. It should make sense in the context of our own experience—that is, it should be plausible.

If the interpretations in the present study fulfill these require-ments, we will have an argument for their validity.

Of course, one could argue that these canons do not offer real criteria since they do not spell out exactly what "sense" or "coherence" or "plausibility" mean. But such an objection misses the point. These canons offer guidelines for interpretation, not *substitutes* for it. Interpretation is a dialectical, human activity, and there are no predictive rules by which it can be "cranked out" automatically. It always occurs in a unique and specific situation and must be evaluated in the irreducible context of the same situation. Ricoeur (1976) has noted that the validation of interpretation has its own logic:

[This kind of] validation is not verification. It is an argumentative discipline comparable to the juridical procedures used in legal interpretation, a logic of uncertainty and of qualitative probability (p. 78).

Ricoeur calls this process of validation—this argumentative discipline—"the method of converging indicies" (p. 79).

This conception brings us back to the dialogue among researchers and critics. This dialogue is indispensible because it provides the "logic of argumentation" which leads to increasing validity and secure knowledge about a phenomenon. We assume that our dialogue will be fruitful, that we will move toward progressive agreement, because we live in a common world and we study phenomena that spring from common sources—social, economic, biological, and physical. As we observe the ways different subjects organize a psychological phenomenon in this common objective matrix, and as we discuss this phenomenon from a number of theoretical perspectives, we cannot help but converge upon its essential structure:

Always and necessarily, through reciprocal correction, agreeing consciousness of the same common world with the same things finally achieves validity (Husserl, 1937, p. 254).

When Husserl wrote this passage, he was referring primarily to physical objects. But his characterization applies just as aptly to human phenomena which are shaped in the object world and which can be systematically studied by interview research and the logic of argumentation. In this respect, the findings of well-conducted multiple-case research can be deemed "objective."

The multiple case study, then, is capable of generating knowledge that is valid and, in the most important sense, objective. Such a study is based on a dialectical process that moves in the direction of greater understanding. Ultimately, we can expect to gain worthwhile knowledge about the social world through this process. This is only an assumption, of course; but so too is the idea that systematic experimentation will converge on the truth. Epistemologically, the interview is just as securely grounded as the experiment. It is only in the area of *quantifiability* that the latter can claim any advantage over the former. The experimental study can offer a specific probability that a particular conclusion has been obtained erroneously. An interview study can make no such claim and must be evaluated on a strictly qualitative basis. Whether it was worth giving up this advantage to obtain the results of the current investigation, only the reader can judge.

Bibliography

Adorno, T. W. [1966] 1973. *Negative dialectics.* New York: Seabury Press.

Bandura, A. 1969. *Principles of behavior modification.* New York: Holt, Rinehart and Winston.

Bateson, G., Jackson, D., Haley, J. and Weakland, J. 1956. Toward a theory of schizophrenia. *Behavioral Science* 1:251-64.

Beloff, H. and Beloff, J. 1959. Unconscious self-evaluation using a stereoscope. *Journal of Abnormal and Social Psychology* 59: 275-78.

Berne, E. 1964. *Games people play.* New York: Grove Press.

———. 1972. *What do you say after you say hello?* New York: Grove Press.

Brenner, C. 1973. *An elementary textbook of psychoanalysis.* New York: International Universities Press.

———. 1976. *Psychoanalytic technique and psychic conflict.* New York: International Univeristies Press.

Brissett, D. 1972. Toward a clarification of self-esteem. *Psychiatry* 35: 225-63.

Carnap, R. [1936] 1953. Testability and meaning. In H. Feigl and M. Brodbeck (eds.), *Readings in the philosophy of science,* 47-88. New York: Appleton-Century-Crofts.

———. 1956. The methodological character of theoretical concepts. In H. Feigl and M. Schriven (eds.), *Minnesota studies in the philosophy of science,* vol. 1, 38-76. Minneapolis: University of Minnesota Press.

Cheshire, N. 1975. *The nature of psychodynamic interpretation.* New York: Wiley.

Chomsky, N. 1957. *Syntactic structures.* The Hague: Mouton.

———. 1959. Review of B. F. Skinner's *Verbal behavior. Language* 35: 26-58.

———. 1966. *Cartesian linguistics.* New York: Harper.

———. 1969. Language and the mind. In *Readings in Psychology Today,* 280-88. Del Mar, Calif.: CRM Books.

Coopersmith, S. 1967. *The antecedents of self-esteem.* San Francisco: W. H. Freeman.

Coward, R. and Ellis, J. 1977. *Language and materialism.* London: Routledge and Kegan Paul.

Diggory, J. C. 1966. *Self-evaluation: Concepts and studies.* New York: John Wiley.

Eckstein, R. 1978. Further thoughts concerning the nature of the interpretive process. In S. Smith (ed.), *The human mind revisited,* 329-48. New York: International Universities Press.

Edelson, M. 1975. *Language and interpretation in psychoanalysis.* New Haven: Yale University Press.

Fenichel, O. [1937] 1954. Early stages of ego development. In *Collected papers,* vol. 2, 25-48, New York: W. W. Norton and Co.

Ferenczi, S. [1913] 1950. Stages in the development of the sense of reality. In *Sex in psychoanalysis*, 213-39. New York: Brunner.

Feyerabend, P. 1975. *Against method: Outline of an anarchistic theory of knowledge.* Atlantic Highlands, N. J.: Humanities Press.

Freud, S. [1900] 1964. The interpretation of dreams. *Standard edition*, vol. 5. London: Hogarth Press.

――――. [1914a] 1964. On narcissism: An introduction. *Standard edition*, vol. 14, 69-104. London: Hogarth Press.

――――. [1914b] 1964. Remembering, repeating, and working through. *Standard edition*, vol. 12, 145-56. London: Hogarth Press.

――――. [1915] 1964. Instincts and their vicissitudes. *Standard edition*, vol. 14, 109-41. London: Hogarth Press.

――――. [1920] 1964. Beyond the pleasure principle. *Standard edition*, vol. 18, 7-64. London: Hogarth Press.

――――. [1921] 1964. Group psychology and the analysis of the ego. *Standard edition*, vol. 18, 67-144. London: Hogarth Press.

――――. [1923] 1964. The ego and the id. *Standard edition*, vol. 19, 3-68. London: Hogarth Press.

――――. [1924] 1964. The economic problem of masochism. *Standard edition*, vol. 19, 159-70. London: Hogarth Press.

Gadamer, H-G. [1960] 1975. *Truth and method.* New York: Seabury Press.

――――. 1976. *Philosophical hermeneutics.* Berkeley: University of California Press.

Gross, E. 1979. *Understanding another person: A life historical investigation.* Ph. D. dissertation, University of Michigan, Ann Arbor, Michigan.

Habermas, J. 1968. *Knowledge and human interests.* Boston: Beacon Press.

Hartmann, H. 1950. Comments on the psychoanalytic theory of the ego. *The psychoanalytic study of the child* 5: 74-96.

――――. 1956. The development of the ego concept in Freud's work. *International Journal of Psychoanalysis* 37: 90-115.

Heidegger, M. [1927] 1962. *Being and time.* New York: Harper.

――――. 1971. *Poetry, language, thought.* New York: Harper and Row.

Horkheimer, M. 1968. *Critical theory: Selected essays.* New York: Herder and Herder.

Husserl, E. [1937] 1970. *The crisis of European sciences and transcendental phenomenology.* Evanston, Ill.: Northwestern University Press.

Jacobson, E. 1965. *The self and the object world.* London: Hogarth Press.

James, W. [1892] 1935. Letter to James Ward. In R. B. Perry (ed.), *The thought and character of William James*, vol. 2, 96-97. Boston: Little Brown.

Kelly, G. A. 1955. *The psychology of personal constructs*, vol. 1. New York: Norton.

Kernberg, O. 1966. Structural derivatives of object-relationships. *International Journal of Psychoanalysis* 47: 236-53.

Kohut, H. 1966. Forms and transformations of narcissism. *Journal of the American Psychoanalytic Association* 14: 243-72.

――――. 1972. Thoughts on narcissism and narcissistic rage. *The Psychoanalytic Study of the Child* 27: 360-400.

_____. 1976. Creativeness, charisma, group psychology. (Reflections on the self-analysis of Freud). *Psychological Issues* 9 (monograph 34/35): 379-425.

Kris, E. [1956] 1975. The personal myth. In *Selected papers of Ernst Kris*. New Haven: Yale University Press.

Kuhn, T. S. 1962. *The structure of scientific revolutions*. Chicago: University of Chicago Press.

Lacan, J. [1953] 1968. *The language of the self*. New York: Delta.

_____. 1966. *Ecrits*. Paris: Editions du Seuil.

Lakoff, G. and Johnson, M. 1980. *Metaphors we live by*. Chicago: University of Chicago Press.

Langer, S. 1960. *Philosophy in a new key*. Cambridge: Harvard University Press.

Lichtenstein, H. 1977. *The dilemma of human identity*. New York: Jason Aronson.

Lorentzer, A. 1976. Symbols and stereotypes. In P. Connerton (ed.), *Critical sociology*. New York: Penguin.

Maslow, A. [1950] 1973. Self-actualizing people: a study of psychological health. In R. J. Lowry (ed.), *Dominance, self-esteem, self-actualization: Germinal papers of A. H. Maslow*, 177-202. Monterey, Calif.: Brooks/Cole.

_____. 1970. *Motivation and personality*. New York: Harper and Row.

Maxwell, G. 1974. Corroboration without demarcation. In P. A. Schilpp (ed.), *The philosophy of Karl Popper*. LaSalle, Ill.: Open Court.

_____. 1975. Induction and empiricism: A Baysian-frequentist alternative. In G. Maxwell and R. Anderson (eds.), *Minnesota studies in the philosophy of science*, vol. 6. Minneapolis: University of Minnesota Press.

McCall, G. and Simmons J. 1969. *Issues in participant observation: A text and reader*. Reading, Mass.: Addison-Wesley.

Mead, G. H. 1934. *Mind, self, and society*. Chicago: University of Chicago Press.

Moore, C. and Ascough, J. 1970. Self-acceptance and adjustment revisited: A replication. *Psychological Reports* 26: 855-58.

Norman, D. A. and Rumelhart, D. E. 1975. *Explorations in cognition*. San Francisco: W. H. Freeman.

Nunberg, H. [1931] 1955. The synthetic function of the ego. In *Practice and theory of psychoanalysis*, 120-36. New York: International Universities Press.

Palmer, R. 1969. *Hermeneutics: Interpretation theory in Schleiermacher, Dilthey, Heidegger, and Gadamer*. Evanston, Ill.: Northwestern University Press.

Peirce, C. S. [1932] 1955. *Philosophical writings of Peirce*. New York: Dover Publications.

Piaget, J. and Inhelder, B. 1966. *The psychology of the child*. New York: Basic Books.

Quillian, M. R. 1969. The teachable language comprehender: A simulation program and a theory of language. *Communications of the Association for Computer Machinery* 12: 459-76.

Ricoeur, P. 1976. *Interpretation theory: Discourse and the surplus of meaning.* Fort Worth: Texas Christian University Press.

Rogers, A. and Walsh, T. 1959. Defensiveness and unwitting self-evaluation. *Journal of Clinical Psychology* 15: 302-4.

Rogers, C. and Dymond, R. (eds.) 1954. *Psychotherapy and personality change.* Chicago: University of Chicago Press.

Rosenberg, M. 1965. *Society and the adolescent self-image.* Princeton: Princeton University Press.

Rothstein, R. and Epstein, S. 1963. Unconscious self-evaluation as a function of availability of cues. *Journal of Consulting Psychology* 27: 480-85.

Rubin, L. 1976. *Worlds of pain: Life in the working class family.* New York: Basic Books.

Russell, B. 1948. *Human knowledge: Its scope and limits.* New York: Simon and Schuster.

Ryle, G. 1949. *The concept of mind.* London: Hutchinson.

Sartre, J.-P. [1943] 1956. *Being and nothingness.* New York: Citadel Press.

————. [1948] 1975. *The emotions: Outline of a theory.* New York: Wisdom Library.

————. [1960] 1963. *Search for a method.* New York: Vintage Books.

Saussure, F. [1916] 1959. *Course in general linguistics.* New York: Philosophical Library.

Schafer, R. 1968. *Aspects of internalization.* New York: International Universities Press.

————. 1976. *A new language for psychoanalysis.* New Haven: Yale University Press.

Silber, E. and Tippett, J. S. 1965. Self-esteem: clinical assessment and measurement validation. *Psychological Reports* 16: 1017-71.

Skinner, B. F. 1957. *Verbal behavior.* New York: Appleton-Century-Crofts.

Sullivan, H. S. 1950. The illusion of personal individuality. *Psychiatry* 13: 319-32.

————. 1953. *The interpersonal theory of psychiatry.* New York: Norton.

————. 1954. *The psychiatric interivew.* New York: Norton.

Taylor, C. and Combs, A. 1952. Self-acceptance and adjustment. *Journal of Consulting Psychology* 16: 89-91.

Videbeck, R. 1960. Self-conception and the reactions of others. *Sociometry* 23: 351-59.

Wells, L. E. and Marwell, G. 1976. *Self-esteem: Its conceptualization and measurement.* Beverly Hills, Calif.: Sage Publications.

Winch, P. 1958. *The idea of a social science.* London: Routledge and Kegan Paul.

Wittgenstein, L. 1953. *Philosophical investigations.* Oxford: Basil Blackwell.

Wylie, R. C. 1974. *The self concept,* vol. 1. Lincoln: University of Nebraska Press.

————. 1979. *The self concept,* rev. ed., vol. 2. Lincoln: University of Nebraska Press.

Zimbardo, P. G. and Ruch, F. L. 1975. *Psychology and life.* Glenview, Ill.: Scott, Foresman and Company.

Index